THE DUNERA SCANDAL

THE DUNERA SCANDAL

CYRIL PEARL

ANGUS
& ROBERTSON
PUBLISHERS

ANGUS & ROBERTSON PUBLISHERS

Unit 4, Eden Park, 31 Waterloo Road,
North Ryde, NSW, Australia 2113, and
16 Golden Square, London W1R 4BN,
United Kingdom

First published in Australia
by Angus & Robertson Publishers in 1983
First published in the United Kingdom
by Angus & Robertson (UK) Ltd in 1983
This paperbound edition 1985

ISBN 0 207 15245 4

Typeset in 10pt English Times
Printed in Australia by
The Dominion Press – Hedges & Bell

FOREWORD AND ACKNOWLEDGEMENTS

This is the story of what Winston Churchill called "a deplorable mistake" and what Major Cazalet, a member of his Government, described as "a bespattered page" of English history.

It is the story of the great wrong inflicted on a number of German and Austrian anti-Nazis who had sought sanctuary in England. It involves two countries — England and Australia. The British Government was quick to realise its mistake, and make amends for it. The Australian Government was less responsive. It sacrificed humanitarian considerations to political expedience, and perpetuated the injustice for many years.

Both countries are still reluctant to make all the facts of the happening known. The Home Office has placed a ludicrous 100-year ban on the relevant files, and successive Australian Governments have slavishly followed Whitehall.

The principal sources of this chronicle have been reports of parliamentary debates in England and Australia, English newspapers and the invaluable diaries, letters and personal recollections of many of the victims of the "deplorable mistake".

I am particularly indebted to: the Australian Archives; the Lord Avebury; Charles Bastian; Bern Brent; Herbert Baer; Professor K. Baier; Dr Brooks; Professor Gerd Buchdahl; Professor Hans Buchdahl; Alfred Clarke; Arnold Ewald; Professor Eirich; Erwin Frenkel; Freddie Festburg; Professor Sir Edward Ford; Julie and Klaus Friedeberger; Professor S. C. B. Gascoigne; Professor F. Gruen; Mrs Hirschfeld; Miss Margaret Holmes; Professor Peter Herbst; Ian Hamilton; Rear-Admiral Hogger; Fred Hopkins; Dr Huppert; Gavin Johnston; Walter Kaufmann; Albert Karoly; Karl Koenig; Heinz Koppel; Professor Ernst Kitsinger; Gilda Lamm; Julian Layton; Klaus Loewald; Bim Meier; Professor Henry Mayer; Elfi and Ernst

Mook; Dr Parkinson; John Pomeroy; Professor Uwe Radok; Professor Rainor Radok; Professor Dr J. Rowher, Bibliothek für Zeitgeschichte, Stuttgart; Miss Patricia Reynolds, La Trobe Librarian; Stephen Rabson (P & O); H. B. Shaye; Captain L. W. Smith; Mrs K. Sternberg; Dr Leon Shirlaw; Fred Schonbach; H. McNeill Simpson; Archdeacon Twigg; Captain P. K. Wieting; Oswald von Wolkenstein, Weiner Library, London; Ursula Wiemann; Professor Wolfsohn.

I am also indebted to François Lafitte's admirable *The Internment of Aliens* (Penguin Special, 1940) and Lord Beveridge's *A Defence of Free Learning* (1959).

CHAPTER ONE

In the seven years from Hitler's rise to power in 1932 to the outbreak of World War II in 1939, about one third of a million Germans and Austrians managed to escape the Nazi terror. When war broke out, less than 74,000 of these (excluding children) were in Britain. There were also about 19,000 Italians and 8000 Czech refugees. Many were awaiting entry visas for other countries, principally the United States. Others intended to settle in Palestine or South America. Some were happily integrated into Britain's professional, artistic, academic and industrial life.

As Sir John Hope Simpson, chairman of the Christian Council for Refugees, observed in his authoritative study "The Refugee Problem" (1939), Britain's record in the admission of refugees was "not distinguished". Since the war of 1914-18, she had pursued "a strictly enforced and selective policy of immigration", Sir John wrote, and had "ceased to be a country of asylum on a large scale".

The refugees who had been admitted to Britain were, for the most part, treated sympathetically by the British people and the Government. Most were regarded, in the semantically quaint phrase, as "friendly enemy aliens".

There were of course a few exceptions to the prevailing mood of tolerance. Lord Beaverbrook's *Daily Express*, for instance, in August 1938 published a series of articles, the theme of which was that it was much too easy for Jews to enter England. The series ended with a tongue-in-cheek leading article headed "The Wandering Jew":

> Dreadful, dreadful are the afflictions of the Jewish people...
> Every warm heart must sympathise deeply with them in their
> plight...Certainly there is no room for the Jews in Britain,
> where we have 1,800,000 of our own people out of work

and biting their nails. But places must be found for the
Jews. There are plenty of uninhabited parts of the world
where, given a touch of the Christian spirit, they may yet
find happy homes.

And Nancy, Viscountess Astor, MP, confided to R.A. Butler
of the Foreign Office that she felt "too many Jews coming to
England was a mistake".

More surprising than this typical *Daily Express* appeal to
xenophobia was a letter sent about the same time by six trade
unionists to the Labour organ, the *Daily Herald*. They wrote:

We appreciate that often the refugees have committed no
crime against the country that harries them; but charity
begins at home, and we shall never... keep the standards
that have been won for us, if the influx of aliens goes on
unchecked.

The Government's policy, the Secretary of State for the Home
Department, Sir John Anderson, told the House on 4 September
1939, "took full account of the importance of distinguishing
refugees from Nazi oppression from other categories of enemy
aliens", a policy, he later declared, that gave him personally the
greatest satisfaction and was "in accordance with his country's best
traditions".

In July 1938, as the Nazi terror increased, the United States
organised a conference in the French spa town of Evian to discuss
the problem of refugees. Thirty-eight nations were represented,
including the United Kingdom, Canada and Australia. The conference listened to many pious speeches but there was more oratory
than action. Delegate after delegate deplored the plight of Hitler's
victims, but regretted that their respective countries could do no
more than they had already done. The Swiss delegate discreetly
refrained from mentioning that he was currently holding talks with
the Nazis with a view to preventing Austrian Jews escaping to
Switzerland. As an English historian, Simon Schama, wrote: "The
hollow proceedings of the conference served only to vindicate the
gloating conviction of the Nazis that no one wanted thousands of
Jews on their hands, least of all Jews left destitute by German
punitive taxation. Goebbels crowed: 'If there is any country that
believes it has not enough Jews, I shall be glad to hand over to it all
the Jews that we have.'"

The leader of the Australian delegation at Evian was Thomas
Walter (later Sir Thomas) White, then Minister for Trade and
Customs in the Lyons conservative Government. (A pompous little
man, White later walked out of the Ministry because he had been

given the wrong order of precedence at a swearing-in. But he had a distinguished record in World War I. As a flier in the Australian Flying Corps, he was twice mentioned in despatches and was awarded the Distinguished Flying Cross. Captured by the Turks, he escaped by way of Russia, and later recorded his adventures in a book titled *Guest of the Unspeakable*.) White was appointed chairman of the sub-committee which heard representations from a number of refugee organisations. In his report, White referred to the "moving stories" they had listened to. They disclosed "a great human tragedy" which called for "early amelioration and co-operative action", he declared. But he qualified these noble sentiments by saying that as Australia had "no real racial problem", she "was not desirous of importing one by encouraging any large scale scheme of immigration". The *Manchester Guardian*, detecting a note of racial antipathy in it, commented that White's speech went so far as to suggest that only Englishmen were wanted in Australia.

Two Australian newspapers, the *Sydney Morning Herald* and the *West Australian*, were equally critical of the speech. "Apart from the humanitarian considerations", the *Sydney Morning Herald* pointed out, Australia had a unique chance "to obtain some of the best stock and finest minds in Europe".

However, the Australian Government on 1 December 1938 announced that it would receive up to 15,000 refugees over the next three years, although, as the Dominions Office was told, if the refugees did not have capital they might not qualify as immigrants, and the Foreign Office was told that "the last thing the Australian Government desired was that their good intentions should become public property".

In making this announcement, the Minister for the Interior, Mr (later Sir John) McEwen said the Government viewed

> with feelings of deep sympathy the sufferings of people both
> of Aryan and non-Aryan races who have become refugees ...
> In arriving at the figure of 15,000 over a period of three
> years, the Government has been influenced by the necessity
> that the existing standards of living should not be disturbed
> and for reconciling with the interests of refugees, the
> interests of Australia's present population and of the people
> of British race who desire to establish themselves in
> Australia.

In 1939, the first year covered by the Evian agreement, 5080 refugees arrived in Australia. At the end of the war, the total population of Jews in Australia was only 35,535. Australia's population was then seven million.

With the outbreak of war on 3 September 1939, tribunals were set up to classify the aliens in Great Britain in two ways. They were to be divided into three categories: "A", "B" and "C". "A" class aliens were interned as possible security risks, "B" class aliens were free but subject to certain restrictions, and "C" class aliens were left entirely free. They were also classified as "refugees from Nazi oppression" and "non-refugees". Of the 73,400 who appeared before the tribunals, 64,000 were put into "C" class, and 55,500 classified as "refugees from Nazi oppression". No fewer than 27 per cent of the men and 17 per cent of the women were professional workers — doctors, dentists, pharmacists, oculists, psychologists, architects, engineers and teachers.

The tribunals did their work well.

Some months later, during a House of Commons debate on refugees, Osbert Peake, Under-Secretary of State for the Home Department, said with justification: "I wish we knew half as much about many of the neutral aliens and many British subjects, as we know about the 'enemy aliens' now in this country."

In April 1940, two eminent British leaders distinguished themselves by uttering sublime idiocies. On 4 April — April Fool's Day would have been more appropriate — the Prime Minister, Neville Chamberlain, asked defiantly: "Why was it that Hitler, despite all his long preparations for war, did not at the outset try to strike a knock-out blow at Britain and France? Whatever the reason — one thing is certain — Hitler missed the bus."

Next day, the Chief of the Imperial General Staff, General Sir Edmund Ironside, told a *Daily Express* interviewer: "Time is against Germany . . . Frankly we would welcome an attack. We are sure of ourselves. We have no fears . . . We are ready for anything they may start. As a matter of fact we'd welcome a go at them."

Less than four months later, Hitler had conquered five countries — Denmark, Norway, Holland, Belgium and France, and the prescient Ironside had been promoted first to the chief command of Home Forces and, after eight weeks, to the rank of Field Marshal. He was then mercifully retired on half-pay.

Chamberlain resigned on 10 May, and Winston Churchill was asked by George VI to form a new administration. London newspaper posters announced: BRUSSELS BOMBED: PARIS BOMBED: LYONS BOMBED: SWISS RAILWAYS BOMBED. The real war, the devastating *blitzkrieg*, had begun. Late at night on 11 May, as Nazi tanks raced towards the Channel ports, British military authorities called on Sir John Anderson "and represented that, in view of the imminent risk of invasion, it was in their view of the utmost importance that every male enemy alien between 16 and

70 should be removed forthwith from the coastal strip which in their view was the part of the country likely, if invasion took place, to be affected". Sir John found it impossible to reject the suggestion and immediately put it into effect. "There was not a responsible newspaper which did not applaud what had been done," he told the House.

A wide coastal belt, from Inverness in the north, to Dorset in the south, was declared "protected", and all male Germans and Austrians, excluding the invalid and infirm, were rounded up for "temporary internment". The round-up, which netted about 2200 men, was indiscriminate. The University of Cambridge and the London School of Economics, which had moved to Cambridge, lost important staff members, because Cambridge was in the "protected" area, and many "enemy aliens" who had the bad luck to be spending the Whitsun weekend by the seaside were included in the bag.

"These measures," declared the Home Office, "are to be considered as measures of urgency applied to areas where for military reasons special precautions are required for the time being." The Home Office regretted that this would involve great hardship "in individual cases", but assured the persons affected that the rigours of the measure would be mitigated "as soon as circumstances permit". But the rigours were soon intensified, not mitigated. On the night of Wednesday 15 May, and the following day, when the battle of the Meuse was raging and Holland had surrendered, all male Germans and Austrians aged 16 to 60 in "B" class, about 2200, were interned in a series of secret raids. *The Times* on 17 May reported that:

> the whole of Scotland Yard's fleet of motor cars from
> headquarters and police stations were mobilised, and chief
> officers were on duty throughout Wednesday night ... The
> greatest secrecy was maintained by Scotland Yard and even
> the officers concerned had no idea of what was afoot until
> they were given instructions when reporting for duty
> yesterday morning. At Sheffield two motor coach loads were
> rounded up and they were accompanied by two lorries
> manned by soldiers.

From the melodramatic tone of this report, with its reference to secret night raids, and lorry loads of soldiers, readers of *The Times* might have concluded that a devilish Fifth Columnist plot had been frustrated by Scotland Yard's vigilance.

In fact, the selection of refugees for internment was often arbitrary and sometimes ludicrous. Eric Schmidt, for example, had lived in England since he was a year old. His British-born mother had divorced her German husband in 1927. His elder brother was serving in the British Army. But Eric joined the heterogeneous community of internees on the Isle of Man.

Among those internees were many distinguished German and Austrian artists, doctors and scientists, and dedicated opponents of Nazism.

For the most part, the police who carried out the round-ups behaved with courtesy and humanity. But there were deplorable exceptions. In a letter to *The Times* (23 July), Dr J. J. Mallon, warden of Toynbee Hall, wrote:

> It is hard to write with composure about the present
> treatment of friendly aliens in East London. How can one
> explain or excuse the internment of elderly men, many of
> them invalids, who have lived here blamelessly for 40 or 50
> years? Men who have not been away from London for 20
> years; men who have occupied a single residence for half a
> century; men who are ailing or who have ailing wives;
> obscure and helpless men about whom the synagogue and
> their neighbours know all that can be known; men of whom
> it is not even pretended that there is any suspicion, are being
> interned or have been interned in scores.

For the first few months of the so-called "phoney war", the high tradition of tolerance which Sir John Anderson had acclaimed was maintained. The friendly and sympathetic attitude of public, press and authorities remained unchanged until the third week of January 1940 when suddenly an apparently co-ordinated campaign against refugees was launched in the "popular" — perhaps "prostitute" is the better term — press, particularly in the *Sunday Express* and *Daily Sketch*. "The fact that the same charges were put forward at the same moment and almost in the same words suggests that the campaign emanated from one centre," commented a writer in the *New Statesman*. The "one centre" almost certainly was the Army, and the purpose of the campaign, to prepare public opinion for a policy of interning all refugees.

Week after week, the *Sunday Express* and the *Daily Sketch* published inflammatory and wholly unsubstantiated stories of refugees acting as spies and saboteurs. In one they were accused of causing an explosion at the Royal Gunpowder Factory at Waltham Cross. Some of these stories purported to give the views of the London police on the refugee danger, an attribution which the London Police Commissioner, Sir Philip Game, twice publicly denied. The virulent anti-refugee campaign continued for months. In the second half of April, Mass Observation, an organisation for sampling public opinion founded by the anthropologist Tom Harrison, reported:

> April has been marked by a campaign against 'The enemy in our midst', the sinister, invisible enemy: the Fifth Column. A campaign against the Fifth Column, led with restraint by MPs, has been whipped up into something rather different in the press: a campaign to intern all refugees. The Sunday press has been particularly active; several papers have ignored the point made by MPs and the serious weeklies, namely that the Fifth Column may be mainly composed of persons in high positions, British born and bred.

On 24 May, Mr Ward Price, a well-known special correspondent of Lord Rothermere's *Daily Mail*, contributed a characteristic diatribe headed: "Act! Act! Act! Do it now." Before the war Price and his boss, the noble lord, had been enthusiastic supporters of Hitler and Mussolini. (Rothermere had also championed Mosley and his blackshirted thugs.) But now Ward Price thundered:

> The rounding-up of enemy agents must be taken out of the fumbling hands of local tribunals. All refugees from Austria, Germany and Czechoslovakia, men and women alike, should be drafted without delay to a remote part of the country and kept under strict supervision ... As the head of a Balkan state said to me last month: 'In Britain you fail to realise that *every* German is an agent. All of them have both the duty and the means to communicate information to Berlin.' Certain 'diplomatic bags' leaving this country are at the disposition both of such people and also of disaffected Britons.

Another fire-breathing patriot, courageously entrenched behind his typewriter, was Mr Beverley Nichols, an authority on Madame Melba, mulching, and Moral Disarmament. Before the war he too had championed Mosley and used his column in the *Sunday Chronicle* to acclaim Hitler and justify Nazi anti-semitism. But the outbreak of war miraculously transformed him. He now denounced the Nazis as passionately as he had acclaimed them, and extended his denunciation to all Germans, including the victims of Hitler who had fled to England. His synthetic frenzy reached a climax in the *Sunday Chronicle* on 26 May 1940:

> 'The Fifth Column.' And what about the spies here? Don't skip this, because you have read before that we ought to have interned the lot. We have not interned anything like

7

the lot. I hate writing this. I have German friends, but I
would very willingly indeed see them all, yes all, behind
bars, and I have told them so to their faces. Why should we
be blown up as we are walking over a bridge, unless it is
strictly necessary? Or poisoned by contaminated water, or
hit on the head by the local gasworks, as it descends to
earth? No, sir. The letters readers send about Germans who
are going free in their own district would make your hair
stand on end. Particularly the women. There is no dirty
trick that Hitler would not do, and there is a very
considerable amount of evidence to suggest that some of the
women — who are very pretty — are not above offering
their charms to any young man who may care to take them,
particularly if he works in a munition factory or the Public
Works.

"You can hardly imagine what discouragement and depression
all that alien-baiting, in which part of the press has indulged lately,
produces in men who have always believed in something like
democratic solidarity," said a writer in the *New Statesman*:

> This is not a question of the personal wellbeing of a few
> thousand refugees. It is a question of honour and of
> common sense. It is deeply regrettable that even the *Daily
> Herald* thought fit to encourage the suspicion that sees a
> Fifth Columnist in every alien and to extend it to men who
> have risked their lives and their freedom in illegal work
> against the Nazi regime. On May 17 the *Daily Herald*
> triumphantly informed its readers of a 'Secret Swoop on
> 30,000 Germans'.

Even *The Times* succumbed to the anti-refugee virus, and
demanded that no chance should be taken with "aliens". Eminent
Tories agreed. When the Secretary of State for War, Anthony
Eden, in July 1940 told Parliament that "enemy aliens" were to be
released from internment camps to serve in the Pioneer Corps, the
gallant Lieutenant-Colonel Acland-Troye, CMG, DSO, shouted:
"Will my right honourable friend bear in mind that you cannot
trust any Boche at any time?"

As the military situation deteriorated and invasion of England
seemed possible, more restrictive measures were taken. On 25 June,
the day France capitulated, an order was issued to intern all "C"
class men under 70 excepting those in a few exempted categories. (It
was assumed that an alien of 71 could not be dangerous!) By mid-
July, about 13,000 "C" class men had been rounded up.

"The press howled from one end of the country to the other, 'Intern the lot'," said Mr Rhys Davies, MP. "There were also voices in this House of Commons that spoke very nearly on the same lines. The Government succumbed and interned the lot...It is strange how man's mentality works. We remember the horror that sprang in this country when Hitler put Jews, Socialists and Communists into concentration camps...but we almost did the same thing to the same people."

The Government had now decided that as Clement Attlee, the Lord Privy Seal, put it, "in the interests of national security, it was desirable to transfer overseas a number of the enemy aliens...in order to reduce the general dangers which might arise from having large numbers of enemy aliens concentrated in a comparative small number of camps in different parts of the country".

Churchill referred to the possibility of invasion, and to the internment of suspected Fifth Columnists, when he made his historic speech to the House on 4 June ("We shall fight on the beaches, we shall fight on the landing grounds, we shall fight in the fields and in the streets, we shall fight in the hills; we shall never surrender..."). The Belgian Army had surrendered, and 335,000 badly mauled British and Allied forces had miraculously been evacuated from Dunkirk, abandoning their equipment:

> We have found it necessary [Churchill said] to take
> measures of increasing stringency not only against enemy
> aliens and suspicious characters of other nationalities, but
> also against British subjects who may become a danger or a
> nuisance should the war be transported to the United
> Kingdom. I know there are a great number of people
> affected by the orders which we have made who are the
> passionate enemies of Nazi Germany. I am sorry for them,
> but we cannot at the present time and under the present
> stress, draw all the distinctions which we should like to do.
> If parachute landings were attempted and fierce fighting
> attendant upon them followed, these unfortunate people
> would be far better out of the way, for their own sakes as
> well as for ours.

The fear of invasion was widespread. George Orwell records in his diary that left-wing intellectuals wanted Scotland Yard to destroy their police records to prevent them falling into Nazi hands. It was rumoured that the Royal Family had gone to Canada. Children whose parents could afford the fare were being evacuated by the thousands. When a Children's Overseas Reception Board was set up in London, nearly 3000 parents queued for admission on opening day. By 25 July, applications for the evacuation of 224,000 children had been received. The Minister of Information, Duff Cooper, was criticised in Parliament and the press for sending his son to Canada — but the ship that carried the boy across the Atlantic also took away the gold reserves of the Bank of England.

There was a general fear of Fifth Columnists — Nazi agents planted among anti-Nazi refugees — and British-born collaborators. This fear was exacerbated by the clamant anti-refugee propaganda of the popular press which the Government made no attempt to counter. When Mr Wilfrid Roberts, MP, asked the House what the Government had done to try to correct the false impression created by this propaganda, he received no answer. In the same session, another MP, Mr Graham White, declared: "It would be well for the Government to make a plain statement that they do not regard every alien as hostile and as an enemy." Again, there was no answer, and the cry of "Intern the lot" became more clamant.

By 2 May, more than 250,000 men had joined the Local Defence Volunteers, later to be known as the Home Guard, and the House of Commons discussed the use of shotguns and sporting rifles. It was told that both were permissible, provided they were used only with soft-nosed bullets. The other equipment issued to the Volunteers consisted of an armband and a forage cap. Some members were sceptical whether men so equipped could resist a large force of German parachutists armed with sophisticated weapons.

In June 1940, Britain faced her "darkest hour". The Norwegian campaign had failed, and Italy had declared war. A chastened General Ironside remarked to Anthony Eden: "This is the end of the British Empire."

Picture Post, a brilliant pictorial weekly, edited by a German refugee, Stephan Lorant, devoted its entire issue of 15 June to advice on how to deal with invaders. It gave expert instructions, graphically illustrated, on methods of immobilising tanks with improvised devices and countering attacks by parachutists.

On 16 August, in a long letter to *The Times*, nine London correspondents of leading newspapers in four neutral European countries pointed out that Britain's traditional reputation for fairness was being damaged by the "indiscriminate internment of refugee aliens":

> In our journalistic work we endeavour to establish a
> favourable picture of Britain's spiritual and moral strength.
> For this reason we deem it our duty to emphasise the

damaging impression created abroad by the spirit and
methods of the refugee internments. Millions of
sympathisers with Britain's case begin to doubt whether the
British ideals of humanity and justice still prevail. The
critical attitude of a number of leading personalities of
British public life raised our hopes...The fact that ample
space had been granted in the column of *The Times* to this
problem gave further nourishment to this expectation...

The Times commented: "The treatment of friendly aliens
continues to be the subject of criticism by many correspondents
who deplore what they consider in many instances to be grave
injustices." In the same issue *The Times* published a letter from a
woman who had worked among refugees, asking a number of
questions:

Cannot some system be arranged to notify relations as to
the whereabouts of their men? What is the exact situation of
aliens in Category 'C' who have been sent to the Dominion
and what means of livelihood will be provided for them? Is
the promise given to these men that their wives and children
will follow by the next transport to be broken? What is
being done to support dependants while they are waiting to
go? What is going to happen to the property of deported
friendly aliens?

The questions remained unanswered.

The sentiments of the nine foreign correspondents were
endorsed in a letter signed by Lord Cecil, Violet Bonham-Carter,
Gilbert Murray, H. G. Wells and Andrew McFadyean, a former
Treasury official, who wrote: "...A complete reversal of
Government policy is the only solution. It involves the release of all
interned friendly aliens, of whose antecedents the Home Office has
information and against whom there is no reasonable suspicion."

CHAPTER TWO

Jews were the principal targets for Hitler's malignity. Eighty per cent of the refugees in England were Jewish, and the cost of maintaining them was borne by Jewish relief organisations. Under pressure from these organisations, the Government in February 1939 sanctioned the establishment of an interim camp for male refugees aged 18 to 45, awaiting re-embarkation. The camp consisted originally of derelict army buildings at Richborough, near Ramsgate, that had been used for training Kitchener's Army in World War I. It was known as the Kitchener Camp. The refugees helped to rebuild it. They were a happy community. A booklet about the camp, titled "Some Victims of the Nazi Terror", stressed this:

> A Union Jack flies proudly overhead. Below thousands of Germans and Austrians work and sleep...Looking up at this flag there is no bitterness in their expression. There is no barbed wire, no armed sentry to be seen...This flag in their hour of need they recognise as their emblem of freedom. Each one of them, Jew or Christian, has been branded as a criminal; the Jew because of his birth, the Christian for his love of freedom. They have been driven from their homes and persecuted...These law-abiding, peace-loving people have endured torture, privation and suffering, almost beyond human endurance. Deprived of their property, destitute and often starving, these people sought sanctuary. They found it in England — in a free and happy land.

When the Archbishop of Canterbury, Dr Cosmo Lang, visited the camp, he told the refugees: "I am proud that this country has had the honour to give you a place of refuge and of hope...It will be a great thing when we in this country can look upon you, not only as refugees whom we have been glad to welcome, but also as fellow workers in a common cause.''

A similar spirit prevailed in the five camps on the Isle of Man.

Internees arriving at these camps were given a pamphlet in English and German expressing England's sympathetic attitude towards them. Dated 1 June 1940, it was signed by the commandant of the camps, Lieutenant-Colonel S. W. Slater, who wrote: ''It is my wish that every man who enters internment on this island shall be assured that nothing avoidable will be done that might add to his discomfort or unhappiness.''

After pointing out that a uniform code of discipline was essential if a community of men were to live together successfully, Slater continued:

> There is, however, a good reason for every order, and there will be no aggression. The officers and troops who are given charge of you are men of understanding. In any case, it is not a British characteristic to oppress the man who is powerless to retaliate... My duty is concerned with your security and discipline but my interest goes beyond this... I wish every permissible measure to be taken that can relieve your internment of its irksomeness... A man's internment is not regarded here as a reflection on his character. He is credited with being a man of good intent until he proves himself to be otherwise. There are among you men of widely divergent political views and religious beliefs. You will neither find favour nor encounter prejudice from us on this account...

''In all events,'' Slater concluded, ''you are assured of justice.''

It is not a British characteristic to oppress the man who is powerless to retaliate... These were stirring words. But in less than two months many refugees were to recall them with bitter disillusion.

The High Commissioner of the United Kingdom in Australia, Sir Geoffrey Whiskard, on 15 June 1940 addressed an ''URGENT AND SECRET'' letter to the Australian Prime Minister, Robert Gordon Menzies, dealing with the custody of German and Italian internees and prisoners in the United Kingdom. The total number of German male internees, he wrote, was over 12,000, of whom 2500 were definitely pro-Nazi in sympathy and allegiance, and were therefore a source of danger in the event, for example, of parachute landings or invasion. There were also 1500 male Italian professing members of the Italian Fascist Party who would have to be interned, together with some 8000 other male Italians whom it would not be safe to leave at large. In addition, there were already approximately 3000 German prisoners of war, including German seamen taken off ships.

"The custody of so large a number of dangerous or potentially dangerous persons imposes a serious burden on the authorities responsible for their custody and immobilises a considerable number of service personnel required for guarding them," Sir Geoffrey wrote. It was therefore considered most important that they should be interned as soon as possible in some area outside the United Kingdom. The Canadian Government had agreed to receive 4000 internees and 3000 prisoners. Would the Commonwealth Government also be prepared to accept internees, and if so, what would be the maximum number it would accept? Any expenditure on account of transport and maintenance would be borne by the United Kingdom. A similar request was being made to the Government of the Union of South Africa.

On 1 July Canberra informed the Secretary of State for Dominion Affairs, Viscount Caldecote, that the Commonwealth was agreeable to accepting 6000 internees and prisoners of war, and asked that particulars of the classification of the persons concerned be supplied urgently. "Provided we obtain quickly particulars of the first 4000, we will be able to make the necessary arrangements to handle them in approximately six weeks' time."

Sir Geoffrey Whiskard advised Menzies on 9 July that the United Kingdom proposed to send to Australia about 2700 men leaving on 10 July and 2600 men, women and children leaving on 15 July. A further ship would be leaving on 16 July which could take 1700 men. Could the Commonwealth Government accept 500 of these men? The New Zealand Government was being asked to accept the remainder.

The second and third ships never left England.

Menzies confirmed that Australia was prepared to receive alien internees from Britain. "Might these internees not become a great problem?" Menzies was asked in Parliament. "Whatever problem they are," Mr Menzies replied, "they would be a far greater problem in Britain." The Labor leader, John Curtin, said this type of question should be discussed by a secret session of Parliament before a decision was made.

The British public knew nothing of the Government's decision to deport internees till the evening of 3 July when the BBC announced that the preceding Tuesday (2 July) at 6 am, the 15,500 ton (15,750 tonnes) Blue Star liner, *Arandora Star*, on its way to Canada with 1500 German and Italian internees, had been torpedoed and sunk by a U-boat off the west coast of Ireland. The news bulletin described the arrogant behaviour of Nazi officers and quoted the ship's crew's description of the young Nazis as "skulking, swaggering louts". The popular newspapers devised lurid accounts of the panic on the sinking ship and everything was done to suggest that she contained only Nazis and Italian Fascists.

In the debates on the sinking of *Arandora Star* it was disclosed that she had no escort as it was not the practice to escort fast ships, and that no compensation could be paid to relatives of the victims because the ship had been sunk by enemy action.

Seven days after the sinking of *Arandora Star* the authorities, with extraordinary insensitivity, re-embarked its survivors on *Dunera* and from the same wharf from which *Arandora Star* had sailed. One of the survivors was Dr Frank Eaton, who said, "When we reached the shore, we were assured we would never be put on another ship again." (Dr Eaton was subsequently Professor of German at Portland (USA) State College.)

One Viennese boy was deported on *Arandora Star* and *Dunera* while his father remained in England making parachutes for the Royal Air Force. The father of another *Dunera* deportee was fighting in the British Army. There were many such examples of bureaucratic bungling.

Hein Heckroth was an eminent German artist and stage designer. When his work was proscribed by the Nazis, he came to England and became head of the Dartington Hall College of Arts. Dartington Hall in Totnes, Devon, perhaps the most celebrated — and most expensive — of England's "progressive" schools, was founded and endowed in 1926 by Leonard and Dorothy Elmhirst. It soon gained an international reputation for democratic co-education and the cultivation of the arts. At the outbreak of war, the College of Arts had some 65 "enemy aliens" working in it. Heckroth was shipped aboard *Dunera* without warning to his wife or his employers. (He had arranged to meet his wife at the Ritz for tea, and could not communicate with her.)

When he returned to England, Heckroth designed the striking sets for *The Red Shoes*, one of England's most successful films. The cast included Madame Rambert, Moira Shearer, Massine, Robert Helpmann and Anton Walbrook.

Heckroth died in July 1970. He was then chief designer of the Frankfurt theatre. Michael Powell wrote: "Hein Heckroth has been an elder brother to me for more than 24 years, ever since we worked together at the ballet *Red Shoes*...I think it was the first time that a painter had been given the chance to design a film including the title and it was a triumph of work and organisation. For the ballet alone he made 600 sketches and they are preserved on film in the Museum of Modern Art, New York. He was a big man in every sense, who thought things out for himself and had a great influence on his friends. He worked hard as an artist and he loved life, food and drink. He was the sort of man who leaves an almost visible gap when he dies...He loved England his adopted country and he loved London."

Heckroth was art director of a number of other notable films — including England's most ambitious production, *Caesar and Cleopatra*.

On 8 May 1940 Peter Stadlen, a young Austrian pianist, gave a very successful recitation in London's Wigmore Hall. He played ancient and modern music, ranging from Schubert to Bartók, and from Mozart to Egon Wellesz. "He is a pianist who can make such a programme interesting because he reacts instinctively to the style and spirit of each work," said *The Times*. And it complimented him on his imaginative handling of the subtle harmonies of Wellesz, a composer then practically unknown in England.

Two months later, Peter Stadlen and his brother Eric were herded on to *Dunera*.

No one in 1940 was better qualified to discuss the refugee problem than Sir Herbert Emerson, a former Governor of the Punjab, who was then Director of the Evian Committee, League of Nations High Commissioner for Refugees, Chairman of the Bloomsbury House Committee, Vice-Chairman under Lord Lytton of the Government's Advisory Council on Aliens, and a member of the Committee of Three assisting Sir John Anderson in "dealing with the problem of aliens of enemy nationality".

His mandate as High Commissioner required him

> to provide for legal and political protection of refugees...to
> facilitate the co-ordination of humanitarian assistance in
> their efforts to promote emigration and permanent
> settlement.

Despite his diverse responsibilities, Sir Herbert found time to send the Australian High Commissioner on 23 July a long and thoughtful memorandum on the treatment of refugees, with a request that it be brought to the notice of the Commonwealth Government. In it, he stressed "the essential fact" that except for "A" class, internment "did not by itself involve any disgrace or moral stigma, or create any presumption whatever that the person interned is disloyal or unreliable":

> The truth is that the great majority of the 'B' and 'C' class
> are decent, well-living persons who have gone through one
> suffering after another, and who have very good grounds

for hating the Nazi system. They belong to the same classes and the same types as provided emigrants to Canada and Australia before the war began.

Sir Herbert assumed that the question of whether all of these deportees would be interned was entirely a matter for the Australian Government to decide. "It would be impertinent for me to make any suggestion on this score," he wrote, especially as he realised that, "apart from the reliability or otherwise of the persons concerned, political considerations are involved."

However, he permitted himself to make a few suggestions, based on his experience of internment camps in Holland, Belgium and France:

It is most desirable to keep the refugees as fully employed as possible. The camp should be as self-contained as possible. While it was probably undesirable to group intellectuals in a special camp, it was desirable that they should have the company of other intellectuals. Interned musicians and actors, etc., should be encouraged to organise entertainments. It was unwise to cut off internees from news of the outside world. This only resulted in alarming rumours. As most of the internees were cut off from friends and relatives, it was most desirable to provide adequate communication facilities.

Finally, although it is understood that the refugees have been deported only for the duration of the war, and are to be returned to England at its termination, Canada and Australia may find that the deportees include many whom they would be willing to retain and who would be glad to stay, who would make excellent citizens, and who would add to the economic welfare of the country. While no hope of this kind can or should be given to the refugees, it may be worthwhile for the authorities not entirely to dismiss this possibility, and to keep their eyes open for individuals who would be a real asset, if ultimately it is possible to allow them to stay.

Sir Herbert's constructive suggestions were soon entombed and forgotten in the files of the Australian Prime Minister's Department.

HMT *Dunera*.

CHAPTER THREE

On 10 July 1940, a low grey ship lay at the Pierhead in Liverpool, loading an extraordinary cargo. The ship was HMT *Dunera*, a 12,615 ton (12,815 tonnes) trooper built in 1937, owned and manned by the British India Company, but under long charter to the British Government. (HMT stood for "Hired Military Transport.") She had a speed of 16 knots, and, as a trooper, a maximum capacity of 1600 including crew, but her "cargo" now consisted of 2542 German and Austrian internees, apart from crew and escort troops. Most of the internees were political or racial refugees, and bitter enemies of Nazism and Fascism.

Many had scarred memories of concentration camps. Nearly all had been classified "C" by the Special Aliens Tribunals. Some had volunteered to go overseas on the strength of certain promises. Others had been compulsorily recruited. They were bound for Australia though none at the time knew this. The general belief was that Canada, or the United States, was their destination. There were also 200 Italian Fascists and 251 Nazi prisoners, "A" class internees, survivors from the *Arandora Star*. These were regarded as dangerous. They included a number of German merchant seamen taken off German ships. The British Government advised that they should be detained under "conditions of strict security". The 200 Italians had been interned as members of the Fascist Party immediately after Italy had entered the war.

The refugees came from various English camps, and the promises made to them were just as various. In one camp, they were told that going overseas meant more personal freedom with the possibility of congenial work, and that their wives and children would follow soon after. In another they were told that they were going to Canada, and that their wives and children would be in the same convoy. Others were told that by volunteering they would get a free trip to the United States, where they would regain freedom of movement.

Each was allowed 80 pounds (36.3 kilograms) of luggage. For many who had fled from the Nazi terror in Germany, Austria, Holland and Belgium, this represented everything they possessed. But it was with high hopes that the men arrived in Liverpool to embark. The high hopes were soon shattered. The ship that was to carry them to "freedom" was, in effect, a floating concentration camp.

As the bewildered refugees filed on to the landing stage, they were subjected to a brutal search. To quote from a report later submitted by the victims to the British Government:

> Everything carried in the hand or in pockets was taken off the internees. All less valuable effects like gloves, toilet utensils, eatables, pipes, etc. were thrown on the ground. Valuables were stuffed into sacks or disappeared openly into the pockets of the searching soldiers. Soon rows of emptied wallets were lying on the deck. Valuable documents, identity and emigration papers, testimonials of all kinds, were taken away, thrown on the ground or even ostentatiously torn up before the eyes of their owners...'You will not need these again as you will be sent back to Germany after the War,' said one of the soldiers. Appeals to the officers standing by were fruitless. Attempts at protests were roughly suppressed...Of all the articles taken away on the landing stage, only a very few were ever seen again...In some cases even toothbrushes, soap, notebooks, were removed...All these searches were carried out without any discrimination, accompanied by acts of violence, and resulted in the loss of an enormous amount of money, valuable articles, toilet necessities, and important documents.

The commander of the escort troop, Lieutenant-Colonel Scott, and First Lieutenant O'Neill witnessed all this but made no attempt to restrain their men. (William Patrick Scott, a World War I veteran, was gazetted Major in the 14th London Regiment, Territorial Army, in November 1934. He was transferred to the Pioneer Corps as a substantive Major in November 1939 and was given the acting rank of Lieutenant-Colonel on his appointment to the *Dunera* command.)

A 58-year-old refugee, Moritz Chlumetski, stumbled up the gangplank carrying a violin case. He explained to the guards that it contained a valuable instrument belonging to his son, also an internee. The guard responded by bashing Chlumetski's foot with a rifle butt. Another seized the violin and Lieutenant O'Neill pushed

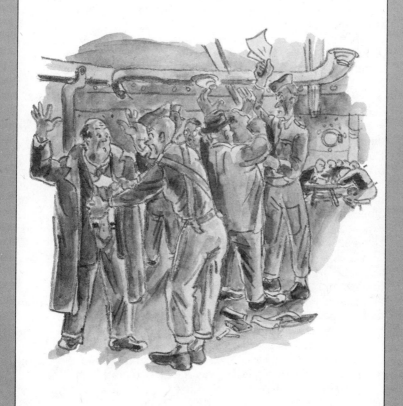

Artist F. Schonbach, who was to capture many such moments during his time as an internee, records the brutal search men were forced to undergo when first boarding the *Dunera*.

(Schonbach Graphics)

Chlumetski with bleeding foot on to the deck.

René von Podbielski, a Junker nobleman, was carrying the manuscript of a novel on which he had been working for years. It was seized by a guard and thrown overboard.

"When I boarded the horror ship," said K. J. Koenig, a Prague solicitor who later practised in Sydney, "I was asked in a friendly way by two commissioned officers to hand over all my valuables. When I requested a receipt, I was smilingly told that I could trust a British officer, and that this was for my own protection. And my luggage was taken into 'safe custody' by a non-commissioned officer. Needless to say, I never saw valuables or luggage again."

Embarkation took place during the day to a rather unfriendly demonstration from all who witnessed it...

During the confusion, a taxi pulled up outside the wharf building and from it stepped a brisk, thick-set man named Sigurd Lohde. He carried a steamer ticket to the Isle of Man and an official document confirming his appointment as a German interpreter in one of the internment camps. To his bewilderment, he was ordered by a British soldier to board the ship lying alongside. Lohde protested. "I have a ticket to the Isle of Man," he explained. The guard's reply, emphasised by the lowering of his bayonet, was a curt, "Get going!"

Uncomprehendingly, Lohde boarded *Dunera*. "It's a mistake, a stupid mistake," was all he could say. His later protests to English and Australian authorities were ignored.

Lohde was a well-known Austrian actor who had appeared in many European plays and films, often portraying military men. His last role in Europe was Napoleon in Mussolini's forgettable play, *Hundred Days*. (Mussolini sent him a telegram congratulating him on his performance.) When the Nazis banned him from acting, he practised for a while in Austria as a radiotherapist, before escaping to England where he was in turn a window cleaner, a film actor (*Night Train to Munich, Sailors Three*) and a BBC announcer on its German service.

According to Heinz Koppel, Lohde was not the only internee to be wrongly shipped in *Dunera*. "I was one of 320 men coming from Lingfield Racecourse...destined for Huyton Camp, near Liverpool. We were redirected on to a railtrack leading to the dockside and promptly bundled on board ship." Later, Koppel learned that 320 evening meal rations had been prepared for men who never showed up.

Dunera sailed at about midnight with a single destroyer escort in convoy with a big Cunarder evacuating children. As well as the internees she carried a guard of seven officers and 309 other ranks.

It consisted of a company of Pioneer Corps and reservists from various regiments. There was also a naval contingent and a Lascar crew.. "The ship was grossly over-crowded," said her First Officer, L. W. Smith. "She was carrying about one thousand men above her permitted capacity."

As the internees shuffled into their gloomy quarters, an officer of the guard with a whimsical sense of humour addressed some of them: "To those of you who have survived the *Arandora Star*, I have some reassuring words: if this ship should be torpedoed, we have made sure that none of you will get out."

Less than 24 hours after leaving Liverpool *Dunera* was attacked by a German submarine. At 9.20 am on the morning of 12 July as she was ploughing through a heavy sea off the north coast of Ireland, the German U-boat U-56 under the command of Oberleutnant Zur See Harms fired two torpedoes at a range of about 1500 metres. What happened to them is not clear. There are several versions of the attack. Scott's account given to Sydney newspapermen was: "We were in convoy with a ship evacuating children and the alarm was given, and the children's ship with our destroyer escort steamed off at full speed. The torpedoes passed underneath. We crammed on full speed and guns were manned." In another interview Scott added that both torpedoes had exploded after passing under the ship.

A member of *Dunera's* crew who signed himself "Semaphore", in a highly coloured and not always reliable account of the voyage which he sold to a Sydney newspaper, wrote in his diary:

> We were plunging through a heavy Atlantic gale today,
> when our convoy destroyer was seen to be rapidly signalling
> to us. The whole ship, by some strange miracle, seemed to
> see it at the same moment. 'Full speed ahead. You are being
> attacked,' the destroyer wig-wagged. Orders were shouted
> from the bridge. Two loud explosions seemed to come from
> under the ship...it swung rapidly, lurched drunkenly. At
> the after end of the ship, the prisoners were running about
> with life jackets on, screaming advice to one another.
> Suddenly, as if prearranged, they panicked. About 50 of
> them dashed on to the deck, crashed through a wooden
> door and on to the barbed wire...The refugees behaved less
> violently, but also with panic. They put on life jackets and
> rushed the boats. Some of them clambered in, but then they
> just sat there as if the boat would lower itself. Others were
> not so anxious, and were held back by the sentries, who had
> fixed bayonets...A private coolly released the safety-catch

of a rifle and faced the maddened, fear-crazed, desperate men. He took aim and fired. The bullet whistled over their heads and passed clean through a thick steel bulkhead. They paused, the private addressed them with grim British humour: 'I have a lot more left, the next one who moves gets a bullet through him.' After a short pause, the prisoners slowly turned back. By this time...there were other guards present all with bayoneted rifles and safety-catches up.

After the first dull explosions the ship began to swerve madly. Observers on the bridge saw the long white trail of a torpedo heading swiftly amidships, and incredibly it passed right under the hull. Another missed by a few feet as the ship swung round. What had happened was in that heavy sea we had been riding on a wave instead of plunging into a trough, the very moment the torpedo was calculated to strike us.

The Cunarder was now far ahead, a spot on the horizon. The destroyer was also rapidly drawing away, dropping depth charges as she went. Both were soon out of sight.

"Semaphore's" extravagant account is not substantiated by Smith, who gave this recollection of the incident:

Off the north coast of Ireland a sudden explosion severely shook the ship and we immediately thought we'd been torpedoed. However, a quick look over the ship's sides revealed no damage and a search for a sabotage bomb within the ship found nothing, neither was the ship taking in any water. There was some slight concussion damage in the engine-room, but otherwise the ship was undamaged. Some panic did occur among the internees, which was not altogether surprising as some of them were survivors of the *Arandora Star*. A sentry in the after part of the vessel had fired his rifle over their heads, as there had been some attempt to break out of the cage. A signal from our escort asked us if we'd been torpedoed, so the shock of the explosion must have been felt about half a mile [0.80 kilometres] away. None of the lookouts, or anybody else had seen an explosion in the water close to the ship, and the whole affair still remains a complete mystery. The Royal Navy afterwards offered the suggestion that it could have been caused by a self-destroying torpedo at the end of its run close to the ship. If this was the case, why had nobody seen the explosion? The same question would have arisen in the case of an acoustic mine or an aerial bomb. These are the facts as I recall them. I have no theories to offer.

Many of the refugees claim to have experienced two heavy bumps. One wrote:

> There was this strong knock against the ship's side, and everybody forgets his sea-sickness...and rushes for the only staircase which leads to the upper-deck, the only one available for eight hundred people to reach freedom. The stairs are completely jammed, and when there is a second, stronger knock, everybody thinks the end has arrived. It is impossible to move up or down. On the Italians' deck, everyone falls to his knees and begins desperately to pray. After about five minutes the 'All Clear' sounds and calm is restored. Later we hear a torpedo raised the keel of the ship.

Rear-Admiral Charles Hogger commented: "It is almost impossible to miss a large steamer with two torpedoes at 1500 metres." His theory is that either the gyro setting was wrong or that the depth setting gear of the "fish" was defective. The Germans, he points out, were having trouble with their torpedoes in the early days of the war. "The torpedoes could so have passed under *Dunera* and gone off either at the end of their run as the British Navy says, or on impact with the bottom of the sea."

The entry in the U-boat's war diary reads:

> 12-7-40, 0940 hours, AM 5345; About 150 degrees steamer in sight in haze, inclination red, Alert!
> After about 20 minutes big steamer sighted, passenger ship, one funnel, inclination green 80.
> 1006 hours two torpedoes fired at range 1500 metres, boat slipped under water during shot. Target changed course immediately after firing, therefore target missed ahead. Destroyer ahead of steamer, second steamer in same bearing but at much greater distance...Two explosions after 8 min. 13 seconds, 8 min. 33 seconds respectively. Sound of explosions as otherwise observed, similar to aircraft bombs (depth charges?) Both explosions accompanied by rattling/pattering noise. Ships' propeller noise starboard abeam well audible, destroyer approaches at high speed, but turns away.
> Size of steamer assessed at 15,000 BRT.

One refugee who retains a unique memory of the incident is Dr Kurt Enderl, later a distinguished Austrian diplomat, with posts in New Delhi, New York, Israel, Poland, Hungary and England. He retired as Ambassador to the Court of St James in 1978. Dr Enderl was occupying one of the much sought-after lavatory seats, when the attack took place. Whatever caused the "bump", it was

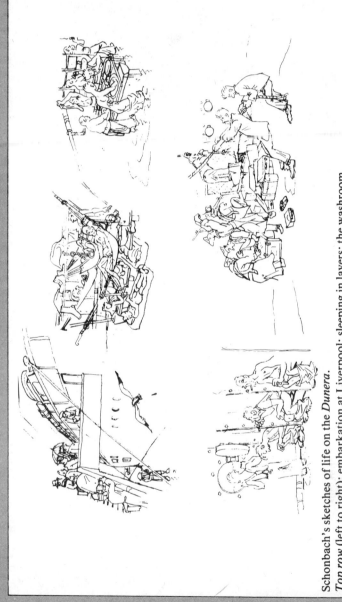

Schonbach's sketches of life on the *Dunera*.
Top row (left to right): embarkation at Liverpool; sleeping in layers; the washroom.
Bottom row: illegal smoking of butts in the latrine; luggage being opened, searched and stowed away.
(Schonbach Graphics)

strong enough to catapult him into the air!

Conditions on the ship were appalling. As the lower decks were at least 50 per cent over-crowded, many internees had to sleep on mess tables or on the floor throughout the voyage. Staircases and every available inch of floor space were constantly occupied. Had a disaster occurred, this over-crowding alone would have made lifesaving impossible, as the ship's captain, Captain Caffyn, confided to the medical officer, Lieutenant Brooks. In any case, no lifebelts were issued and no emergency drill was carried out. Prisoners of war had barbed wire enclosures on the aft deck where they could enjoy the luxury of fresh air. Most of the internees were kept below decks.

On the first night at sea, it was forbidden to visit the latrines. Buckets were provided for urine. These soon overflowed, and as the ship rolled and pitched, sewage flooded the decks. In the midst of this, men on the floor were trying to sleep.

"What do I remember about the *Dunera* voyage?" asked H. B. Shaye. "There was that single bucket in our hold that was supposed to serve as our latrine. I remember it mainly because of the stink and the spillage due to the movement of the ship. But, stink or no stink, I had my eye on that miserable utensil for use in the event of the ship going down. I had an idea of upending the thing and trapping air in it like a diving bell, thus outlasting most others, and, hopefully, making it out of that barbed wire gate. All sounds a bit naive now, but at least it was an idea which I was mentally going over repeatedly, trying to include every possible negative and positive eventuality."

For weeks all hatches were battened down, and neither daylight nor fresh air ever reached the decks below. The atmosphere was noisome. The portholes remained permanently closed, except, during certain times, in the galley, the washrooms and latrines. When these portholes were open, men queued around them, trying to breathe a little fresh air. No inoculations for typhoid and cholera were given, and medical supplies were inadequate.

On one deck, about two dozen toilet seats were provided for 1600 men. Because the salt water flushing was too violent, some of these seats became smeared with a mixture of salt water and excrement, making them unusable. Long lines of men, many suffering from violent diarrhoea or sea sickness, queued outside the remaining seats. In rough seas, the latrine floors were a hideous lake of sewage. There was a constant shortage of toilet paper. The usual daily quota was two sheets per person.

Shaving materials, combs and brushes had been confiscated,

First Lieutenant O'Neill, VC.
(John Fairfax & Sons Ltd)

and unkempt beards produced an epidemic of skin diseases. At first, the internees were without towels or soap. Later, one towel was issued to every 10 men. (Most of these towels came from the rifled suitcases.) And a piece of soap was issued once or twice a week to every 20 men.

Food was monotonous, when it was not inedible. It consisted mostly of smoked fish, sausages, potatoes, with a spoonful of melon and lemon jam a day. Often the bread was maggoty and the butter and margarine rancid. Fred Schonbach said: "I remember sitting on the floor with a mug of soup, carefully removing the bodies of little white maggots before I drank it. Everything else tasted too awful, and the greatest delicacy was an occasional raw onion." Klaus Loewald recalls "the battles for the last prune in the tapioca".

Chess sets were made from inedible bread, and loaves hollowed out to hide possessions in. Wooden spoons were the only cutlery permitted. When spoons were lost, the internees replaced them by whittling substitutes from wooden packing cases. One day a carving knife was found to be missing from the galley, and an intensive search was carried out. During the search a wooden spoon was discovered with a message written on it: "HMT DUNERA PRISONERS ABOARD." How this inscribed spoon, even if picked up by a vigilant U-boat, would threaten the safety of *Dunera* is not clear, but the military reacted to the discovery violently. Internees were threatened that their food and light would be curtailed unless the culprit confessed. The culprit did not confess.

The *London Gazette* on 26 December 1918 announced that Sergeant John O'Neill, MM, 2nd Battalion, Leinster Regiment, had been awarded the Victoria Cross for "conspicuous gallantry" in France near Moorseele, on 14 October 1918. The citation read:

> When the advance of his company was checked by two
> machine guns and an enemy field battery firing over open
> sights, at the head of eleven men he charged the battery,
> capturing four field guns, two machine guns, and 16
> prisoners. Again, on the morning of 20 October 1918,
> Sergeant O'Neill, with one man, rushed an enemy machine
> gun position, routing about 100 enemy and causing many
> casualties.

O'Neill behaved with less conspicuous gallantry when, as First Lieutenant O'Neill, VC, he boarded *Dunera* as an officer of the escort troop. Encouraged by the Lieutenant, most of his men behaved with a conspicuous brutality that would have won approval from the late Otto Streicher.

During one of their periodic searches, Jewish religious vestments, prayer books and phylacteries were seized. Some of these vestments had been saved from burning synagogues in Germany. When an internee, Chief Rabbi Ehrentreu, complained, Lieutenant O'Neill threatened to "hang him at the mast, swing him by his beard round the mast, and throw him overboard". On another occasion, two internees found out of bounds were tied to a post by O'Neill, who was apparently very drunk and called them "German Jewish swine", and "sons of German Jewish dogs". One was beaten until he bled. "His screams of pain could be heard from afar," said an eye witness. At Cape Town, O'Neill returned to the ship with some of his men, all very drunk. He repeated several times *"Du bist ein Schwein und dein Vater ist ein Schwein"* ("You are a pig and your father is a pig") and challenged one of the young internees to box with him. He hit one of the boys so hard that the boy collapsed. On another occasion he tied two boys together, back to back, pretending to strangle them, tying a rope round their necks, and had them sent to the bunker.

Among the men who staggered back to the ship, heavily freighted with South African liquor, was an assistant troop cook who, aglow with bonhomie, entered a latrine and kissed one of the internees. He had previously been twice cautioned; the first time for fraternising with internees, and the second for causing a disturbance. He had also tried to obtain cigarettes for trading with internees, in strict contravention of the Master's orders. When these grim facts were read over to him, he replied: "Please don't ruin my discharge."

Kicks, blows from rifle butts and savage beatings by the troops were a daily occurrence. Complaints only resulted in more ill-treatment.

During the early part of the voyage the internees were not allowed to use the gangway to the lavatories. One who endeavoured to reach the lavatory was stabbed through the barbed wire with a bayonet. He was taken to the hospital on a stretcher, bleeding badly. Lieutenant Brooks found that a muscle was pierced, but luckily the stomach was not hurt. In consequence of the lack of cleaning and washing facilities, many skin diseases, impetigo, furunculosis, etc., occurred, but much worse were the violent attacks of diarrhoea from which only a small percentage escaped. One internee who complained to a sergeant that a guard had been stealing from the internees' clothing was handcuffed, beaten with fists, and hit on the feet with a rifle butt. "Now you will be fucking sorry you spoke," the sergeant said during the beating. Another who complained that an officer of the Royal Tank Corps had taken from him a pair of diamond earrings and a diamond brooch, was told by the sergeant-major, "You cocker! Don't talk so much or you'll be into the bunker. Get away now." The jewels, of course, were never returned.

There were three cells in the bunker. Early in the voyage a boy allegedly made disparaging remarks about the food and was locked up for 30 days. Other internees were capriciously imprisoned for varying periods and beaten at the same time.

Dr Fleischer, who had seen a corporal take a valuable platinum watch from a refugee, made a written statement to the commandant. He was told by Scott, after being intimidated by a police sergeant and some NCOs several times, that he, Scott, would not take proceedings against the corporal, who had denied the charge. It would amount to believing the words of an enemy alien instead of a British soldier. Scott added that he did not wish to be bombarded by internees with letters "regarding their alleged property" and he could not act as amateur detective.

P. W. Johnson, who came to England as a schoolboy, maintains that Scott was the biggest thief of them all, and claims to have seen him pocketing items from rifled suitcases.

One morning at about 1 am a soldier entered the deck where a young internee, Leo Roth, was sleeping and noticed a gold signet ring on his outstretched hand. The soldier woke Roth and demanded the ring. When the young man explained that he was unable to remove it, the soldier angrily took him to the washroom and, with the aid of soap and water, painfully forced it off. In doing so, he injured the finger and next day Roth had to attend hospital. Brooks asked what had caused the injury and made an official report of the incident. He also sent a sardonic note to Scott: "If one of your soldiers wants to remove a ring, I will do it aseptically and surgically in my room. Don't tear it off skin and all."

As befitted an English officer and gentleman, Colonel Scott generally remained aloof from his scruffy foreign passengers, leaving the dirty work of administration to his subordinates, especially Lieutenant O'Neill. But on two occasions he condescended to address some of the internees.

His first oration, delivered to the deck leaders of the foredeck on 19 July, was mercifully short. "I have to speak to you," he said, "but do not want to be asked by you any questions. I have been called to the War Office in order to receive precise orders concerning your treatment. The safety of the transport is my first task and my foremost concern. I have to carry out this task. You will be treated according to instructions received. As to your belongings, all your property will be restored." The following day,

Scott addressed all the deck leaders of the aft deck, except the leaders of the Nazis. This time he was more eloquent, if a little obscure:

> Pay attention [he began], I have to speak to you but I do
> not want to be asked any questions. I do not want to be
> bombarded with individual applications and especially I do
> not want my officers to be bothered by you. I am in charge
> of this transport and I have found out that quite a number
> of people amongst you are refugees. But it also has come to
> my knowledge that some of you claim to be such refugees,
> but who are not. I and my officers have definite proof in
> my possession that there are dangerous people amongst
> you... There are genuine cases. I know that it is not for me
> to decide who is a genuine case, and who is not. I was also
> told that some of you have come to my country seeking the
> hospitality of it and who after having been granted this
> hospitality have abused it by volunteering to go and running
> away from my country when the war situation looked bad. I
> give you my word that my country is far from being in a
> bad way and further I promise you that my country will win
> the war. I have also been told that some of you were
> promised that they will be shipped to the USA. I know
> nothing about this. As regards your valuables I can tell you
> that there are a lot of them in my safe and they will be
> returned to you. If a watch goes astray here and there, you
> as intelligent men will understand that my officers cannot
> have their eyes everywhere and this is no concern of mine.
> You have been led up the path. I am not like the
> commandant of the IOM [Isle of Man], and what I promise
> I keep. I was told a different story as I have received
> definite instructions as to your treatment. In order to clarify
> the whole position, I have made a report to the War Office,
> which will be posted in the next port, and in which I have
> made a recommendation that the genuine cases be re-
> shipped to the USA.
> I warn you my officers have complained that you are
> running after them with requests, applications, complaints.
> If you do not stop this I shall have to consider what steps I
> shall have to take against you.

About the same time as he delivered these homilies, Scott paraded his troops and addressed them in a somewhat different vein: "I am only too aware that were we in the position of our guests [the internees]," he said, "after being searched, we would be lucky if we had our belly buttons left." And he continued:

So therefore, I close an eye to any little petty offence of purloining articles. I'm an old soldier, and I know that the British Tommy looks upon a time like this as an opportunity to help himself to any unattended trifles. When I inspected your company the other morning, I could not help seeing little articles, which I'm sure did not come aboard with you, but it has reached my ears that a certain number of people have started to loot cases. This must immediately cease, but I'm damned if I'm going to punish any man, unless this really ought to be done.

One internee, Fred Gruen, devised an ingenious way of safeguarding two English pound notes — his sole capital — by concealing them in the lining of his tie, which he never removed even when sweating fearfully in the tropics. (Vienna-born Gruen was a student at Hern Bay College, Kent, when he was deported. In 1946 he graduated from the University of Melbourne and later held many important academic posts including the Chair of Agricultural Economics at the Australian National University. From 1973 to 1976 he was Senior Agricultural Consultant to the Australian Government.)

Equally ingenious was the way some internees safeguarded their watches. Assuming that the looting soldiers would not make an intimate search of their bodies, they suspended the watches from the buttons on the inside of their flies.

After some days of incarceration in the mephitic bowels of the ship, small parties of internees were compelled to take exercise on the upper deck. Brooks had insisted on them having a ration of fresh air. They had to run or walk fast with bare feet around the deck for from 10 to 15 minutes. At each end of the deck Lewis guns were kept trained on them. Those who did not move fast enough were driven along by blows from rifle butts or fists. A Roman Catholic priest and a rabbi were among those assaulted. On one occasion a sergeant playfully threw an empty beer bottle among the exercising internees. The bottle broke, and the internees were driven over the splintered glass, to the amusement of the watching Lascars. Dr Koenig recalled the ordeal of this compulsory exercise: "We were treated in a most undignified manner by mostly drunken commissioned officers, NCOs and soldiers of the guard. I was one of the party forced to run over the broken bottle. There was no one in the party whose feet were not cut and bleeding after the run."

Koenig offered two explanations for the soldiers' monstrous behaviour. "The first is that the transport was arranged shortly after the evacuation from Dunkirk. Our guard, who, I understand,

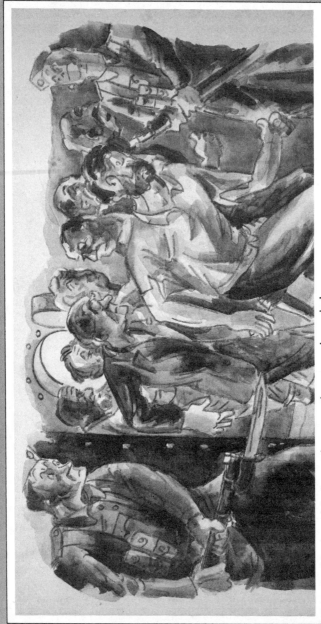

Schonbach's view of the harrowing compulsory exercise period.
(Schonbach Graphics)

had all been involved in this shattering experience, probably thought that the war was lost and wanted only to have a good time in their own way by heavy drinking and by sadistic treatment of defenceless people who were in their hands.''

The other explanation was that "on occasions when Army units were requested to make personnel available for special duties, commanding officers took the opportunity of getting rid of undesirables, and so it happened that the scum of the British Army became the guards of internees on board a ship''.

"There are some extraordinary people among the refugees on this ship," "Semaphore" wrote in his diary.

> An Austrian lawyer tells me that there are altogether 14 lawyers, several with degrees in British law. There is a reporter from the *Berliner Tageblatt* who is proud of his friendship with a Turkish pasha whom he never fails to mention in conversation.
>
> There is a man who was once a leading variety agent in Berlin with an interest in La Scala Opera House and the famous circus Sarasani. There is 'Zeppi', a famous acrobat, Tyrolese dancer and strong man. There are a number of men whom the others address as 'Doctor' — it is difficult to know what kind of doctors. There are four or five professors, an artist of great distinction, and a world famous psychologist.
>
> But I think more typical is a young boy with only one arm who helps in the cook's galley who never says anything. I asked him: 'Where do you come from?' 'Vienna,' he said. 'Gay Vienna,' I said. 'I was in prison there,' he said. 'Have you been in prison?' I asked in surprise because he seemed so young. 'Yes, nearly everyone was when Hitler took Austria,' he said. 'What did you do then? You must have done something.' 'Well, you see, I am a Jew, and...' He did not finish.

CHAPTER FOUR

Two writers have published descriptions of what life was like below deck. Walter Kaufmann was born in Berlin in 1914. At the age of two he was adopted by parents who 13 years later were killed by the Nazis. He escaped to England and was attending the Herrlingen School in Kent when he was shipped to Australia. In his novel *The Turn of the Spiral* he writes of an obviously autobiographical character, whose world on *Dunera* "has been reduced to a dark corner in the tween-deck":

> Somewhere between the hammocks burns a feeble bulkhead
> light, and when the hammocks sway, as the ship sways, even
> that is intermittently obscured. Darkness. Time drags. Is it
> night or day? No one knows for certain. Way up above, the
> square of the hatch has remained covered so long that nights
> and days have begun to merge. There is no perceptible
> division between morning, noon and night. At last the
> weather breaks — how much later, one week, two weeks
> later? — and now, for a period each day, the guards remove
> the covers from the hatch. But his corner of the tween-deck
> remains in darkness. Only the far edge of the table under his
> hammock catches enough light for reading. And that edge is
> constantly claimed by others, by those older, stronger...

Werner Isaac Pelz was born in Berlin in 1921, of middle-class Jewish parents. His father had been a Prussian soldier, an extra at the Staatsoper and the Staatstheater, and the owner of a chain of cinemas, which he lost during the Depression. When Hitler came to power, he was a shop assistant in a fashionable Berlin men's store. Leaving his parents, Werner went to England in July 1939 and was working as a farm-hand at Sutton Bank, near Beverley, when he was interned. He was one of the few who volunteered for the

Dunera. "I was convinced that no one would dream of sending us half-way round the world just to put us in another camp," he wrote in his autobiography, *Distant Strains of Triumph.* "I discovered too late that the logic of war follows its own rules." He describes "the large dim womb" that bore him into a new world:

> We slept in four layers. On hammocks, on the tables, the
> benches, the floor. The first night was unkind. Rhythmically
> and spasmodically the ceiling attracted and repelled our
> hammocks. In the dim haze beneath us, bodies rolled and
> moaned and then one here and one there and more and
> more exploded in true wretchedness. The sultry air turned
> thick and sour.

Next to him hung a lean, angular Jewish youth with an Oxford accent. In a few heavings of their hammocks, he took Pelz through the philosophies of Locke, Berkeley, Hume, Spencer, Spengler, Russell and Whitehead, criticising their systems and outlining his own. "Hegel is bunkum," he said, as they climbed out of their hammocks.

> For hours that night we walked backwards and
> forward...past bodies straining towards the evil-smelling
> latrine, past bodies returning, tottering, hopeless; over
> bodies rolling under our feet.

Sanitary conditions in another part of the ship were described by a prisoner of war, Captain P. K. Wieting, an officer of the German merchant marine and a survivor of the *Arandora Star*:

> ...there were far too few lavatories and these could only be
> reached via the one flight of stairs to the main deck. The
> only way to overcome this was to organise a roster system,
> by which the refugees were queued up in front of the stairs
> and then let through in groups of 10 at a time.

Captain Wieting and his colleagues occupied deck space aft on the starboard side, from which they could look down through a hatch on the appalling conditions of the refugees below:

> The smell coming from the lower deck became nearly
> unbearable...We merchant seamen were ordered to clean it
> up...with hoses, brooms and squeegees.

Captain Wieting recalls a revealing incident that took place five or six days out of Liverpool:

> We were led in groups into a hold in the other part of the
> vessel. There we found large piles of clothing in separate

37

heaps of coats, trousers, shirts, etc. These were the suitcases confiscated by the guards from the refugees...We were told we could take anything we needed...

After the war Captain Wieting joined an Australian oil exploration ship.

Despite their squalid living conditions, the internees managed to preserve some intellectual and cultural life. Professor Peter Meyer composed a *Dunera Mass*, and organised a choir to sing it. There were lectures on music and counterpoint, on literature, economics, agriculture and geography. There were language classes, vocal concerts and debates.

Compounding the suffering of the internees was the complete blackout on news which Scott imposed. An internee who had retained a school atlas attempted to plot the ship's course, but their first contact with the outside world took place at Cape Town when a crew member was induced to smuggle them a South African newspaper. This was given to Dr Franz Borkenau, who spent hours collating and interpreting the news items.

Borkenau, one of the fortunate occupants of a hammock, lectured from it, as from a university podium, on contemporary politics. The internees could have had no more distinguished mentor than this eminent Austrian historian and sociologist. From 1921 till 1929 he had been a member of the German Communist Party, and in the last months of his membership an active agent of the Comintern. But he gradually became disillusioned. "I had already doubted for some time the correctness of Communist policy," he later wrote. "Closer contact with its machinery made me decide to break with it." He became an influential anti-Communist and anti-Nazi propagandist. He twice visited Spain during the civil war, was imprisoned briefly, and in 1937 published what George Orwell described as "the best book yet written about the subject", *The Spanish Cockpit*. The following year he published *The Communist International*, an authoritative exposé of Russian duplicity.

An equally distinguished lecturer in a different sphere was Dr Ludwig Hirschfeld. Born at Frankfurt-am-Main in 1899, he had served as an officer in World War I and had been decorated with the Iron Cross. After the war, he graduated at the Munich Academy of Art, and became a student apprentice and part-time teacher at the Bauhaus, the cradle of modern architecture, where Walter Gropius harnessed such diverse talents as Kandinsky, Moholy-Nagy, Joseph Albers and Paul Klee.

After leaving the Bauhaus, Hirschfeld taught in various

German schools until 1936. Hitler had come to power, and Hirschfeld's grandmother was Jewish. No longer able to work in Germany, he sought refuge in England and joined the Peckham Institute, where he developed his "Colour Band". This was a device in which instruments such as xylophones and guitars had their different keys and strings painted different colours. The conductor displays a colour disc, and the players follow by playing keys or strings of the same colour.

In Wales he taught crafts to unemployed miners, and when World War II broke out he was Art Master at Dulwich College, until his internment.

Gerd Buchdahl, who had managed to smuggle a copy of Joad's *Guide to Philosophy* on board, gave philosophy lectures, reading from the sections on Plato and Aristotle to a packed and enthusiastic audience. Buchdahl also arranged English lessons, and was the co-author, with Peter Herbst and a lawyer named Laske, of the famous *Dunera* "constitution" (a scheme of self-government for the internees). This historic document, which occupied a large part of a roll of toilet paper, became the basis of the organisation subsequently adopted in the Australian internment camps.

Buchdahl, who recalled the persecution he had suffered as a schoolboy in Germany, found that internment produced an attitude of defensiveness. "I knew exactly how to adjust myself to people whom I regarded as persecuting."

Peter Herbst went to school in England, but his Cambridge studies were cut short by lack of money. He was then accepted for the Officers' Training Corps, but was not called up in the first year of the war because equipment was lacking. He was studying full-time at London University when he was interned.

"Perhaps the greatest hardships were suffered by orthodox Jews," said Asher Joseph. "The food itself was *treif* [not conforming with Jewish dietary laws] and the *kosher* people had only some dried vegetables, onions and fruit available. Ship's biscuits were consumed only by the very ill. Many of the devotional objects and religious books had been thrown overboard." But there were "true spiritual leaders among us who projected cheer and encouragement. Scholars gave talks on Torah learning, and whoever had managed to save a little book or a few pages of *Chumash, Mishnah,* or *Gemarrah* in his pocket, taught from them. A few pairs of tephillin which still held together served about 200 religious Jews on board. The rabbis also decided who among the sick people should eat what, in order to survive."

Looking back on his fellow-internees many years after the

nightmare voyage, Dr Peter Huppert, a Sydney psychiatrist, recalled the diverse groups "sometimes formed on the spot, sometimes already cohesive before embarkation":

The largest group appeared to be the one of the orthodox Jews with their small skull-caps and beards, who had somehow managed to hang on to their Talmuds and Bibles and throughout appeared oblivious to all hardships. Then there was a group of Sudeten German Communists, all gentiles, a rough and intimidating lot who immediately organised a latrine cleaning and deck cleaning service and coerced others into participation. The next group appeared to be a snobbish band of university youngsters sporting Oxford accents and behaving as if they were at Henley. They throughout maintained that the way the British treated us was perfectly understandable and would no doubt be rectified once the muddle had been sorted out. The rest of us would be the amorphous bunch of men between the age groups of 16 and I believe 65, Jewish, half-Jewish, gentiles, with a sprinkling of Nordic types, whom we vaguely suspected of being U-boat prisoners.

To pass the time, I joined the bridge playing section as well as an ad hoc debating society and what we termed the 'Staff Conference'. My particular group of bridge cronies took the view that the British, with their usually deficient organising methods, had muddled us up with German POWs and were, at the moment, treating us as such. Hence our disgust and despair with their notorious muddle-headedness or what we regarded as such. The people worried most were holders of USA affidavits, an irreplaceable document, which our unspeakable Pioneer Corps guards had thrown holus bolus overboard. There was deep gloom and even despair amongst these men.

By contrast to the gloom merchants, there were some extraordinarily cheery, physically fit and helpful youngsters, some of whom had been at sea before and helped us to sling our hammocks and find our sea legs. To this day I admire these 'unquenchables', as I termed them, and take my hat off to them. Some of these lads managed to get themselves jobs as stewards with the officers on deck and so supplied us with scraps of information as to the course of the ship, the state of the war and such like. They supplied the 'Staff Conference', a bunch of self-appointed experts who met around the mess table attempting to plot our course and hypothesising about the state of the war. I can recall the person of Franz Borkenau, and was most impressed with the

seemingly profound speculations as to the Battle of Dakar
which was being fought as we rounded West Africa.

The next shock came when our so-called expert declared
we were definitely not bound for America, but quite
possibly for South Africa. Most of the volunteers on the
ship had hoped America was their destination.

Talk of suicide was not uncommon, but, surprisingly, only one
internee took this way out. On the morning of 21 August, as
Dunera was encountering a strong head-wind and a heavy sea, an
elderly internee, exercising on the upper deck, dashed to the side of
the ship and threw himself over. He was particularly depressed
because his passport, with an Argentine visa, had been torn up and
thrown overboard.

The ship's siren sounded "Accident stations", her engines
were stopped and reversed, and lifebelts thrown out. But there was
no sign of the man.

The official account of the suicide reads:

21.8.40: *Dunera*, 9.38 am.
Lat. 32 degrees, 36′ S.
Long. 83 degrees, 02′ E.
At this hour the alarm was raised of 'Man Overboard'.
The emergency boats' crew were mustered, extra lookouts
posted and vessel manoeuvred to Master's order. As at
10.30 am there was nothing visible of the man, the life
buoys (three) were picked up, and 10.38 the vessel
proceeded on her voyage.
Private W. Lamb said, 'I was on duty near the ship's
dispensary door whilst internees were exercising. 30 men
were coming aft. After about 10 men had passed me, one
jumped on the rail, and went overboard. The other internees
stood spellbound. I attempted to get to him, but was too
late and shouted "Man Overboard". I looked over the side
and saw that the man made no attempt to swim.'
Siegfried Fiegelstock (an internee): 'We were exercising
as usual, when Jakob Weiss, who was following, pushed me
on side and vaulted over the ship's side.' Fiegelstock
volunteered that he had heard there were suicidal tendencies
in Weiss's family, also that Weiss had been depressed during
the past week, thinking of the future and his inability to get
work.

An elderly Jewish refugee, Walter Meyer, described the voyage as
"disagreeable but not dangerous". He was an old soldier, and
stronger than most of his co-religionists, he said. Confronted by

one of the "Dunkirk heroes", he exclaimed, "Try to touch me and you will go overboard with me." And the "hero" went away. "This is always the same," said Meyer. "Prison guards and similar types attack only the weak and helpless."

Meyer summed up philosophically: "I learned a lot about living together with a crowd of human beings, and now understand the 'white apes' better. You see everything has 97 sides. This is the story of an old man. The young men had trouble with sex and suffered from internment more."

Other internees held the opposite view. It was the aged who suffered most, they argued. The young were more adaptable and had a sense of adventure. For example, Fred Schönbach, who was 20, recalled: "There was mixed in with the terror of being searched and robbed by the soldiers, a feeling of being very much alive, maybe of getting away alive at a time when all of Europe was about to be swallowed up...Someone who had led a very sheltered life, suddenly competing for *lebensraum*, sleeping gear, scraps of fresh food, cigarette butts and latrine seats."

If Lieutenant-Colonel Scott and Lieutenant O'Neill were the principal villains of this sombre odyssey, its hero was unquestionably Lieutenant A. Brooks, a Scottish doctor who in World War I had served with the Seaforth Highlanders, was captured in France and escaped while acting as interpreter to Allied prisoners of war.

He qualified as a doctor in Aberdeen in 1925, and after a few years in the Colonial Service with the rank of Acting-Colonel, went into general practice in Monmouthshire, Wales. At the outbreak of World War II, he rejoined the Army and was attached to a field hospital at Ormskirk, near Southport. On 9 July 1940, at the invitation of his commanding officer, Brooks volunteered for secret service abroad, "destination undisclosed". He was issued with a tropical kit and 24 hours later found himself in Liverpool, about to board *Dunera*. He thought they might be bound for Egypt, but that night when he opened his "Q" instructions, he learned their destination was Australia.

"The first thing that struck me on the wharf at Liverpool," he says, "was a colonel — it was Scott — standing on the brig like Nelson, or some other admiral taking the salute, supervising a crowd of civilians with battered suitcases as they trooped on board. I wondered, what the hell is this!" Brooks's wonderment increased when he saw the way the troops were treating the internees.

On board *Dunera*, Brooks found himself with more than 2500 internees, one assistant — an RMC sergeant — and a hundred-bed hospital, inadequately supplied. He was able to recruit three internee doctors, including the distinguished heart specialist

Lieutenant Brooks, the medical officer aboard the *Dunera*.

Dr P. Schatzki, and some medical students. It is a tribute to their skill and dedication that there was only one death from natural causes throughout the appalling voyage. A 53-year-old Austrian judge, Hans Pferrern, died from myocardial failure, following influenza, despite strenuous efforts to save him. "We didn't have M & B [an early antibiotic] which had just come in," says Brooks. "The internees comprised a cross-section of all types and ages, with complaints such as dysentery that one would expect among older people, so the 100 beds were always fully occupied, and there were the operating theatre and dispensary to look after." Captain Frederick Caffyn, a warm-hearted Cockney, accompanied Brooks on his daily hospital rounds. Brooks fought hard to give the internees fresh air. With the co-operation of the captain, and his first officer, he was able to have a chute rigged up to force fresh air down below. Caffyn and First Officer Smith both tried to help the internees, but were frustrated by the military over whom they had no authority "We, the ship's officers, did what we could to alleviate hardship and unnecessary suffering," says Smith, "but usually our efforts were countered on grounds of security which, of course, was outside our responsibility."

The internees had no change of clothing during an eight-week voyage, much of it through the tropics. What they had was soon reduced to rags as a result of constant washing with salt water. When Brooks tried to relieve the shortage of clothing by getting access to what remained of the internees' baggage, he was stopped by an Army captain.

CHAPTER FIVE

In England, the Army had surrendered to panic. The Government
had surrendered to the Army. But the mother of Parliaments was
not silenced. As stories of the internment muddle emerged,
pertinent questions began to be asked in the House by members of
all parties.

In the 39 days on which Parliament sat between June 1940 and
August, there were only four in which "enemy aliens" were not
mentioned. They were the subject not only of questions about
individuals but, between 10 July and 3 December, of four debates.
Three ran respectively for six, three-and-a-half, and four hours.
"Nearly 14 hours of parliamentary time," Lord Beveridge wrote,
"devoted to the interests of enemy aliens in the year of greatest
danger that Britain had ever known."

Two outstanding critics of the Government's internment
policy were Eleanor Rathbone (Independent, English Universities)
and Major Cazalet (Conservative, Chippenham), who for years
had championed the cause of refugees.

On 10 July 1940 — the day *Dunera* sailed from Liverpool —
they initiated a full scale debate on the recent treatment of refugees.
"I know enough about the subject to realise something about the
hardships, miseries and sufferings these people have endured
during the past four years," Major Cazalet told the House. "It has
been the historical policy of this country for many centuries to give
asylum to refugees, and I do not believe that England has lost by
this policy."

"As a result of the tremendous influx of refugees in recent
months," he continued, "coupled with fears of invasion and Fifth
Column activities, there had been a tremendous public demand for
the internment of practically everyone whose family had not lived
in England for 100 years, in complete disregard of the individual

merits of the cases concerned — a totally un-English attitude to adopt. I fear that the authorities have been somewhat stampeded against their own better judgement...Alas, all unwittingly, they have given some material to German broadcasters.''

Major Cazalet made it clear that the safety of England was the paramount consideration, but he asked for a review of the cases and the release of those whose loyalty was not in question. "War must bring many injustices,'' he concluded. "Do not let us therefore add unnecessarily to those injustices by mere administrative muddles and confusion. Let us not add to the sum total of human misery through which the world is passing today...I appeal both to the Home Office and to the War Office to maintain that tradition which we have always followed in regard to refugees.''

Major Cazalet said that the man responsible for putting the internees on the *Arandora Star* was the Lord President of the Council, Mr Chamberlain, who was not present at the debate though he must have known it would be taking place. He had deported not only Nazis and prisoners of war but men who had fought "for our cause in Spain, for our cause against Mussolini'':

> How much longer will our Government refuse to realise that
> this is not a war between the nations, but the last stand of a
> people who love freedom enough to die for it. You put our
> friends into concentration camps but you allow Mosley's
> gang...to go free and untouched.

There were many protests about Chamberlain's absence from the debate, which Sir Percy Harris (Labour, South West Bethnal Green) described as "an insult to the House''.

In the same debate, Miss Rathbone told of the fate of a German professor of chemistry, who had taught for 23 years at a German university:

> He is 62 years old. He is an international authority on
> dyestuffs, and at this very moment his book on that subject
> is being translated by Harvard University. He was kept in
> Germany so that other countries could not profit by his
> knowledge; he was thrown into the most brutal
> concentration camp, suffered tortures for 17 days, and
> finally, when he was released, came to this country. He was
> permitted to do research work with a research grant, and for
> the last year has been employed by a company where he has
> been developing a process for utilising sisal waste
> particularly for use in submarines. Is that work of national
> importance?

His firm applied to the Home Office for his exemption. A week ago the police called at his flat, he showed them his application to the Home Office, he asked them to wait until that application had been investigated; they refused, and told him that they would come back shortly. He warned them that he could not endure another internment. They came back in two hours, but he had escaped from the stupidity and the malice of others — he had taken a quick poison. When the inquest was held, one of the two police officers asked the widow whether her husband was a Jew, and she said, 'No, he was of Jewish origin, but baptised a Christian'; whereupon, the police officer turned to the other, and said, 'What a pity. If we had only known before.' The policeman thought that the man's Jewish origin was a reason for not exempting him from internment.

And what of his widow? "Much as I sympathise with the widow," Sir John Anderson told Commander Locker-Lampson, "I regret that it is not possible to make any grant to her out of public funds."

Mr G. Strauss (Labour, Lambeth North) asked what possible public purpose could be served in interning aliens who were known to be keen anti-Nazis. He gave a few examples:

> I understand that a very famous author who has for long written books against Hitler and has been struggling against Hitler for many years, has been put into an internment camp. He is Rudolf Olden and he wrote a book balled *Hitler, the Pawn*, as well as other books. His position cannot be in doubt. Now he can no longer carry on his anti-Nazi propaganda. There is another man called Haffner who has written a book entitled *Hitler — Jekyll or Hyde?* exposing the Nazi machine and suggesting methods by which we can beat it. He has been put into internment, where he can no longer use his brains or experience in helping to fight Nazism. These are category "C" people.

"To intern these people, great fighters for democracy, was contrary to common sense and to England's finest traditions," Strauss added.

The House was told many stories of husbands being arbitrarily separated from their wives, and children from their parents. In the debate of 13 August 1940, Mr S. S. Silverman (Labour, Nelson and Colne) raised the case — typical of many — of Walter Oscar Hollar, aged 18, who had recently left the Highgate School, "having attained the School Certificate with five distinctions and twice been awarded first prize in all-English music competition from among 11,000 competitors". He had been interned with his father on 1 July, was taken away four days later, and had not been heard of since. Silverman asked Sir John Anderson where the boy was and how long his family had to remain in ignorance of his whereabouts? Ten days later, Mr Osbert Peake said he thought the boy had gone to Australia, but was not sure. When Silverman asked who had decided that Hollar should be deported, Peake replied disingenuously: "Practically all those who went to Australia went as volunteers." In the same debate, Strauss asked what decision had the Home Secretary come to about sending Sir Oswald Mosley and other Fascist sympathisers, to the Dominions? The Government had said on 4 July that they were considering this matter. Peake regretted that he could add nothing to his previous answers — which had said nothing.

In his review of the progress of the war on 20 August, Churchill said: "We may be able to show the enemy quite a lot of things that they have not thought of yet. Since the Germans drove the Jews out and lowered their technical standards, our science is definitely ahead of theirs." But many of these Jews, together with equally gifted non-Jews, were soon to be isolated behind barbed wire in distant Australia.

And in the privacy of the Cabinet room, Churchill repeatedly advocated the internment of refugees. His first Cabinet, on 11 May 1940, approved the first large scale arrests. Cabinet minutes reveal him as the architect not only of the internment policy, but also of the policy of deporting refugees. "He was strongly in favour of removing all internees out of the United Kingdom," says a minute of 24 May 1940.

There were, of course, a few members who defended the Government's internment policy. Earl Winterton (Conservative, Horsham and Worthing) had been the British Government representative and chairman of the Evian Committee, and had demonstrated his sympathy with the refugees by accommodating nine — seven Belgian and two German-Jewish — in his "comparatively small" London house. But he believed that refugees had aided the Nazis in their invasion of Europe, and declared during the debate on 22 August: "If I got up before any public meeting of constituents in this country and asked, 'Which do you put first, the safety, honour and welfare of the realm, or the interest of foreigners, however badly treated', there would be one shout in reply, 'England'."

Colonel Wedgwood (Labour, Newcastle-under-Lyme) was more realistic when he said in the same debate: "If I was asked from where the danger will come if the Germans invade this country, I would not say from the German Jews. One cannot conceive it coming from them. The danger would come from the Fascist Party, from people who were defeatists, and from people who had nothing to lose if Hitler comes here. Those are the natural dangers.''

Government apologists for the refugee policy often misled the House, knowingly or unknowingly. Thus on 9 July 1940, when the Minister for Shipping, Mr Ronald Hibbert Cross (Conservative, Lancashire) was asked how many of the deportees on the *Arandora Star* were known Nazis and how many anti-Nazi refugees, he replied: "I am informed by my right honourable friend the Secretary of State for War [Anthony Eden] that all the Germans on board were Nazi sympathisers and that none came to this country as refugees. None had Category 'B' or 'C' certificates or were recognised as friendly aliens.'' Whether or not Eden deliberately misinformed his colleague, or whether he merely showed an extraordinary ignorance of the facts is not clear. In fact, the *Arandora Star* carried at least 200 German and Austrian refugees many of them well-known anti-Nazis. These included: the German Social Democrat Franz Leberecht, who had been arrested by the Nazis for laying a wreath on the grave of the murdered German socialist, Rosa Luxemburg; Karl Olbrisch, a former Communist member of the Reichstag who was caught by the Gestapo doing underground propaganda and spent three years in prison (in 1937, he escaped from a concentration camp to Czechoslovakia, and later to England); Louis Weber, a leading anti-Nazi in the German Seamen's Union; Valentin Wittke, a German trade union leader with a long record of underground anti-Nazi struggle; Kurt Regner, a distinguished Austrian socialist lawyer, who had defended many working-class people (he was one of the organisers of an anti-Nazi demonstration near Vienna in March 1938, was beaten up, and escaped to Czechoslovakia, and later England); Rudolf Schenk, another anti-Nazi fighter who had married in England and was being trained as an agriculturist in Cornwall when he was interned; and D. Anzani, secretary of the Italian section of the League of the Rights of Man, a resolute anti-Fascist who had lived in England for 31 years. Anzani, Olbrisch, and Weber were among the drowned. "I consider that whoever was responsible for those men, and after their internment, for their transportation, is answerable for their deaths,'' Lord Faringdon told the House of Lords.

Eden was still maintaining on 16 July that all the men on the *Arandora Star* were Nazis or Fascists.

Parliament was again misled during the debate on 13 August. Osbert Peake, when asked who decided that a refugee be deported to Australia, replied: "Practically all those who went to Australia went as volunteers." He repeated this untruth in the following debate on 22 August, when he said: "There is perfectly conclusive evidence that 90 per cent of those who went there were anxious to go there." There was, of course, no such evidence. And he continued: "The Australian authorities have informed us that a considerable number of those who are on their way there are those whom they have been refusing to admit for many years past." In fact the "Australian authorities" had no knowledge of who was on *Dunera* and were later to complain that they had received only twelve dossiers for the entire shipment.

The fourth debate was opened on 3 December by George Latham (Labour, Sheffield), who said: "Indiscriminate internment brought to light evidence of what looked like double persecution, first by the Nazis and Fascists and secondly by ourselves." Latham was followed by Colonel Wedgwood, who said: "Home Secretaries think they are responsible for law, order and security. They are, but they are responsible for something more than law, order and security. They are responsible for the traditions and honour of our country, more than any other minister, and it is only by balancing those duties, security and the old decencies of English culture and law, that we can win through."

England's general internment of "C" class males which had started on 25 June lasted only three weeks and stopped as suddenly as it had begun. Many Germans and Austrians who lived in districts with large proportions of aliens were not interned because the police had not been able to deal with their cases within the three critical weeks. Those whose cases were by chance dealt with in these three weeks were to remain in internment unless they came within one of the categories of certain White Papers.

• The first White Paper, published about three weeks after internment ceased, permitted release in cases of special hardship, and in 16 categories of employability.

• A second White Paper issued shortly afterwards permitted the release of persons who had played a public and prominent part in opposition to the Nazi system.

• A third White Paper added categories for the release of those who could make contributions to science, learning, literature and art. A further category was added permitting persons ineligible for the Pioneer Corps (a non-combatant labour unit) to be released if they could prove they were friendly to the Allied cause.

No such provisions were made by the Australian Government for the release in Australia of any of the internees.

When Miss Rathbone asked the Home Secretary, Herbert

Morrison, whether he agreed that it was a waste to keep men of high quality in internment in Australia, Morrison replied: "That would be a proper question for the Parliament of Australia. I would not like to give an answer to it."

Colonel Wedgwood asked if it were not possible that if the Australian Government was approached by Morrison, they would release and use these people? Morrison replied: "Naturally, there was a clear understanding that the immigration policy of the Australian Government was their business, and I do not feel it is possible for me to intervene in any way."

Under the heading: ENEMY ALIENS SENT TO AUSTRALIA, the *Sydney Morning Herald* on 14 August reported: "Mr Attlee told the House of Commons that 9120 Germans, Austrians and Italians had left for Australia, including a number who were considered dangerous. The Under-Secretary for the Dominions, Mr Shakespeare, said they had been treated in accordance with the Geneva Convention relating to prisoners of war." Both Mr Attlee and Mr Shakespeare were ill-informed. Only 2542 internees were on their way to Australia, and their treatment was certainly not in accordance with the Geneva Convention.

Three days later, the *Sydney Morning Herald* reported that "a large concentration camp, laid out in three compounds, has been built at Hay to accommodate internees being sent to Australia by the British Government. The huts in which internees will be housed are about 60 feet x 18 feet [they were in fact 60 feet x 20 feet (18.3 metres x 6 metres)] with rows of bunks down the centre, separated by partitions. Powerful electric floodlights will be installed around the compound." Internees would be guarded by members of garrison battalions recruited by men of the first AIF.

Each compound consisted of 37 cypress pine huts on piers, with white-grey asbestos roofs. The bunks had straw palliasses and army blankets. Each compound had its kitchen, messing and administrative huts, latrines and lavatory buildings. The compounds were surrounded by a triple fence of barbed wire. (To many of the internees, barbed wire evoked hideous memories of Dachau or Buchenwald.)

A third garrison battalion was being recruited in New South Wales to cope with the additional demands, with 40 vacancies for men under 55 who served with the Army Medical Corps.

On 19 August 1940, His Majesty's Government in the United Kingdom suggested "for the consideration of His Majesty's Government in Australia", that steps should be taken to segregate, in different internment camps, category "A" Germans and

Austrians from the category "B" and "C" Germans and Austrians, and also, if possible, to intern the Italians separately. And it was hoped that when further information about individuals was available

> the Australian Government will feel able to undertake the classification of the civilian internees and to consider whether it would not be possible, while keeping potentially dangerous enemy aliens under strict custody, to apply a less rigid custodial treatment to genuine refugees from Nazi oppression.

His Majesty's Australian Government emphatically rejected this suggestion. In a cable approved by Menzies to the Australian High Commissioner in London, the Department of Defence Co-ordination replied on 13 September:

> The effect of this suggestion is presumably that, after classification, certain internees might be released by the Commonwealth Government, subject to restrictions such as reporting periodically to the police as are considered necessary in the interest of national security.
>
> The Commonwealth Government only agreed to accept prisoners of war and internees for internment in Australia. To release certain persons on arrival here would be undesirable on grounds of national security and would also involve questions including employment, sustenance and ultimate repatriation of such persons even though it is assumed that any expenditure in respect of them would be borne by the United Kingdom Government.
>
> Would you kindly point out above difficulties to the United Kingdom Government and indicate that persons should not (repeat not) be embarked for Australia unless —
> (A)   Interned in the United Kingdom: and
> (B)   On the understanding that they will remain interned until returned to the United Kingdom for release.
>
> In effect, this means that the Commonwealth is not (repeat not) prepared to accept for internment in Australia any aliens who would not, in ordinary course of events, be considered sufficiently dangerous to warrant internment in the United Kingdom.

Similar conditions applied to the entry into Australia of the wives and families of internees:

> Commonwealth Government not (repeat not) prepared to

receive non-interned wives and families of internees even
though prepared to come to Australia at their own expense.

The cable also complained that as only 12 dossiers had been
supplied by the United Kingdom Government there was no adequate means of identifying the expected internees.

(Five months later Australia agreed to permit the entry, under
certain conditions, of wives and children of married internees. Sir
Stanley (later Viscount) Bruce (Australia's High Commissioner in
London) reported that while England had expressed gratitude for
this, lack of shipping and "other considerations" presented serious
difficulties and the Minister for Home Security had concluded it
was not practicable "or in the interests of the parties concerned" to
take advantage of the offer.)

CHAPTER SIX

Dunera reached Freetown, Sierra Leone, on 24 July; Takoradi, Ghana, on 27 July, and Cape Town, South Africa, on 8 August. The Australian coastline was sighted on 26 August, and *Dunera* reached the Port of Fremantle (Western Australia) the next day. Customs officials who inspected the baggage were indignant at its condition and said they would make an official report about it.

Each internee was issued with a Certificate of Registration, for which he was finger-printed, and photographed with his internment number hanging round his neck.

W. Eddy was boarding officer in the Customs Department in Fremantle when *Dunera* arrived. The internees, he said, "certainly looked a very motley mob, and appeared to be underfed". There were numerous complaints about the food and treatment, some of which reached the ears of the Department of the Army, and on 31 August when *Dunera* was crossing the Great Australian Bight, two days' steaming from Melbourne, Scott received a wireless message from the OC, Prisoner of War Information Bureau, Australian Imperial Forces. No copy of this message is to be found in the Australian archives, but it must have dealt with the allegations of theft and brutality by Scott's troops, for his reply, dated "At Sea, 2 September 1940", was a long essay in hypocritical self-justification. It began:

> *Subject:— Your Memo dated 31st August 1940.*
> With regard to the disembarkation of internees I wish to stress the following points:—
>
> *1. Baggage*
> As there are over 2000 bags and a like number of document cases, all unlabelled, it is absolutely and completely impossible to sort out the property of any internee going

ashore at Port Melbourne. This will be appreciated when I inform you that embarkation at Liverpool was made in such inadequate time that to tabulate this baggage was out of the question. Moreover, as the voyage progressed, bags had to be forced open in order to obtain linen and clothing which after fumigation and washing, was distributed piecemeal to the internees. This was an urgent necessity owing to large numbers becoming lousy.

It will be a simple matter for detention authorities at Sydney to distribute baggage on identification by internees when the balance may be returned to Melbourne.

2. Valuables.
The same applies in this paragraph. Valuables have been placed in a sack and sealed. Two valuable items of jewellery are under separate cover. As I have already pointed out to Captain Heighway, search of internees was commenced on shore by the Dock and Military Police in conjunction with my command, but there being such urgency to sail owing to escort and convoy anxiously waiting, that it had to be continued to the best advantage on board ship.

It will be appreciated that in the difficult circumstances of sorting out internees in their respective groups, that certain articles are possibly missing, but in my opinion this of course is unavoidable. I have asked Australian authorities to support my urgent request to the British authorities that they should in no circumstances permit internees to have more than one kitbag per head and that all valuables should be handed by conducting officers in a sealed parcel for which receipt may be demanded.

To this farrago of lies and half-truths, Scott added a wildly irresponsible but very revealing postscript. It read:

I would now like to give my personal views on (a) Nazi Germans, (b) Italians and (c) German and Austrian Jews.
(a) Having warned this group prior to sailing of my methods should trouble arise through them, their behaviour has been exemplary. They are of a fine type, honest and straightforward, and extremely well-disciplined. I am quite prepared to admit however, that they are highly dangerous.
(b) Italians. This group are filthy in their habits, without a vestige of discipline, and are cowards to a degree.
(c) Can only be described as subversive liars, demanding and arrogant, and I have taken steps to bring them into my line of thought. They will quote any person from a

prime minister to the President of the United States as personal references, and they are definitely not to be trusted in word or deed.

Scott was not a consistent liar. In a message addressed to the Reception Officer, Australian Imperial Forces, also dated "2 September, At Sea", Scott gave another explanation of the rifled baggage:

Complaints may be made by Jewish internees that they have lost articles of value and money. I disclaim all responsibility if this is found to be correct.

Conducting Officers assured me that internees were permitted to bring up to £2 per head, out of the country, and that their baggage had been searched on two occasions. This I found to be untrue and had to have each man searched before coming abroad, recovering lethal weapons and petrol in large quantities.

The search was performed in the main by the Military and Dock Police in conjunction with my command. Baggage room not being available internees' baggage was stacked on the lower deck where it had to remain overnight. The following morning it was reported to me by the Chief Officer that the baggage had been pilfered by the Lascar crew, which on personal inspection I found to be only too true.

Report on this matter was forwarded to the War Office from Freetown, Sierra Leone, in which I stressed the most urgent necessity for camp authorities to embark internees with one kitbag, and all valuables to be collected before departure and made into one packet, checked, and receipts given, so that this packet may be put in the ship's safe prior to sailing.

I understand that large sums of money have been credited to internees in Australian banks. From experience I suggest that great care should be observed that they should not be allowed to have on their person any sum of money over £1 as I have had many instances on this journey of their bribing or attempting to bribe sentries or members of the ship's crew.

Dunera reached Port Melbourne on 3 September 1940, but news of her arrival was not released by the censor until the day after she reached Sydney. "Some days ago, a low grey-painted liner moved silently to a berth in Port Phillip," reported the Melbourne *Argus*

— a now defunct morning paper — on 7 September:

> The ship brought to Australia the first shipload of German
> and Italian prisoners captured at Dunkirk and other fields
> of battle...At Port Melbourne a large number disembarked
> and entrained for a prison camp [at Tatura]. Some sick
> prisoners were taken off in an ambulance.
> Word that the Tommys were in town passed round
> quickly. It was the first time Australians had seen the British
> Army dress of World War II. With short business-like tunic,
> knee pockets, and ankle-length gaiters, the men looked
> ready for instant action.

Among those who disembarked at Melbourne were 251
German and Austrian "A" category internees regarded as
dangerous or potentially dangerous, 94 "doubtful" Germans and
200 Italians interned as members of the Fascist Party in England.
Both groups were survivors of the *Arandora Star*.

Constance Duncan, secretary of VIREC, who was to become
one of the most resolute fighters for the rights of the internees, met
Dunera at Port Melbourne. VIREC — the Victorian International
Refugee Emergency Council — was inaugurated in Sydney on 13
December 1938. Represented on it were five Protestant Church
organisations, the Australian Jewish Welfare Society, the Dacome
Relief Committee, the Council for Civil Liberties, YMCA, YWCA,
National Council of Women, Australian Women's National
League, Women's College and surprisingly, the Chamber of
Manufactures. Prominent people associated with it included writer
Nettie Palmer, Professor H. Woodruff, Archbishop Head and
Judge Foster.

Miss Duncan was appalled by the accounts of the voyage,
describing it in letters to the German Emergency Council in
London as "almost unbelievable" and "deplorable". "Men
arrived in camp in a ghastly condition," she wrote, "unshaven and
unwashed with all kinds of makeshift clothing and some so weak
they could hardly walk." Details of their vicious ill-treatment were
also given in a report sent by the Society of Friends in Australia to
Colonel Wedgwood, whose daughter, Camilla, was a member of
the Society of Friends in Sydney, and principal of the Sydney
University Women's College (1936-1940). She, like Miss Duncan,
became an active champion of the *Dunera* internees.

At Port Melbourne several Australian officers came on board to
enquire about the well-being of the internees, but Lieutenant
O'Neill's presence prevented the internees from talking freely, the
over-crowding speaking for itself. Towards midnight when most of

the escort troop were drunk, Australian officers inspected the decks and bunkers and got the true picture of conditions.

After departure the following day Lieutenant O'Neill summoned the deck leaders to tell them that two telegrams to the Archbishop of Melbourne had been smuggled ashore (which archbishop — Protestant or Catholic — was not specified). He gave the culprit until the next morning to confess. There was no confession and nothing further happened.

As the ship lay tied up at Port Melbourne, a diminutive German internee who had suffered from mental disorder during the voyage made a ludicrous attempt at escape. Borrowing a uniform of the escort's 15-stone (95 kilograms) regimental sergeant major, obviously very much too big for him, he crawled through a porthole, slid down a steel hawser, and jumped a short distance to the quay. He was immediately seized by Sergeant Arthur Helliwell and another sergeant who was standing by the gangplank, and dragged back, struggling ineffectively, on board.

An officer who directed Helliwell to confine the internee to the ship's cells noticed no substantial injury to him, but five hours later, another officer inspecting the cell, the key of which Helliwell retained, found the internee in a shocking condition. He was lying on the floor clad only in a blood-stained shirt. His eyes were puffed and black, his nose injured, and his face covered with blood. His right leg was also injured. He was without water or blankets, though an officer had ordered Helliwell to supply these. Captain Burton showed the blood-stained shirt to Scott. "It was horrible," says Lieutenant Brooks. "They broke his nose and cut his lips. I stitched him up and wrote a strong letter about it to the CO."

On 6 September, H. A. Rorke, State Publicity Censor for New South Wales, sent this instruction, conspicuously stamped SECRET, to Sydney newspaper editors:

INTERNEES FROM OVERSEAS

1. Newspapers will be permitted to publish photographs or letterpress in regard to the arrival of internees from overseas after midnight 6th, 7th instant.
2. The number and destination of all or any section of the contingent must not be published.
3. Articles of an alarming character such as might cause reprisals against Australian internees in Germany must not be published.
4. All photographs and letterpress must be submitted for censorship.

Shortly after 10 o'clock on the morning of 6 September — 57 days out of Liverpool — *Dunera* steamed through the rugged heads that flank the entrance to Sydney Harbour, and took on the pilot and shipping officials. Internees struggled for portholes to glimpse the famous harbour which, despite man's vandalism, remains one of the most beautiful in the world. After health and customs authorities had completed their formalities, *Dunera* was towed to her berth where a long train was waiting. She tied up at 11.48 am. The internees were given a hasty lunch and disembarkation began. Their last act was to forcibly open porthole covers that had remained fastened throughout the voyage. It was an affirmation of their new freedom.

Before the internees left *Dunera*, Brooks handed out fifteen copies of this testimonial:

> The undermentioned medical men and others have all
> worked in the hospital and I have found them exceptionally
> willing, well disciplined, and they have been of very great
> help through the voyage. They can all be trusted.
>
> I trust that they will all be usefully employed in their
> new sphere of activities. They are all men of undoubted
> probity and full of desire to help in the common cause
> against Nazi-ism.

BOAS. B.	EIRICH. F.	SIMON. E. L.
COHN. S.	JACOBSEN. E.	STERN. K.
DANZIGER. H.	MARX. A.	WEISS. J.
DANZIGER. R.	SCHATZKI. P.	DRONBERGER. M.
DURRHEIM. G.	SCHORR. R.	RUHSTADT. K.

In his novel, *The Turn of the Spiral*, Walter Kaufmann describes a remarkable incident of the disembarkation:

> Called out on deck, the men of number two hatch file out
> of the ship's belly and the glaring sunlight causes them to
> totter as if they had suddenly been blinded. A tumult, a
> general disorder ensues, and the Lion Hunter [so called
> because he always carried a loaded revolver], a burly British
> sergeant, smashes the butt of his rifle down on the foot of a
> young boy. A shriek pierces the air.
>
> From out of that motley crowd of tattered men, a man
> emerges, jumps forward, tall and dark and rough, and
> armed with only his fists — and punches the sergeant in the
> mouth...
>
> On the other side of the world, in Germany, in Nazi
> Germany, prisoners died, were murdered, were tortured to
> death for less.

Sydney newspapers were permitted to describe the elaborate security precautions taken as the internees left the ship. "The 1984 prisoners filed off between British guards and proceeded to the train between files of Australian soldiers," reported the *Sydney Morning Herald*. "Every 30 feet [nine metres] along the wharf were men armed with revolvers, and the entire wharf was surrounded by a cordon of police, while the police speed-boat *Nemesis* cruised around the boat." The inference was, of course, that the internees were dangerous and desperate men. No report mentioned that the dangerous men had been taken off at Port Melbourne.

Sydney's two morning papers, the *Sydney Morning Herald* and the *Daily Telegraph*, both gave considerable space to the *Dunera* story — which owed much to the imagination of Scott and his cronies. Differences in the two accounts must be ascribed to their mendacity.

"The internees," said the *Herald*, "varied greatly in type. Some — usually the younger ones — laughed gaily as they landed; others were grave. Others surveyed the new land with a sneer. It was stated that Hitler had arranged for the men, on arrival in Australia, to receive £2 each. Two of the internees refused to receive this bonus and asked that it be paid into a fund for the purchase of Spitfires for Britain."

> One internee was a well-known designer in Germany before the war and was interned in England on the outbreak of War. On the voyage to Australia he did 20 paintings and also sketches of the officers on the ship. It was stated that he had completed designs for a ballet which might be produced in Sydney this year.
>
> Most of the internees seemed very young and they smiled as the train pulled out of the wharf into the sunshine as though they were delighted at arriving in a safe country. Many gave the thumbs-up to the onlookers. A number of the older men, however, frowned and scowled through the train windows, looking like cartoons of dangerous conspirators, as they shrugged back into their carriages, out of the sunshine. As the train pulled out, faces wreathed in open smiles, dour faces, stolid faces, thin lipped, sneering arrogant faces, framed in the carriage windows, flashed by the knot of guards at the wharf gate.

"The internees were better fed than any British troops," said Colonel Scott. "By the time they reached Australia they had filled out and were dashing round the deck like two-year-olds." The *Herald* report continued:

The *Sydney Morning Herald* (6 September 1940) captioned this photograph, "Prisoners disembarking from the *Dunera*".

(John Fairfax & Sons Ltd)

This picture was published in Sydney's *Daily Telegraph* (6 September 1940) with the caption, "One of the prisoners brought to Australia in the prison ship".

(Consolidated Press)

The guard consisted mainly of Norfolk and Suffolk men who were in the evacuation of Dunkirk. The commanding officer of the troops, who are officially designated as 'Q' troops, as indicative of the mystery of their assignment, is Lieutenant-Colonel W. P. Scott, an impressive kilted figure. Colonel Scott has had three brothers killed during the present war and two are interned in Germany.

The *Daily Telegraph* report was more sensational and more imaginative: "Tragedy and wild excitement marked the voyage to Australia of a British troopship carrying German and Italian prisoners which reached Sydney yesterday," it began. "Among the internees were parachutists, other prisoners of war, and hundreds who had been carrying out subversive work in England. There were no women."

Two torpedoes fired by a submarine passed under the ship and exploded on the other side.
A Nazi announced that he was going to die for the Fatherland. He then leaped overboard and drowned.
A prisoner was killed in a brawl with another Nazi.
A third man died from natural causes.
One guard said: 'There's nothing to choose between the Germans and the Italians except the Germans eat more meat. The German Jews wouldn't eat the meat and were given special food all the way out.' Some soldiers said the prisoners were better treated on the ship than they would have been at home in Germany. 'At one meal they ate piles of sausages and they consumed many pounds of fresh fish between Fremantle and Port Phillip.'

Sydney's afternoon paper, the *Sun*, added a few more items to the stories in the morning papers: it told of the attempted escape by the internee at Port Melbourne but did not mention that he was brutally beaten after recapture and it revealed, as neither of the morning papers had done, that there were refugees among the internees.

Some of the refugees and internees were really heartbroken because they had not seized the chance to get naturalised. One of them was a German who had not been in Germany since he was three months old. He talked Cockney better than a lot of Londoners, and he can't believe that Germany is going to win the war. Nor can any of the refugees, but the Nazis don't want to give an opinion, one way or the other.

The Norfolk, Suffolk and Gloucester guards were fine specimens of British soldiers. Less wiry than the digger, they were stocky and muscular, bronzed and fit. Most of them were reservists.

At the outbreak of war they were called up and before the end of September last, were sent to France.

'We were a bit lucky,' said one. 'We were just ahead of the concentrated German bombing in the breakthrough in France, and we were evacuated from Le Havre a fortnight before Dunkirk.'

This was not consistent with the *Herald* story that the guards were heroes of the Dunkirk evacuation. But consistency was not a virtue of Scott and his men.

Pale and emaciated, the internees shuffled down the gangplank on to Australian soil. A few sang, as they landed from what they had christened with grim humour the "pick-pocket battleship", and the "luggage-destroyer":

My luggage went into the ocean,
My luggage went into the sea.
  Bring back, O bring back,
  Bring back my luggage to me.

Some were driven away in ambulances. Their treatment had been well below the standard laid down by the Geneva Convention, which requires that clothing, underwear and footwear shall be provided and regularly replaced. Many arrived in rags, and remained in them until the Society of Friends, or some other welfare organisation, provided clothes.

As the first train pulled out, another took its place. The disembarkation continued throughout the afternoon. The fourth and last train pulled out at 5 pm and reached its destination, Hay, about 19 hours later.

"We arrived at Sydney physically and mentally exhausted," says Dr Fleischer. "The chapter of the *Dunera* came to an end when we were for the last time threatened and beaten when leaving the deck." And he added:

It would be unjust not to mention that some of the officers and men were well disposed and felt strongly about the treatment to which we were subjected, but they were not in a position to help us as they wished. We are particularly grateful to the Medical Officer, Lieutenant Brooks and Captain Caffyn, also to Lieutenant Mallaney and Sergeant Stanley (RAMC). Also quite a few officers and men of

whom we do not know the names, expressed their
sympathies. And we do know that those officers and men
who maltreated us did not act in accordance with the true
British tradition.

After their harrowing experiences on the voyage, the internees were
moved by the friendliness of the Australians, old "diggers" from
World War I. One internee recalls his amazement when a guard
said to him: "Hey, mate, hold my rifle while I roll a cigarette!" At
various stations along the line, the men were given a food box
containing sandwiches, fruit and a tomato. Coffee was served en
route, and as the long trains clattered westwards, the atmosphere
became more and more relaxed. Guards offered internees cigarettes
and tobacco, which many desperately craved, and joined them in
games of cards.

"After all, this internment of ours is but a side-show of the
war, and a rather insignificant one at that," an internee later wrote.
"There are, however, little glimpses of this life which for human
interest would be remembered with a smile":

> Take for instance that feeling of relief we sensed when
> coming off the boat, that feeling of a nightmare coming to
> an end...Cigarettes offered by the new guards and gladly
> accepted by us are symbolic of that change of
> atmosphere...And the psychological, apart from the
> gastronomic effect of that cup of milk coffee accompanying
> a delicious supper, appetisingly packed, has to be
> experienced to be appreciated.

Some of the British guards accompanied the Australians to
Hay, and O'Neill had the effrontery to show himself to the
internees. He was received with jeers, whistling and cries of,
"Where's our luggage?" He retreated hastily, to the amusement of
the Australian soldiers.

Oswald Volkmann, an internee, commemorated the incident
with a poem, the first and last verses of which read:

> *Oh! Oh! O'Neill, my dear O'Neill*
> *I wish you'd only know just how we feel,*
> *You don't know how much we love you*
> *For the kindness we got of you*
> *Man of steel*
> *Oh! Oh! O'Neill.*
>
> *Just landed in Australia*
> *What did we bad boys do*

Sydney welcomed Scott and his troops warmly. Lieutenant-Colonel Scott (centre) and Captain Collie (left) are seen here as part of a Sydney theatre party, 11 September 1940.

(John Fairfax & Sons Ltd)

Lieutenant-Colonel Scott (left) paraded his men at the Sydney Showground, September 1940.

(John Fairfax & Sons Ltd)

Australia's Governor-General, Lord Gowrie, inspects members of the *Dunera*'s escort troops at the Sydney Showground, 9 September 1940.

(John Fairfax & Sons Ltd)

They welcomed you from all their hearts
And shouted boo, boo, boo.

According to some Hay residents, Scott also visited Hay, and attended a concert given by Hay schoolchildren at which, it was alleged, he handed out as gifts watches stolen from the internees.

During the ten days *Dunera* was in Sydney, Scott played the part of the stalwart patriot. He laid a wreath on the Cenotaph, addressed Legacy — an organisation that looks after the widows and families of Australian servicemen — and paraded his men before enthusiastic crowds at the Sydney Showground. His imagination was as fertile as ever. He told the Legacy audience that "in the early days of the war British motorists were found guiding German bombers to anti-aircraft guns and searchlight emplacements by headlights, but that had now been dealt with".

Sydney acclaimed him, O'Neill and the troops as conquering heroes. Commonwealth and State Governments, municipalities and many local individuals, business organisations as well as the military authorities, vied with one another in welcoming them. Fleets of cars were put at their disposal. They were given free travel on trams, ferries and trains, and free admission to the cinemas. Some were taken on excursions to the Blue Mountains, where the Mayor of Katoomba, Councillor Freelander, thanked the British forces for keeping Australia safe. The mountain town of Katoomba took an unofficial holiday when the 266 members of the escort troop arrived.

Australia's Governor-General, Lord Gowrie, was among those who welcomed Scott. The 68-year-old Gowrie had a distinguished military record. Awarded a Victoria Cross in 1898 in the Sudan, he later served in Somaliland, Gallipoli and France, where he won the Croix de Guerre. He was a man of wide human sympathies and was soon to be shocked when he learnt of Scott's behaviour on *Dunera*.

At the request of the British Government, 13 internees were re-embarked on *Dunera* when she left Sydney for Bombay on 16 September. Their names remain undisclosed by the Home Office or the Australian Archives. None had money or a passport. The Australian Government gave each a suit, a greatcoat, underclothing and £2 to spend on the voyage. On 20 December, the Home Office requested that four other internees be returned. One was the pianist Peter Stadlen, the other, the sociologist Franz Borkenau who was wanted for important work in London.

The second request was not acceded to. It was not until 2 June 1941 that any other internees were returned to England.

CHAPTER SEVEN

The New South Wales internment camps were 750 kilometres west of Sydney in the midst of a vast area of almost treeless, semi-arid grazing country. They were immediately adjacent to Hay, a typical sleepy Australian township that then had a population of about 3000. Administrative and headquarters buildings occupied most of Hay's showground and race-course. There is a saying in New South Wales, "Hell, Hay or Booligal", implying that both towns — Booligal is 77 kilometres from Hay — are fairly hot places. Certainly none of the internees had ever seen such a forbidding landscape, but all were not dismayed by its harshness. Hans Buchdahl, Gerd's brother, later professor of theoretical physics at the Australian National University, Canberra, recalls his delight at the shimmering sunshine, the sunsets, even the dust storms. "This is the country I am going to live in," he decided. Other internees recall their first sight of kangaroos which sometimes raced alongside the train, even overtaking it.

The camp complex was surrounded by a triple fence of barbed wire, and guarded by four watch-towers equipped with machine guns and searchlights. (One tower later did duty as the judge's stand on the race-course.) The internees were divided into two compounds, Camp 7 and Camp 8. Each housed about a thousand men in 32 wooden huts and had its big mess hut or assembly hall and necessary offices. Camp 7 was entirely Jewish. Camp 8 had a mixed population of Catholics, Protestants, Communists and a few Jews. The camps were close to one another but the military in its mysterious way adamantly prohibited any communication between them.

Above all, the internees had a desolating sense of isolation. For obscure "security" reasons a 40-day embargo had been placed on mail. It was many weeks before any had news of their families in England.

As soon as they had sorted themselves out, the internees set about organising a system of self-government, based on the toilet-roll constitution. An alternative and less democratic constitution had also been drawn up, and after a long debate in the camp, a compromise embodying the more democratic clauses of the Buchdahl-Herbst-Laske constitution was agreed to. Each camp functioned under the direction of a camp spokesman who was assisted by the equivalent of a cabinet, made up of people responsible for different activities. It included the camp bank manager, the chief of the labour force, the kitchen manager and the entertainment manager. In addition there were the hut captains, one each for the individual huts. Each also had a deputy. The hut captains met in a *Hutcaptainversammlung*, a kind of parliament, which had a speaker, a deputy speaker and a secretary to keep the minutes.

Following the acceptance of the constitution, a court of arbitration which became known as the "camp court" was set up. It became necessary, an article in the camp's roneoed paper *Boomerang* explained, because of the enforced crowding together of people of the most divergent nature:

> Its foremost aim is to safeguard peace and order in the camp. The origin of the camp court can be traced to the *Dunera*. At that time, a court was created and several cases were dealt with. The cases falling under the jurisdiction of the court are as follows: settlement of disputes, civil and constitutional, ascertainment of criminal offences...Its paramount and most salutary work is the settlement of differences out of court. Between September 1940 and April 1941, 44 cases were dealt with. January being the hottest month of the year, it is only natural that the inmates of this camp were unusually irritable and minor clashes and disputes were more frequent. The cooler season brought improvement.

About 200 orthodox Jews (the *Chassidim*) were allocated separate huts, a kitchen and mess-hut, enabling them to sleep and eat, pray and learn on their own. After some months they were able to supplement the vegetable and dairy foods with mutton, killed at a nearby abattoir, in the necessary *kosher* manner.

"Joint Torah studies hardly ever stopped for a day," said Asher Joseph. "People huddled in corners, always eager to learn and debate. By the end of two months, there already emerged a regular time schedule which, for instance, in my case was as follows: three times a week *Talmud Ketubbot*, four times *Pessahim*, twice *Hummaeh*, three Bible lessons, one hour Jewish

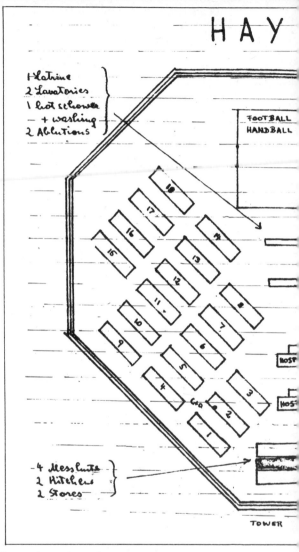

H A Y

1 Latrine
2 Lavatories
1 hot schower
— + washing
2 Ablutions

FOOTBALL
HANDBALL

19
17
16
15
18
13
12
11
10
9
8
7
6
5
4
3
C.O
2
1

HOSP

HOS

- 4 Mess huts
2 Kitchens
2 Stores

TOWER

A diagram of Hay Camp, drawn by an internee.

CAMP.

FROM : Sept.7ᵗʰ, 1940;
TO : May 20ᵗʰ, 1941.

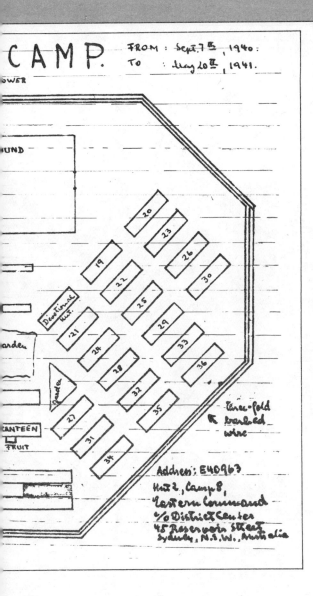

Three-fold
barbed
wire

Address: E40963
Hut 2, Camp 8,
Eastern Command
℅ District Center
45 Reservoir Street
Sydney, N.S.W., Australia

73

Schonbach illustrates scenes from disembarkation to camp life at Hay.
(Schonbach Graphics)

history, two hours Hebrew language and the same for English."

Another glimpse of Jewish life in the camp at Hay is given in an article published in Jerusalem in 1943. "There were two communities organised," it said, "one orthodox and the other liberal. A *Yeshiva* was set up by one community in the camp, and the other celebrated *Oneg Shabat* regularly...The Zionists organised celebrations of Hertzel's and Bialik's memorial days and celebrated *Hanukah* [feast of the candles]. We put lights in the *Hanukah* Lamp which sent out its rays of light over the Australian desert where Jewish feet had never before walked. We also organised choirs for Jewish singing."

Pelz describes the *Chassidim* in the camp ("the late epigoni of a great Polish religious revival") unsympathetically:

> They emerged from their hut surreptitiously. All the young, pasty faces, spongy-yellow under incipient blond whiskers, taut-sallow under black beards, had the same bedazzled eyes. Their eyes were shocked by the sun, since they were used to pore, for hours on end, over pages and pages of the huge Talmud volumes they always carried under their arms while they were not reading. They reminded me of the prisoners in 'Fidelio' as I had once seen them come out of their dungeon in the Staatsoper. They were always in full dress, their caftan-like cloaks buttoned to the neck, old felt hats, crushed over oily locks. Only their eyes, absorbed, defenceless, were startlingly naked...

"The religious societies soon got active and internees who had declared themselves to belong to Catholic, Protestant or Jewish denominations became the lucky recipients of the odd toothpaste, pants, footballs, etc.," said Bern Brent. This inspired a German poem which circulated in the camp. A literal translation of one verse reads:

> *Retain under all circumstances*
> *Your childhood faith,*
> *Religion is everything,*
> *If you get into difficulties,*
> *It doesn't matter if you're Jew or Christian,*
> *The main thing is — you belong.*
> > *By professing any faith you might be rewarded with*
> > *sandals, pants and shirts.*

Before long, canteens, banks, workshops for repairing clothes and shoes and a recreation department had been established, a handball ground levelled, and handball and fistball tournaments organised.

Schonbach depicts a camp soccer game.
(Schonbach Graphics)

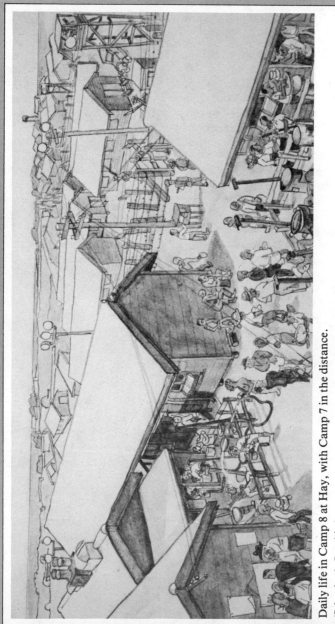

Daily life in Camp 8 at Hay, with Camp 7 in the distance.
(Schonbach Graphics)

An emigration department handled problems of communication with relatives and friends. (Often it took months to get news from England.)

A watch-repair shop struggled to keep the few watches that had escaped the attention of the *Dunera* guards free from the camp's pervasive red dust. In the shoe repair shop, six cobblers worked around the clock with inadequate tools and materials patching up decrepit footwear. Soles and heels were cut from old motor tyres, worn boots converted to shoes, metatarsal supports improvised for those who needed them.

Most importantly, a camp university was set up. There was no lack of talent to staff it. Borkenau and Regner lectured on politics, Hirschfeld, Heckroth, Kitsinger and Franz Philipp on art, Hugo Wolfsohn on philosophy, Leonhard Adam on anthropology, Frederick Eirich on inorganic chemistry, Father Koenig on Goethe's *Faust*, Richard Ullman on German poetry and Doc. K. Sternberg on film making. Henry Mayer taught English and Dr George Herzog, a former master at Bryanston School, Dorset, French language, literature and history in three classes, preparing young internees for matriculation. Rainor Radok and Felix Behrend taught higher mathematics, sometimes working out complex problems on the back of jam tin labels. Other experts lectured on atomic research, astronomy and theology.

The language classes were the busiest. They taught English, Chinese, classical Hebrew, Spanish, French, Italian, Russian, Czech, Brazilian, Portuguese, Latin, classical Greek, modern Greek and Japanese.

Berlin-born Behrend was a graduate of Berlin and Prague universities, and had held posts in Berlin, Cambridge, Zurich and Prague and was at London University when he was deported. He later became Professor of Mathematics at the University of Melbourne. His son, F. A. Behrend, deported with him, became associate professor.

Dr Richard Ullman, a saintly poet, philosopher, humanist and tireless worker for international understanding, was born in Frankfurt-am-Main in 1904 and brought up as a Lutheran, though he had some Jewish ancestry. He took his PhD at Frankfurt University and from 1927 to 1930 conducted a German language school in Serres, Greece. Returning to Germany, he was arrested and sent to Buchenwald concentration camp, from which he was rescued by the Society of Friends. He reached England as a refugee shortly before the outbreak of war and was later interned on the Isle of Man. After his return to England he joined the Society of Friends and, until his death in 1963, worked in adult education at

Woodbrooke and in various Quaker activities, writing, lecturing and preaching the gospel of peace and tolerance. Among his writings were *German Parliaments* with Sir Stephen King-Hall (1954), *Friends and Truth* (1956), *Between God and History* (1959) and the Swarthmore Lecture for 1961, *Tolerance and the Intolerable*. Pelz described him with "his face gleaming with perspiration...his sad eyes, puzzled, sarcastic, mischievously naive, looked out of a pasty, undefined face through dark-rimmed glasses", as he discoursed on Hölderlin, Eichendorff, Mörike, Heine, Lenau, Storm and Droste-Hülshoff, in the mess-hut, "surrounded by the stale memories of disembodied food and the buzz and bump of insects on the window panes".

Franz Philipp was one of those brilliant alumni of the School of Art History in the University of Vienna who were driven out of Austria by the Nazis. He was a world authority on Italian art. After the war he became an ex-service student at the University of Melbourne, subsequently played a principal part in the establishment of the Department of Art History, and became reader in fine arts. He was the author of several studies of Australian art. He died in London in May 1970 while on sabbatical leave.

Hugo Wolfsohn, born in Berlin in 1918, had worked for the Fiat Company in Italy as technical interpreter before going to England in 1939, where he was interned. After the war he studied history at the University of Melbourne, graduating with honours and filling many academic posts until 1966 when he became foundation Professor of Politics at the newly formed La Trobe University (Melbourne). He worked for the Indian Government, did field work in India, received fellowships from many American universities, and was visiting professor at Munich. Pelz acknowledges his debt to Wolfsohn, who while in camp induced him to study economics, sociology and politics, commentaries on Kant's *Critique of Pure Reason*, Freud and McDougall. "He loved truth in all its diverse, unpoetic shapes and hues, with dry enthusiasm," said Pelz. Wolfsohn died in 1981.

Rainor Radok, one of the three brothers rescued from *Arandora Star*, became professor of oceanography at Flinders University, Adelaide, and of mathematics at Brown University on Rhode Island, USA. Uwe Radok became head of the Department of Meteorology at the University of Melbourne, and later at the Boulder University, Colorado, USA. Jobst Radok became a technical executive for the Volkswagen organisation, first in Australia and later in Germany.

Kurt Sternberg, known in Australia as Doc. K, before the war produced films for UFA in Germany and Gaumont British in England, before becoming an independent producer at the Hammersmith Studios in London. After the war he made documentaries for the Commonwealth Film Unit.

Berlin-born Dr Leonhard Adam studied ethnology, law and sinology at the University and Oriental Seminary of Berlin, making a special study of primitive material culture and art at the Berlin Ethnographical Museum. After taking his degree of Doctor of Laws he was called to the bar, was employed in the administration of justice, and later became a judge. He was also a reader in primitive law at the Institute of Foreign Laws, Berlin University, and a member of the Board of Experts of the Ethnographical Museum. Adam was a friend of Malinowski, who wrote to Lady Masson on his behalf (Lady Masson was the wife of the professor of chemistry at the University of Melbourne). In Margaret Holmes's words, "Lady Masson and I yanked him out of the camp." Dr Adam was given special residence at Queen's College, Melbourne, and granted a fellowship by the university to study and classify Aboriginal artefacts at the museum. He had worked on a second edition of his Penguin Special *Primitive Art* while in camp, and had been allowed out to see these artefacts. He had published books and articles in German, French and English on primitive law, tribal organisation, and other ethnological subjects, and on American, Indian and Chinese art. He spent the last years of his life as lecturer on cultural anthropology at the University of Melbourne, where he became curator of an ethnographical and archaeological museum of his own foundation. He died in 1960.

One of the most assiduous students at the camp university was a 20-year-old Austrian Jew, Hans Kronberger, the son of a prosperous Linz leather merchant and a mother "terribly ambitious", as he put it, for his intellectual achievement. He could read, write and play the piano at the age of four, and began learning English at the age of five.

When the Nazis overran Austria in 1938, he managed to flee and six months later arrived at London's Victoria Station with £10 in his pocket, a bicycle, two suitcases, and his very flattering school leaving reports. He was determined to attend a university — any university, in any faculty. With combined naivety and determination, he went from registrar to registrar seeking free admission. He even wrote to President Roosevelt telling of his flight from Nazi-controlled Austria and asking in vain for admission to the United States. Finally, he succeeded in persuading King's College, Newcastle — then part of the University of Durham — to accept him for a course in mechanical engineering though his Austrian matriculation was in mathematics, Latin, Greek and German.

When the round-up of aliens took place in 1940, he was classified as a "friendly enemy alien" and interned on the Isle of Man. Here he met Herman (later Sir Herman) Bondi, the noted mathematician, who tutored him in higher mathematics. Before long, they were separated; Bondi was shipped to Canada, Kronberger to Australia. But there were many other distinguished academics in the camp university, and Kronberger attended their courses from eight in the morning until 10 at night.

Kronberger was allowed to return to England in 1942, travelling on an ammunition ship. He arrived penniless and a policeman in the Liverpool immigration hall gave him half a crown, put him on a train and farewelled him with, "The best of British luck to you." It was a far cry from the sadism of the *Dunera* guard, and Kronberger never forgot the incident. It contributed to his enduring affection for the British.

Back in Newcastle, Kronberger transferred to a physics course. He had been so well taught in Australia that he found the work relatively easy, and he was able to earn money by lecturing on physics at a technical college. Two years later he took his honours degree in physics. From then on, his story is the story of British atomic research and development, to which he contributed immeasurably.

He was a member of the famous "Tube Alloys" team (as Britain's wartime atomic bomb project was code-named) and went to Harwell shortly after its establishment, then to Capenhurst, where he was primarily responsible for the development of diffusion plants for the separation of uranium isotopes. Later, he became chief physicist at the UK Atomic Energy Authority's Industrial Group, scientist-in-chief of the Reactor Group and the authority's member for reactor development.

Kronberger received many honours — OBE, CBE, Fellowship of the Royal Society, and the Royal Society's Leverhulme Tercentenary Medal "in recognition of his many distinguished contributions to nuclear reactor research...and for his outstanding leadership in all branches of this field". But his private life was darkened by three tragedies. Soon after the end of the war he learned that his mother and sister had been murdered in an Auschwitz gas oven. He married in 1951 and within a year found his wife was suffering from a slowly-growing brain tumour. She was progressively disabled and, despite three operations, died in 1962.

Kronberger had a boisterous love of living. Apart from his dedication to his work, he enjoyed with gusto the company of friends, good food and wine, music, mountaineering, skiing and sailing. But even his remarkable resilience failed at last. He had a deepening sense of loneliness, and on 30 September 1970 *The Times* reported:

> Dr Hans Kronberger, aged 50, one of the country's
> outstanding scientists, was found hanged in the garage of his
> home in Wilmalow, Cheshire, yesterday. His chauffeur
> found him when he reported for work...He made an
> outstanding contribution to developments in nuclear energy.

Before the war an organisation called Youth Aliyah was formed in Sydney to raise money to send German and Austrian refugee children in England to Palestine. A number of these young people reached Australia in *Dunera*. Another internee, Franz Stampfl, undertook their training. Stampfl was the Austrian javelin and discus thrower at the 1932 Olympics and national coach at the Olympics in 1936. He had been a parachutist in Austria, and was an athletic coach at Queen's University in Belfast when the war broke out. He had lived in England before the war and returned to enlist in the RAF. A friend advised him to "have a comfortable war in Ireland...they'll grab you as soon as you land". They did.

In 1946 he returned to Queen's and in 1951 became coach at Oxford. He trained Dr Roger Bannister, the first man to run a mile in less than four minutes. In 1955 he accepted a lectureship in Melbourne's Department of Physical Education and two years later the directorship of the Beaurepaire Sports Centre at the University of Melbourne.

A camp officer who had played table tennis for New South Wales was astonished when an internee beat him effortlessly, 21-5, and 21-3. He asked how long it was since the internee had played. "Not since the world doubles championship in 1939," was the reply. "And how did you get on?" "I won." The internee was the Hungarian champion, G. Viktor Barna, who had won the world men's doubles championship eight times!

"In spite of all difficulties," said Father Koenig, "a rich cultural life had developed in the camp." Erwin Fabian, a pupil of Heckroth, conducted an art school, using boot polish watered down with methylated spirits for paint. When the Heckroth school held an exhibition, a critic wrote in *Boomerang*: "The bleakness of our surroundings has proved an asset rather than a disadvantage...Only aesthetic imagination can make them enjoyable." Fabian was praised for his "Still Life Round an Old Stove", a composition of battered tins, logs of wood, ash and rubbish.

There were regular concerts, dramatic performances, debates and revues. Peter Stadlen's choir gave a performance of Handel's "Israel in Egypt". Soloists were Hans Edelman, tenor, and

Professor H. A. Wolfsohn beside a painting by fellow internee Erwin Fabian.

(The Age)

Gunther Hirschberg, baritone. The orchestra included O. Silberstein, A. Landauer, I. Nagler, M. Pietruschka and Dr Poltschak.

The National Security (Internment Camp) Regulations, which applied to refugees as well as to prisoners of war, were a formidable document of many pages. Here are some extracts:

9-(1) As soon as practicable after the arrival of an internee at an internment camp —
(a) particulars relating to him shall be recorded, and a serial number shall be assigned to him;
(b) he shall be searched and any property (including money) which he is not permitted to retain in his possession in the camp shall be taken from him, and particulars thereof shall be recorded;
(c) he shall be medically examined and a statement of his medical condition shall be recorded; and
(d) he shall be given a notice setting out such of these regulations, the Internment Camp Orders and the Camp Rules as he is required to comply with, printed or typed in a language which he can understand.
The Commandant may, if he thinks fit, direct that —
(a) photographs of the internee; and
(b) prints of his fingers or thumbs or any of them shall be taken and the internee shall permit such photographs and prints to be taken.

16-(1) An internee shall be allowed to write and receive letters and other postal articles, subject to censorship, and to such restrictions and conditions as are imposed by the Internment Camp Orders: provided that communications from an internee to an official visitor shall not be subject to censorship.
(2) An internee shall not be permitted —
(a) to send cables or wireless communications overseas, either direct or through a third person; or
(b) to send telegrams within Australia unless exceptional circumstances exist, and then only with the approval of the camp commandant.

18. An internee shall not converse with, communicate with or signal to, any person outside the internment camp, except with the permission of the camp commandant.

20. An internee shall not —
(a) treat with disrespect any official visitor, any officer

or soldier, or any other person employed in connexion
with the internment camp;
(b) swear, curse or use any abusive, insolent, indecent,
threatening or other improper language;
(c) commit any indecent act or make any indecent
gesture;
(d) create unnecessary noise or disturbance.

For contravention of these regulations the offender was
subject to one of these "disciplinary punishments":

(a) Detention for any period not exceeding 28 days during
which period the internee may be confined in a place
specially set apart for the purpose;
(b) confinement to quarters for any period not exceeding 14
days, during which period the offender may be required to
answer his name at uncertain hours throughout the day, and
may be employed on extra fatigue duties, or
(c) suspension of any privileges.

The camp's first news-sheet, published a few days after the arrival
of the refugees, was hand-written on small squares of brown toilet
paper. It was called *The Sun-and-Monday Gazette*, and attractively
priced at "three farthings" — later increased to "three haypenny"
— but because of paper problems the edition was limited to two
copies. Contents were lively and varied. Under the heading "The
Mystery of the Latrine Buckets", the paper reported:

After the roll-call we decided to go for a short trip to the
latrines. What terrible experiences we had there! All the
badly needed buckets were gone. We saw desperate faces
around us, but the penetrating smell indicated that some
unfortunates could not have stood it any longer...
The article speaks for itself. But we ask the responsible
person, "Where are the buckets?"

Other stories in subsequent issues were:

NEW TYPE OF FOOTWEAR
...has been invented. Instead of the uncomfortable old-
fashioned boots the new ones have an open front to enable
the toes to get more and better air...

THE RAINS CAME
As the first herald of spring rain has come. Some people,
unaware of the fact that we are still on English soil, and
therefore have to be provided with the proper English
weather to which we got used already, forgot to take their
life-belts with them and were drowned. Our editor's famous
right shoe has been scuttled for lack of leather...

BIG ROUND OF DOUBLE EATERS
This morning without any previous warning, the police
made a raid at several mess-huts and got hold of a lot of
people who are under suspicion of eating in two or more
shifts...and some are still at large.

Disaster struck with the issue of 22 September which reported:

The editor regrets to announce the destruction of his latest
publication by superior enemy forces...at the cost of four
pieces of government property 36 square inches each.
Although we will not minimise this severe blow, we
nevertheless retain the superiority in brain-power, and
nothing can break the excellent spirit of our collaborators.

Perhaps because of this disaster the paper changed its name to
the *Desert Hayrald and the Views of the World*, but the unknown
saboteur struck again. In its issue of 6 October, the *Desert Hayrald*
reported:

...The gentlemen used the darkness to destroy both our
copies. As spirit is our only weapon, we realise that we
expose ourselves to every cowardly attack.
    But this is not the only trouble we have to take into
account. Our stock of paper is nearly exhausted, our editor
must waste hours of his valuable time to get a pencil or
some ink...Already we have been compelled to amalgamate
our two editions. But we will not give in. Fully aware of the
difficulties which lie ahead we will carry on with our policy
of good humour and with the help of our common sense we
will not fail. When after our release people will speak of the
struggle of this paper, they shall say: that was their finest
hour.

The frivolous *Desert Hayrald* was succeeded by *Boomerang*, a
more sober publication of 14 roneoed foolscap pages, published
weekly. It contained serious articles, reports on camp activities,
and poems by internees, some in German, others in English.

About 16,000 Austrian refugees had been admitted to Great Britain
before the outbreak of World War II. Of these, fewer than 300 had
been classified after thorough investigation as "enemy aliens" and
interned. The interests of the others, accepted as refugees from
Nazi oppression, were looked after by a "Council of Austrians in
Great Britain". On 25 July 1940, the council wrote to the
Australian High Commissioner in London, pointing out that the
"overwhelming majority" of the Austrians on board *Dunera* were

refugees. "We are most anxious," the letter continued, "that the Australian Government is aware of this fact and that the Australian public should be given information about it. We feel sure that once this fact is established the great tradition of the British people of offering asylum to victims of persecution will be alive and will assure our unfortunate compatriots the elementary rights of human beings and the rights of civil liberties which a democracy can offer them." The letter ended with a request that the council be permitted to send a representative to keep contact with the refugees and "work for their welfare on the spot".

The council's reasonable request was for some arcane reason referred by the Prime Minister's Department in Canberra to the Department of the Army in Melbourne. How Australia's security would be imperilled by the presence at Hay of an Austrian welfare representative is not clear, but after brooding over the vital question for nearly six weeks, the department, through its secretary, J. T. Fitzgerald, informed the Prime Minister and the High Commissioner that as "the accommodation provided for and treatment accorded to internees" was in accordance with the Geneva Convention, and as "official visitors" would be visiting the internment camps "for the purpose of ensuring that the treatment and welfare of internees shall regularly be reported upon, it is considered that no useful purpose would be served by the Council of Austrians in Britain sending a representative to Australia".

The heavy hand of military bureaucracy was manifested in many ways. An Austrian internee who made silk bags — they were called pompadours in the old days — found he could sell them for three shillings and sixpence each outside the camp. But, incomprehensibly, this was not allowed. Two postal notes to the total value of seven shillings were impounded by the camp commandant and returned to the sender. "I could make up to two dozen a month," the bewildered internee wrote to the Society of Friends. "It would help me to *earn* money, which I need for buying food, clothes and books necessary for my study."

As for the civil liberties of the internees, and whether or not the Australian public knew that they were refugees, neither the Department of the Army nor the Prime Minister's Department was interested. And both departments showed a similar disinterest when the Home Office, four days after *Dunera*'s arrival in Sydney, requested the Australian Government to change the name "Prisoner of War Information Bureau" to "Internees' Information Bureau". It was a small enough concession but the Department of the Army firmly rejected it: "As Prisoner of War Information Bureau known internationally by this name...regret unable to agree change which would be associated with practical inconvenience." The "inconvenience" suffered by the internees being labelled "prisoner of war" was not important.

Letters could be sent to enemy countries through two recognised intermediaries — Thomas Cook and Sons, and the Australian Red Cross — but for some months many internees had no writing material. A typical letter written to the Society of Friends by an internee in October 1940 reads:

> We are allowed to write two letters a week. This is not much
> if you have to write over great distances. But even these two
> letters I am unable to write, simply because I have not got
> money to buy writing paper, envelopes, ink, pens. Besides
> of that, some of the letters I would have to write are very
> urgent ones, I cannot however send them all airmail for the
> reason just stated. As nearly all of the internees here arrived
> without money it is impossible to get a sheet of notepaper or
> an envelope lent to you. The authorities, it seems, are not
> willing to supply us with stationery or writing utensils.

Letters to internees had to be endorsed "Services of Prisoners of War" and letters from them were stamped "Prisoners of War". In December, internees were issued with official notepaper, ruled with 22 lines to which their letters had to be restricted. "You cannot imagine how depressed the men are about this measure," Eric Stadlen wrote to a sympathiser. "They fail to understand why this hardship should be inflicted on them." And Norbert Leight, a 16-year-old Austrian, wrote: "Although leading Cabinet Ministers like Mr Churchill and Mr Morrison have repeatedly declared that regrettable mistakes have been made regarding internees in Australia, we are compelled to use this paper designed for prisoners of war." And the letters of internees were subject to a capricious and irritating censorship and to long delays.

The notepaper on which internees had to write carried this injunction in three languages:

NICHT ZWISCHEN DIE ZEILEN SCHREIBEN!
NON SCRIVERE TRA LE RIGHE!
DO NOT WRITE BETWEEN THE LINES.

Ulrich Boschwitz was a young German writer who had the manuscript of an unpublished novel taken from him on *Dunera*. He wanted to resume writing but his first concern was to get in touch with his mother. In October 1940 he wrote to the Society of Friends (on YMCA notepaper endorsed, "THINK CLEAN, TALK CLEAN, LIVE CLEAN, PLAY THE GAME!"):

> Ever since I was interned at the end of June, I don't know

anything about the present address of my mother. Until the
end of June, she was interned on the Isle of Man...Would
you be so kind as to help me find out her present
whereabouts. Could you let her know at the same time that
I am in this camp and am keeping well.

Nine months later, his mother wrote to the Society of Friends:

He needs writing paper, one thousand sheets, and
typewriter, maybe a second-hand one. Please over there can
you manage it that my son who has had good success with
his last book, *The Fugitive*, in France and in England, can
work in his profession as writer. His first book published in
Sweden he has written at 21 years. He wants nothing more
than to work as a writer in the internment too, so that when
he will be free again, he has not lost his whole time, sitting
and lounging round. I am a painter and a writer too and I
don't waste my time. I can do it here but the poor boy there
is handicapped — no paper, no typewriter, no money at all.
It is necessary that useful work is done even in a prisoners'
camp.

The *Manchester Guardian* on 6 March 1941 published this
extract from a letter written by a 19-year-old internee in Australia
to a friend in London:

I hope father is released by now. We hear that so many
people are being released there [in England] whereas we
have to sit here. I tell you that I would rather be a thousand
times there, in spite of all the bombs...Release in Australia
is impossible...I am lying in bed nearly all day long because
it is too hot to get up, only at night do I get a bit of air.
Many of us are very bitter about our transport here...We
were told we would go to a permanent camp in England.
Instead we found ourselves here. We were not asked and did
not volunteer. I would never have volunteered. By the way,
do not let yourselves be deceived by the stamp "prisoner of
war". You know best that we are not prisoners of war, but
refugees from Nazi oppression, and that we before all others
were fighting against Nazi methods. Apparently that has all
been forgotten.

Three *Dunera* internees widely differing in background and belief,
the German Jesuit Father Koenig, the left-wing novelist Walter
Kaufmann, and Werner Pelz, published accounts of their
experiences in Australia.

Father Koenig was one of a number of German Jesuits who in 1939 were expelled by Hitler from their college of St Aloysius at Bad Godesburg, on the Rhine. Some remained in Germany; others, including Father Koenig, sought refuge in England, where he was welcomed by the English Jesuits. He was teaching in a college near Sheffield until he was caught in the alien round-up of May 1940, and joined *Dunera*. In May 1963, when he was over eighty, he contributed an article to the Catholic quarterly *Twentieth Century* which gives a vivid picture of the Hay camp:

> It wasn't the luxury camp we had been told about during the trip through the Indian Ocean — set on an island in the sea, in the shade of waving palm-trees and provided with a sandy beach and every modern comfort! We found ourselves completely isolated, on the edge of a boundless, almost treeless, plain. On the far-off horizon, the air trembled in the heat. Over on the left stretched the fringe of trees bordering the Murrumbidgee. On the right, and a little closer, was a lonely and deserted sheep farm...Apart from this, there was nothing but burnt desolate land as far as the eye could see. The camp itself gave a not unfavourable impression of strength and neatness. With its strong double-barbed-wire fence and four watch-towers equipped with machine guns, the 32 wooden barrack huts with their white-grey asbestos roofs, the two big mess-huts or assembly halls and the offices, it resembled a little fortress. You could see that the barrack huts were arranged in fan formation so that their entrance could be easily controlled from the camp gate.

Escape was impossible. "There was nowhere to go," Father Koenig wrote. "One homesick boy who nevertheless made the attempt was caught climbing the fence at night and saved from a lonely end on the dusty plains." Each hut contained 24 bunks. Father Koenig's hut companions included two religious, a university lecturer, a high court official from Czechoslovakia, a professor of music, a commercial traveller and "a somewhat eccentric professor" from Berlin. There were also a number of young people, among them Father Koenig's mass servers, the two young Counts von Wolkenstein.

Father Koenig estimated that three per cent of the refugees were Catholic, seven per cent Protestant, and the remainder Jews "of most varied religious opinions". The men were divided into two camps of roughly equal numbers, a right and left wing, known officially as Camp 7 and Camp 8, and unofficially as the *kosher* and communist camps. Father Koenig chose "the socialistically inclined" Camp 8, which contained most of the Catholics.

One of the camp huts.

(Uwe Radok)

The Camp 8 guard tower (south), at Hay.

(Australian War Memorial, Canberra)

Gradually the heat rose, and the summer we feared began. Strange mirages built up around us. Towards midday we clearly saw the Murrumbidgee overflow and with its blue waves play around trees on the river banks. Towards evening the mirage disappeared. Then suddenly ghostlike 'willy-willies' [Aboriginal name for a rapidly rotating column of air] whirled through the camp and subsided in the distance. With summer came dust-storms that changed day into night, and temperatures of 100 degrees [38°C] and more. Enormous masses of black topsoil and red sand suddenly filled the air, were torn in a whirl high into the air and were carried...thousands of miles away. The fine sand penetrated our huts and was in everything, clothes, books and palliasses...We thought we would suffocate...At night we lay on the ground to get air.

Kaufmann's account of his arrival in Australia appeared in *Meanjin*, an Australian literary quarterly, in 1954. It begins with the disembarkation of "Stefan Hermann", a 16-year-old internee, in Sydney:

Stefan Hermann turned his head and looked hard at the burly British sergeant from the Royal Norfolk Regiment. For an instant their glances looked and there was no mistaking the hatred in the boy's eyes.

...Come on, the sergeant said in a heavy accent. Git going. The boy hesitated. The sergeant raised his rifle and shoved him forward with the butt.

Break *my* toes, too, said the boy. Here, he held out a foot which was protected only by a rubber sole cut from an old car tyre.

Git, the sergeant shouted again. Move! and he banged his rifle on the ground.

Kaufmann describes how the internees "emerged like moles from the bowels of the ship", most of them carrying nothing but a bundle of bare necessities. Their other possessions had been either looted or tossed overboard by "the hostile English guards". Stefan carries not even a bundle. He wears baggy trousers held in place by a string and a collarless army shirt. Around his neck is a woman's woollen scarf that has belonged to his mother. He boards the "prison train" and gazes sullenly through a window secured with bolts.

As the journey continues, he looks at the slouch-hatted Australian guards, leaning heavily on their rifles, "their feet wide apart, their tunics open at their throats, hats pushed back, stubs of cigarettes stuck in the corners of their mouths". One, "a tall, scrawny man in his fifties with a bony face, and spare, wiry eyebrows", sits down and stretches his legs while he holds his rifle carelessly, like a stick. At length, he asks in a slow drawl, "Where'd they catch yer, mate?"

> The boy started and shrugged his shoulders. It was the first time since his internment that anyone in uniform had attempted to speak to him.
> — Talk Australian?
> — English, Stefan asked. Yes, a little.
> — Well, where did yer get nabbed? The guard's grey eyes blinked impatiently. The boy shook his head.
> — All right, never mind. You one of Hitler's mob?
> — No, said Stefan emphatically. No, I am a Jew.
> — Ah yeah, said the guard somewhat surprised. And what about yer cobbers?
> — Same, said Stefan Hermann not knowing what cobbers meant but guessing that it referred to the other internees.
> — What the hell youse all doing here then? asked the guard. No point in locking you up. Had the idea you was all prisoners of war.

Sympathetically, the guard continues his inquiry. He learns that Stefan is 16 and that his relatives are still living in Germany. In an effort to be friendly, he tells Stefan of a Jewish dental mechanic he had met in Sydney who had made him a set of false teeth. He takes them out and exhibits them. "First-class job," he says. "Clever bloke that Jew in Sydney."

He tells the other guard, Danny, that the internees are not Huns but Jewish refugees. "Open the bloody windows down your end, Danny," he says, "They're not going to make a break for it." With that, in defiance of all rules and regulations, he proceeds to knock down with his rifle butt the special bolts that hold the windows up. Then he and Danny toss their rifles on to the luggage racks and squat down to roll themselves cigarettes, not failing to offer their pouches to the internees, many of whom crave tobacco as starving men crave food. The atmosphere grows jollier and friendlier with every mile.

> At length the guard named Danny asked Stefan how the *Pommies* had treated him. The boy looked up questioningly.
> — You know — the guards on the ship, Danny explained.
> — Ah...not good, said Stefan pointing to a man across from him, whose foot was in plaster. One of their sergeants, we called him Lion Hunter, broke his toes. Danny spat disgustedly.

— Never known a Pommy that was any good yet, he said
with emphasis.
— Cut it out, said his mate. Don't go puttin' ideas like that
in their heads. There's a war on, you know, and it ain't agin
the Pommies.
— Sure, sure, I know, placated Danny, tapping the man
with the broken toe good-naturedly on the shoulder. You'll
be all right here, son. Great country this. Best in the world,
Australia.

Kaufmann describes how the dawn spreads over "a vast and
silent land, barren and unchanging", and how when towards noon
they reach Hay, travel weary, "the singeing sun had reached its
summit and the ground reflected unsparingly the heat and the
brightness that engulfed them like a burning blanket". He and his
companions had never seen such country in their lives.
"Sure...sure, one step from hell, this, one step from hell, hot and
dusty," Danny announces. "But you'll get used to her — in time."
The internees are met by an escort of mounted troops. A
sergeant, "his face burnt the colour of earth", shouts the order to
march. The column struggles slowly through a cloud of powdery
dust towards the camp.

And then behind the last of their column three barbed wire
gates closed slowly...A dog began barking as a bugle
sounded. Inside the roll was called by the sergeant with the
tanned face. He counted them by stepping swiftly along
their flank, two men for every step. One more, one less,
what matter; none would be missing — for where in this
desert could they go? The captain read out the camp orders
in a voice that lost itself over the vast parade ground and in
the pulsating heat. Few grasped his meaning. Somewhere,
inconspicuous among the 2000, stood Stefan Hermann. He
was not listening to what the Australian captain was trying
to explain. He was watching a hawk circling in the blue sky
high above the camp. The hawk circled twice, then swooped
in the direction of a gnarled tree and vanished from sight.
The bird's freedom impressed itself on Stefan, poignantly.

Pelz, in *Distant Sounds of Triumph*, writes:

For two years the treble barbed wire was my second skin. It
defined my life exactly...I had started to walk round and
round it...when the camp was still covered with yellowish-
grey puddles. The cold slimy mud squelched through my
toes, oozed through the corroded shoe leather...I walked
through the Australian spring, when the sun monopolised

the sky, sucked up the puddles and turned the soil into warm glasspaper. . . I walked into and through the summer, while the temperature climbed beyond 110 [43°C] in the shade, the palliasses rotted under sweltering bodies . . . Around us was the desert, blind, cracked, birdless, treeless, dust merging into dust, flatness into flatness, all into the haze of an indistinct horizon where sky and earth were neither severed nor joined.

Round and round you walk, easily circling the whole of the world granted to you, 20 to 30 times a day. The sun fries all unnecessary fat out of you and tans your skin deep mahogany.

And while he circled the camp. . .

men, women and children were burned to death in London, Moscow and Cologne; were tortured to death in concentration camps. In Burma men died of tropical diseases and Japanese brutalities. They died of exposure in the Arctic sea. . .

A poem by Henry Mayer is equally evocative:

RAINY DAY
Outside, bleak showers have transformed
The soil to squelching quicksand
And a reticulated hand
Tries drawing you below. The graph
In year-book later on, will show
The slight increase. The isobars are sunk to naught.

CHAPTER EIGHT

Major McCahon from Army Headquarters visited the Hay camps and reported that they were all sited on flat, dusty ground, carrying no vegetation, because of the drought. "It can be expected," he wrote, "that during the next four months severe dust-storms and high temperatures will make conditions for the garrison and the internees extremely unpleasant. In the event of heavy rains falling...the camps in their present undrained condition would become areas of sticky mud."

Commenting on Major McCahon's report, the chief engineer of the Australian Military Forces, Eastern Command, wrote, "The selection of Hay has been criticised...but many factors governed this, and it is so situated as to give the maximum assurance of retention of those interned. This aspect it is suggested should not be overlooked."

No doubt the refugees had overlooked the Army's solicitude for their "retention".

Local conditions required that each member of the garrison be supplied with a pair of close-fitting, tinted goggles for protection against dust-storms. The eyes of the internees were not given this protection. Snakes, mosquitoes and ubiquitous squadrons of flies added to their discomfort. In a petition, they made an "earnest request...at least for a temporary release, or, if this is not possible, for a move to a more suitable and healthy camp". Five had been taken to hospital, suffering from an imprisonment psychosis, and about 40 suffering from lung and heart complaints were moved to Orange, a pleasant town 260 kilometres west, north-west of Sydney. One, "a highly gifted boy", had tried to open the veins in his wrists.

Dr Richard Ullman expressed the mood of his fellow internees in English verse. The first two stanzas read:

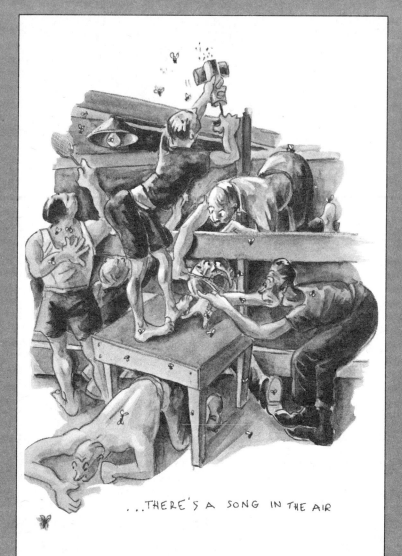

...THERE'S A SONG IN THE AIR

In summer, flies were tormenting at Hay, as shown here by Schonbach.
(Schonbach Graphics)

They walk about and talk and play
They even smile and laugh and sing
But in their voices sounds a ring
As from an organ far away.

It is a tune abrupt and strange
And by their laughter sadly torn
It tells of gardens long forlorn
Through which their yearning spirits range.

"I understand there is at present very little prospect of any of the internees being released, although in the majority of cases there is nothing else against them but their nationality," Alfred Clarke, a member of the Society of Friends, wrote at the end of September, in reply to an inquiry about one of them. And he added, "If they were released there would no doubt be a public outcry, which the Government is desirous of avoiding." It was a perceptive observation.

An article in *Boomerang* (14 April 1941) discussed the health of the Hay internees philosophically:

> The climate is certainly a hard one and thoroughly unpleasant but it is not unbearable. In fact our main problem is to adapt ourselves to the rapid changes in temperature. Sunburn was prevalent soon after our arrival. Some of us suffered from heat exhaustion, with giddiness, nausea, headache and a general feeling of weakness. Conjunctivitis was not uncommon. One of the least pleasant Australian surprises has been a microbe to which we Europeans are not accustomed. This microbe has settled in all our throats causing anything from slight malaise to severe tonsilitis... This microbe produces a poison with a tendency to damage the heart muscles of quite a number of our young community. At first this epidemic was called rheumatic fever but it now seems fairly firmly established that it is a sequel to tonsilitis... a long period of physical rest will improve most cases.
>
> Lastly the chronic skin disease tinea has played havoc with some of our feet. However, tinea dislikes cold weather and with the coming winter months the future looks brighter... Generally our health is good in spite of the exacting climate. If you don't believe it just look at the rosy cheeks of the man next to you.

Fred Hopkins was an old "digger" of 44, a veteran of the Palestine campaign in World War I. He re-enlisted in 1940 when there was a request for World War I men with medical experience to serve at the internment hospital, situated in the old Hay jail.

> Here I saw the strangest assortment of humanity...All you have heard of their treatment by the guards on the ship is true. They robbed them of all their family heirlooms, and you can imagine what that meant when they 'flogged' these around the pubs and posed as heroes of Dunkirk. They told the internees that it was nothing to what the Australians would do to them, and were surprised to find the average 'digger' a kindly soul even if he was anti-semitic in many cases. I loved talking to them, their knowledge of the arts, music, books, etc...For this I was court-martialled. A nasty piece of work said I was a spy, but I got out of it. One of the most remarkable characters was Professor Robert Hoffman, a Viennese. He had been a court painter in Vienna, knew all the Hapsburg gossip, had been a major in charge of a Turkish regiment. And as I was fighting with the Light Horse on the other side, I liked to talk to him.
>
> He told me when he got to London he did portraits in crayon, Harrods charged the clients £100 and he got £50, and if I got the crayons he would do me. It's my proudest possession. After that officers came to get theirs done, but they didn't offer any payment.

When Hopkins left for Darwin in 1941, the young patients lined up and gave him a letter of thanks for his understanding and help. "You can't help much on five shillings a day," he said. One day, flocks of galahs flew across the sky, and Hopkins asked an internee if he had seen such birds before. "Yes," said the internee, "they were in cages, and now we are in cages and they are looking at us."

Soon after the arrival of the internees at Hay, Lieutenant Chapman, with the assistance of an interpreter, Sergeant Masurier, and a number of "selected internees", under instructions from Army Headquarters, made a search for "valuables etc.", in the internees' luggage. His report, dated 9 October 1940, was accompanied by 33 sheets of foolscap listing 2234 names.

In the report, Chapman wrote: "The condition of baggage generally shows ample evidence of interference presumably during voyage from England, and the number of bundles with loose linen, clothes, shoes etc. may also be taken as further evidence of the rough treatment accorded to the luggage." The report continued: "In some cases notes of original content were furnished by owners."

Chapman listed one case where jewellery, valuables and £50 in English bank notes were removed before he opened the locked bag. "This bag showed where the lid had been sufficiently strained to allow the insertion of a man's arm." Among the missing papers were addresses of prominent British people, and a treatise on vulcanising marked "secret" in German, about which the owner had expressed concern.

"It is stated by internees," the report concluded, "that about 10 per cent had received no luggage and about 20 per cent only portion of their luggage."

Accompanying the report was a statement by an internee written at Chapman's request:

> Numerous occurrences where soldiers and NCOs took property such as money, rings, fountain-pens, from internees, resulted in a great number of complaints addressed to the Commandant, Lieutenant-Colonel T. W. Scott. The Commandant thereupon summoned various group leaders, myself included, on deck and delivered a short speech, in which he blamed the authorities in the internment camps in England for allowing internees to leave the camps with money and valuables. He then added that it was naturally impossible for officers to have an eye everywhere and that he did not wish to hear any further complaints. The officer of my part of the ship, Mr Tinning, then informed me, in my capacity as group leader, that facilities would now be given for internees to deposit all valuables, which they did not wish to fall into the hands of the NCOs, in safe keeping, and added a soldier's promise that they would be returned before our arrival at our destination. I, therefore, advised the internees in my group to trust the word of a British officer and to deposit everything of value, properly labelled, in my presence, in a bag, which was then handed to Mr Tinning.
>
> My advice seemed to be justified, because, shortly afterwards, a number of NCOs with a few soldiers, but without any officers being present, made a raid on our quarters, in which everything of value was pocketed, and in which practically all papers were torn, this in spite of an assurance given that it was allowed to keep valuable papers, such as passports, manuscripts, address books, letters of recommendation etc. All this was done in a most brutal manner.
>
> We have to point out that there was no necessity for this searching of our cases as we all came from internment camps where our cases had already been examined...But

chiefly we object to the fact that our cases were forced or
split open and of course damaged, that the search did not
take place in the presence of officers, that our cases were not
returned to us after the search, and they were not stored
safely.

(Cases distributed through three camps in Australia often
were impossible to identify.)

The Department of the Army suggested to the Prime
Minister's Department that copies of Lieutenant Chapman's
report, copies of Colonel Scott's imaginative memoranda, and a
copy of the internee's statement be sent to the British Government.

The Army made a curious comment: "It will be seen that,
owing to baggage not being searched prior to embarkation, money,
valuables, prohibited articles and perishable articles were included.
The OC 'Q' Troops claims that it was necessary to breach the bags
to obtain clothing; but it would appear that adequate steps were not
taken to safeguard the property of the internees which, as it now
transpires, invited theft.

"Similarly, the secretion by internees of valuables on their
persons must have presented a temptation to the guards which
could not have been foreseen by the OC Troops."

The wholesale theft of rings by *Dunera* escort troops inspired
one internee, L. Bernhardt, with the theme of a sardonic short
story. It told how one of the guards returning to England has a
reunion with his fiancee, Joan, who is overjoyed at the prospect of
their early marriage. Suddenly Joan, with tears in her eyes, says,
"Are you a bigamist?" and walks away.

> He stares after her and slowly lowering his gaze notices a
> golden ring on his third finger. 'Good Lord yes,' and
> remembers taking it as booty from one of 'these damned
> internees'.

On 18 September 1940, Mr Roehrs, leader of the German internees
in No. 2 Internment Camp, Tatura, sent this message to Mr J. A.
Pietzcker, consul for Switzerland, the "protecting power" in
Melbourne:

> Question whether prisoners of war or internees leading to
> greatest difficulties and embitterment. Immediate settlement
> and your visit most essential. Wire date arrival.

Mr Pietzcker sent a copy of this message to Captain T. K.
Maltby, DAAS, Southern Command, Melbourne, and wrote:
"Kindly advise me of the decision arrived at by the Department of
the Army regarding their status":

Are they to be looked upon and treated as 'internees', the same as civilian internees from Australia, or does the department intend to differentiate with regard to these newly arrived internees from England?

An early decision on this subject will oblige.

The Adjutant-General replied that the internees from overseas were to be regarded as civilian internees and not as prisoners of war. Their status was the same as that of Australian internees.

But, in effect, they were treated as prisoners of war. They had not the right (as civilian internees had) to appeal to a tribunal against their internment, and their mail was endorsed "Services of Prisoners of War".

On 5 October Mr Justice Gavan Duffy of the Victorian Supreme Court, as an official visitor, reported on his visit to the *Dunera* internees at Tatura. "I was given several accounts of the treatment of these men during the voyage," he wrote. "If even part of these accounts is true, the authorities on that ship seem to have taken the *Altmark* as their model." (The *Altmark* was a German naval supply ship boarded on Churchill's orders and captured in a Norwegian fjord by the destroyer *Cossack* on 16 February 1940. The boarding party overpowered the German crew and liberated 299 prisoners of war, captured by the *Graf Spee*. They had been badly treated.)

> I pointed out, however, the difficulties — time and space and differing authorities — put in their way, and without encouraging them in much hope of redress however real their grievances, advised them if they desire to go on with the matter, to prepare a detailed case, which could, if necessary, be supported by affidavits. If such case is prepared, I suppose it will be forwarded to the English authorities, as it would hardly rebound to our credit to leave definite charges of theft and ill-treatment without inquiry.

A few weeks later, Sir Frederick Jordan, Chief Justice of New South Wales and official visitor to the New South Wales camps, reported on his visit to Hay. The internees complained of the atrocious treatment they had been subjected to on *Dunera*:

> On my asking why complaint was not made to the officers of the guard, I was told that officers were present when ill-treatment and pilfering took place, and that it was thought protest would be futile. I was informed also that shortly before the arrival of the transport in Australia, a letter

signed by representatives of the internees was sent to the commanding officer of the guard. This asked for the restoration of money, valuables and documents, and for compensation for damage to luggage and for anything not restored. Some days later, they were informed...that the commander regarded the letter as the limit of impudence, and if this should happen again, the signatories would be put in irons and handed over to the Australian authorities in that condition.

Sir Frederick's report ended cautiously: "I am unable to offer any opinion as to the correctness of these allegations."

I should think it more than likely that some, if not all, of the charges made are exaggerated, perhaps very greatly so...I am, however, of opinion that there is at least sufficient substance in the charges to warrant their being investigated. I am led to this conclusion by two considerations. First, several officers at the camp at Hay who saw the internees upon their arrival...remarked particularly on their cowed and abject appearance, of which certainly no trace now remains. Second, I am informed that the luggage of the internees...bears signs of having been broken open, apparently by bayonets. It is not easy to see why forcible opening should have been necessary for the purpose of making legitimate search.

Sir Frederick explained to the internees' representative that he had no authority to investigate the matter, but suggested that full and detailed statements be prepared by all complainants...with a view to the complaint being communicated to the English authorities. "I might add," his report concluded, "that I have been informed that Sir Geoffrey Whiskard is interesting himself in this matter; and it might be thought fit to bring this memorandum to his notice."

The internees considered their basic problem was to convince the authorities that they were not Fifth Columnists or prisoners of war. Ignorant as they were of the Australian Government's attitude to them, they thought once their status was established, release from internment would follow.

An example of the way the authorities were misinformed was the fact that soon after the arrival of the internees at Hay, the Swiss consul appeared with an offer to help them. Switzerland was the "protecting party" for interned German nationals and the authorities did not distinguish between Nazi nationals and anti-Nazi refugees. The consul's well-meaning offer was, of course, politely but firmly refused.

A memorandum submitted to Jordan from Compound 2, Camp 7 stated in part:

> As people who had been recognised by British judiciary authorities to be refugees from Nazi oppression, and as loyal supporters of the British cause, we are placed in the difficult position of having to ask for an independent investigation to be conducted, whilst wishing to avoid any publicity useful to the enemy...
>
> We submit that quite apart from promises made we should be granted privileges identical with those prevailing in other dominions...
>
> There are among us scientists and specialists (viz. toolmakers, engineers, etc.) highly skilled in trades and professions, who could go a long way to supplement the general war effort. Many of them had been engaged in England in ministries, engineering works, chemical factories, industrial plants, working under government orders for the export trade and the forces.

The next official visitor to Hay was Mr Justice Davidson of the New South Wales Supreme Court. He, too, received a memorandum from Camp 7, which pointed out that their existing conditions in no way corresponded with the promises made to them in England. The statement continued:

> We particularly mention the severe climate, the primitive sanitary arrangements, the entire lack of any comforts in the sleeping huts, the unwarranted attitude displayed by the district censor in dealing with our correspondence, inflicting additional unnecessary hardships. For instance, attempts to communicate with the officially recognised refugee committees in London were frustrated by the censor stopping our letters. Many other letters from internees were returned after four to six weeks because of 'communication to third parties'.

And, most importantly, they still did not know which authority was competent to review their status, particularly as many of their fellow refugees in England had already been released.

CHAPTER NINE

The Rt Reverend Venn Pilcher, Bishop coadjutor of Sydney, represented the Archbishop of Sydney as chairman of the Inter-Church Committee for Non-Aryan Christian Refugees. In conjunction with three other organisations, the Australian Jewish Welfare Committee, the Continental Catholic Migrants Committee and the European Emergency Committee, Bishop Pilcher in June 1940 sent a lengthy petition to Menzies, asking for the constitution of an appeal tribunal presided over by a judge after the manner of the tribunals dealing with refugees' appeals in England. The petition pointed out that naturalised aliens interned in New South Wales had the right to appeal to a tribunal presided over by Mr Justice Davidson. Refugees however, not being naturalised, had no such right.

The petition made these other points:

> The cases with which we are concerned are those of refugees who have escaped to Australia from the persecution of the Nazis in Germany and Central Europe. All have suffered at the hands of Hitler. Some have suffered and undergone cruelty of treatment which is almost unimaginable...The internees themselves maintain that they have no idea at all as to why they have been interned and their one request is that their cases may receive a thorough and impartial investigation. In other words that the principles of British justice may be extended to them...If the Australian people were told that an Australian citizen could be imprisoned on the basis of a dossier made up by the police without opportunity of defence or the protection of the legal procedure of the court, there would be an immediate outcry from one end of Australia to another. This, however, is the

system to which these unfortunate people are subjected — people who have fled from the Nazi Gestapo to what they believed to be the freedom of our British constitution...In the National Security Regulations the rule is laid down that the onus of proving his loyalty must be on the alien. Under present conditions the alien has no court before which he could prove his loyalty. It seems inconsistent to require that an alien shall afford such proof and then to refuse him any facilities for so doing. This clause in the National Security Regulations definitely implies the existence of an appeal tribunal...The loyalty of refugees serving in England and in the Pioneer Battalions was decided by tribunals before their enlistment. Once again we ask that, if such testing be considered necessary here, the English example be followed. Several refugees, at present interned, have offered or desire to offer their services in this way.

Menzies' reply to these logical and humanitarian submissions is not on record, but the Government took no action. Bishop Pilcher, however, a man of great compassion and fortitude, was not discouraged. He continued to press for an appeal tribunal, next addressing himself to the Army Minister, Senator P. A. McBride, in a letter dated 28 September 1940. Even by the standards of political double-talk, Senator McBride's reply, emitted some weeks later, was an egregious compound of mis-statement, evasion and naivety. "As you are aware," he wrote, "no person is interned unless there are grounds for believing that, if left at liberty, he might act in a manner prejudicial to the defence of the Commonwealth. Internment is thus a precautionary measure in the interests of national security."

His letter continued:

...To sum up, it is not always possible to establish beyond doubt whether a person is a genuine refugee or not, and even a genuine refugee may constitute a menace to the national security on some occasions...I would suggest, further, that it is not practicable in time of war to rely entirely on the judicial methods suitable and desirable in times of peace, in order to safeguard the nation against persons whom responsible authorities reasonably suspect to be dangerous...In conclusion, I should like to say that the suggestion mentioned in your letter, that an appeal tribunal should be set up to deal with enemy alien internees other than those from overseas, is at present under consideration. The further suggestion, that genuine refugees be allowed to serve in the military forces, was considered some time ago but rejected as dangerous and undesirable.

Bishop Pilcher continued his struggle on behalf of the refugees, but found the New South Wales State Government as unco-operative as the Federal Government. On 26 March 1941, he was reported in the *Sydney Morning Herald*:

> People in Australia are playing Hitler's game by persecuting
> refugees who come here, said Dr Pilcher....Refugees in
> Sydney today bear on their bodies marks of Nazi torture,
> and wake at night screaming in terror dreaming of their past
> tortures...The committee of which I am chairman has been
> trying to secure British and Christian justice for them. A
> body representing every religious denomination in New
> South Wales asked to be allowed to speak to the State
> Government on this subject. We have been persistently
> refused. I rather wonder whether any government has ever
> treated the representatives of all the churches with such
> discourtesy. These people want nothing more than joining
> the State and yet we insist on classing them as enemy aliens.
> Is this British or Christian?

Later, writing in a camp paper, George Berger analysed Australia's attitude towards Jewish immigrants and concluded that:

> ...the leaders in New South Wales who swayed public
> opinion against the refugees on anti-semitic grounds or on
> possible disloyalty of refugees were the then premier,
> Alexander Mair and his deputy, Colonel M. F. Bruxner.

VIREC also wrote to Senator McBride asking for a tribunal for classifying refugees. The council had to be satisfied with a reply from the Senator's private secretary, P. T. Hayter: "I am to say that the Minister will see that all consideration is given to the matters referred to in your letter."

No consideration, full or partial, was forthcoming, and Bishop Pilcher on 9 September — three days after *Dunera*'s arrival in Sydney — appealed once more to the Prime Minister:

> I think I ought to let you know that I have written to the
> new Minister for the Army, Senator McBride, telling him
> of our appeal for a tribunal, and explaining to him the
> reasons for that appeal. I have added one reason that I have
> not yet put before you. I learn that the National Security
> Regulations place the onus of proof as to his loyalty upon
> the alien. It seems strange to do this, and then to refuse him
> any means of so proving his loyalty. The present
> refugees...are ignorant of the charge against them and have

no means of making their defence. The situation seems strangely anomalous. I have heard that among these internees are many students for the Jewish Rabbinat together with a few rabbis. It seems psychologically impossible that these men should be disloyal to Great Britain or could favour the Nazis, persecutors of their race.

Menzies' reply, dated 13 September 1940, occupied four lines. "I have your letter of 9 September, regarding the establishment of a tribunal for internees. I know Senator McBride is looking into the matter, and you may be sure he will give it every consideration." Menzies sagaciously refrained from expressing his personal views on the Bishop's proposal.

Bishop Pilcher next wrote to Menzies asking his permission to visit Tatura. Menzies, for a reason that remains obscure, replied that he would be grateful if Bishop Pilcher did not press his request.

On 18 October the Bishop again wrote to Menzies: "I notice that you tell me that you would be grateful if I did not press my request to visit Tatura. I do not wish to do anything that would embarrass you in any way, but I feel that it is only right to explain to you at greater length my reasons for desiring to visit the internment camps."

The Bishop explained that not only was his inter-church committee anxious for him to gain some personal knowledge of the camps, but "the great English Inter-Church Committee was extremely interested in the internees who had been sent to Australia from England". The presidents of this English committee were the Archbishop of Canterbury, Cardinal Archbishop of Westminster and the Moderator of the Presbyterian Church of Scotland.

A quite new situation has been created by the arrival of refugee internees from England [the Bishop wrote]. Many of these reached Australia in a deplorable condition without adequate clothing, shoes, etc. etc. The church committees are anxious to do what they can to relieve this shortage and to co-operate in every possible way with the commandants of the various camps...It is necessary for me to speak as one who has witnessed and talked matters over with the officials in charge...as I have said. I do not press a request that might embarrass you, but I do feel that a visit permitted to a person like myself, who happens to represent church communions, is on rather a different basis from a request made by a private individual.

The Bishop added that the Governor-General, Lord Gowrie,

had given permission to use his name in making this request. The letter concluded: "I notice that the Government of New Zealand has constituted tribunals. I hope this will make the path easier for you and for the members of the Cabinet who feel with you on this point."

What Menzies felt remains unclear, nor is it clear why a visit to the camp by Bishop Pilcher would have embarrassed him. His answer to the Bishop's letter has disappeared from the files.

A week later, however, his mood had changed and on 24 October, Bishop Pilcher, accompanied by the three representatives of VIREC — Miss Constance Duncan, Miss Marjorie Ballance and Miss L. M. Larking — visited the camps at Tatura and Hay.

Miss Duncan, reporting on her visit to Tatura, wrote:

> The men had a long list of questions prepared to ask me, and were most business-like. Their first concern was regarding the wrong impression given to Australians about their status, and behaviour on *Dunera*. Colonel Scott, of the *Dunera* guard, was reported in Sydney and Melbourne papers as saying the men had mutinied on the way out — which was a lie — and Australians think of them as 'dangerous aliens' instead of 'friendly victims of Nazi persecution'. In case the way should be opened for their release in Australia and their eventual settlement, the men fear that public opinion would be against granting them release or landing permits. They ask for every possible co-operation from the welfare organisations in helping the public to appreciate their true position.

Miss Ballance interviewed Dr Felix Gutmann and Uwe Radok. Both had lost everything on the *Arandora Star*. Radok was wearing shorts made of a palliasse cover and a ragged singlet. Both were in a state of "great destitution":

> They had absolutely nothing [Miss Ballance reported], not even a handkerchief, and asked at least for a brush and comb. Sixty-three men were in a similar state. Dr Gutmann was the secretary and Mr Uwe Radok the brother of the leader of the camp university. Both men said, 'If you haven't got enough money for both clothing and books, send us books — books — books!... They say the food is excellent and can't speak highly enough of their treatment by the officers in the camp. But absolutely nothing is being done to occupy them and they are desperate for this help from us.

By contrast with Tatura, Hay, which she, Miss Duncan and

Bishop Pilcher visited the following day, was "very frightful".

> No grass, no shade, no green thing, a wilderness of blowing
> dust...Colonel Thane asked if we could supply shoes for
> the men...He had asked for 2000 pairs and received 150 or
> 250. Seemed to think it is hopeless.

At Hay Miss Duncan found internees "all spruced up, and
were dressed in various items of borrowed clothing in order to look
their best...they were quite gay in spirit, and we had a very happy
conversation. The adjutants of the two compounds, Captain
Carrington and Lieutenant Bass, were extremely popular with the
internees, and relationships between the guards and internees
seemed excellent."

Eric Stadlen had prepared a very careful memorandum
representing the viewpoint of all the men, Jews and Christians
alike. The memorandum dealt extensively with the three groups of
internees:

(a) Those who had their papers in order to go to America
(about 370 in number), and who wanted our assistance
in obtaining the transfer of the papers from the US
Consulate, London, to Sydney, and our co-operation in
getting the British and Australian Governments to grant
them release once they got on board a ship for America.

(b) A relatively small number who wished, upon their
release, to return to England and live there.

(c) The majority, who would like to settle in Australia.
Amongst these is a large group who had either secured
landing permits for Australia or were in process of doing
so when war broke out. This group greatly fears, as do
the men in (a) group, being returned to England before
they are released. They understand that the policy at
present is that they can only be released in England, and
they do not want to face a journey back again, both
from the point of view of the dangers of sea travel and
because of the extremely unhappy conditions which they
suffered on the journey out on HMT *Dunera*.

The married men had all volunteered for *Dunera*, which they
understood was bound for Canada, because they were told that
their wives and children would follow them, and they would have
the chance of a new life. As the wives were not being sent to
Australia, they felt that the authorities had not kept faith with
them. Questioned by Bishop Pilcher about the treatment on
Dunera they said that over a thousand had had their watches

stolen, and that many others had money and other valuables stolen; some even lost their clothes. The luggage that they had not seen since their embarkation had just been distributed at Hay but there was little of it left and it had been denuded of all valuables, documents, bankbooks, etc. Some had not got any luggage at all, consequently there was a great need for clothing and toilet articles.

Miss Duncan explained that the Victorian council could not be responsible for the Hay camp, but they would be glad to keep in touch with the men and forward their communications to England, as well as working on their behalf with the Australian Government.

The visitors were very impressed with the plans of the camp commandant, Colonel Thane, to bring irrigation water into the camp and to develop a mixed farm for pigs and poultry, vegetables, etc.

Miss Duncan's report finished: "The heat, red dust, flies and mosquitoes will make camp life at Hay unbearable in the summer, and we hope that the New South Wales committee can do something to provide the men with a few of the amenities of life to offset these hardships."

While politicians and most religious leaders were indifferent to the fate of the internees, their cause was championed untiringly not only by representatives of VIREC, but by three members of the Society of Friends: Margaret Pierce, a British-born teacher of housewifery at Melbourne's Emily Macpherson College of Domestic Economy; Margaret Holmes, secretary of the Students' Christian Movement and Alfred C. Clarke, a Sydney-born science teacher who in 1942 was chosen by the Department of Labour and National Service for training as an industrial welfare officer.

Some sleuths of military intelligence in Melbourne now behaved with a singular lack of intelligence. Making no effort to find out the true status of the *Dunera* internees, they decided that all were Nazis and anyone taking an interest in them, Nazi sympathisers. VIREC was therefore singled out for harassment.

Constance Duncan and Marjorie Ballance both reported on the pitiable condition of the internees in letters addressed to the Society of Friends in London. "The men had arrived in a destitute condition," Miss Duncan wrote, "and did not possess a razor blade, much less a change of underwear."

Miss Larking (known as "Chips") made a similar report in an article for the *New Statesman*. The letters and the article were intercepted by the military censor, and Miss Ballance and Miss Larking were summoned to Melbourne's Victoria Barracks for interrogation. What followed is best told in Miss Ballance's own words:

Though we demanded to be interviewed together, this was refused. 'Chips' was had in first and we think got the better of them, had an answer to every question, asked them several they couldn't answer, and left them pretty mad. So when my turn came, they took it out on me. Three of them shouting and yelling and banging the table and refusing to allow my letter to go, not because its contents ought to have gone through an official channel, which I should have thought reasonable, but because every word about the *Dunera* was a lie and because I was spending my time working for Nazis and was pro-Nazi in my attitude.

When she returned to her office, somewhat shaken by the accusations, Miss Ballance sent a full report of the interview with a letter of complaint to Sir Geoffrey Whiskard and Dr Pilcher. Copies were also sent to Lord Gowrie at Government House, and to the Minister for the Army, who ordered an inquiry.

Miss Duncan, too, was summoned to Victoria Barracks but, profiting by the experience of her colleagues, went accompanied by her solicitor, Mr Menhennitt, of Alexander Grant, Dickson and Menhennitt. She was questioned by a high-ranking intelligence officer, Captain Hatton, and treated courteously.

Captain Hatton wanted to know whether Miss Duncan had taken steps to inform the Australian authorities of the facts concerning the *Dunera* as well as writing to London. She replied that Bishop Pilcher had talked the matter over with the new Minister for the Army, Mr (later Sir Percy) Spender, in Canberra, and that Lord Gowrie and Sir Geoffrey Whiskard had asked her to let them have all the available information concerning conditions on *Dunera*. "At no time did he query the truth of the statements contained in my letter," Miss Duncan later wrote, "but it was some time before he understood my motives in writing it."

Before the interview ended, Miss Duncan raised the question of the way her colleagues had been bullied and slandered. She pointed out that they were not allowed to be interviewed together, or to have witnesses, whereas each of the interrogators had two witnesses. She considered this to be unjust procedure, and thought the least intelligence could do would be to apologise to her colleagues. Captain Hatton promised to inquire into the incident, which he attributed to a misunderstanding. There is no evidence that the apology was made. Lady Gowrie arranged for Miss Duncan to meet Spender at Government House, but she refused the invitation, believing that any further action would damage VIREC.

Despite Captain Hatton's conciliatory tone, harassment of VIREC continued. Its representatives were forbidden to visit Tatura, letters to and from the camp were held up on the ground that they contravened regulations, but when VIREC asked for a copy of these regulations, this was refused. Miss Ballance's account continued:

> We were beginning to think our only plan was to down tools and go, we weren't able to be useful and we weren't getting any backing in our fight. Then one day suddenly a Major Walker from the Intelligence Department appeared at the council and interviewed Constance and Mr Bainbridge and asked a lot of searching questions about me! We had asked them to come to VIREC and see what we were doing but they replied that they were too busy! Then this man was appointed and found the whole department seething with the subversive activities of VIREC and huge dossiers piling up about us all. Asked who and what we were, found no one really knew and came down to smell out the land for himself, was very suspicious and antagonistic at first and we had to prepare and send a statement of our functions and activities and when we asked for a copy of the regulations, this was given us at last. Gradually things improved...We had tea in the officers' mess and met Major Sproat for the first time who greeted me with, 'Oh, yes, I've heard a great deal about you!!!'

While Army intelligence in Melbourne was pursuing its bumbling policy, its counterpart in Sydney showed enlightenment in allowing VIREC's representatives to visit the Hay camps more freely and to shop for the internees, an amenity forbidden at Tatura.

CHAPTER TEN

A not uncommon Australian view of refugees had been expressed by Sir Frank Clarke, President of the Victorian Legislative Council, a distinguished Victorian pastoralist. Under a conspicuous heading, "Menace of the Refugee — Sir F. Clarke is Outspoken", the Melbourne *Age* in May 1939 reported his speech to the Australian Women's National League when he described refugees as "shrinking, rat-faced men, under five feet [1.5 metres] in height and with a chest development of about 20 inches [50 centimetres], who worked in backyard factories and other localities in the north of Melbourne for 2/- to 3/- a week and their keep. It was horrible to think that such people would want to marry Australian girls or even bring their own under-nourished and underdeveloped women, and breed a race within a race..."

Refusing to apologise for his violent language, Sir Frank later explained that he had two objectives — the preservation of Australia's standard of eugenics and its standard of economics. But he modified his racist attack by conceding that his aim was not to discredit all refugees or all Jews but certain types of Eastern Europeans, Jews and non-Jews, whom he considered "deficient in some of the qualities that made citizens of the British Empire".

Sir Frank's views on racial purity were echoed by an eminent medical man, Queensland's Director-General of Health, Sir Rafael Cilento, who in 1940 informed the State Minister for Health of a sharp increase in syphilis in Queensland and other states during the previous twelve months... because of an influx of large numbers of refugees... especially from Vienna, which he said was "the most dangerous of great capitals in the prevalence of venereal disease".

Another stalwart xenophobe was the Victorian statesman Major A. G. Cameron, a member of the War Cabinet, and of the Intelligence Corps (in charge of censorship) who said:

Numbers, '47 (33 in the Original).

"And ye shall dispossess the inhabitants of the land, and dwell therein: for I have given you the land to possess it."

"Large numbers of refugees from Germany and other European countries have left Sydney for towns such as Bowral, Katoomba, Mittagong and Bathurst. They are paying high rents, and houses have been sold at boom prices in these centres."

— "S. M. Herald," whose post-scriptural authority has been questioned.

POSTSCRIPT TO EXODUS.

Two examples of anti-semitic cartoons from the Sydney Bulletin in the 1940s.

(National Library of Australia, Canberra)

> One of the best jobs Adolf Hitler ever did for Germany was
> when he drove some of these [the Jews] out of his country.
> Yet we welcome them here. We should not go to a great
> deal of expense over people who come here to save their
> own skins.

And the *Bulletin*, a once radical paper that had fallen into the
hands of Fascist sympathisers, had no time for "foreigners who
after all were getting free board and lodging".

In 1944 when a Liberal MHR, W. J. Hutchinson, referred to
the Labor Party "followers of the filthy Jew, Karl Marx", the
fastidious editor of *Hansard* censored the offensive epithet. But as
late as 1947 another "Liberal" politician, H. B. Gullett (later
Australian ambassador to Greece), said that German Jews "in a
very large part, brought upon themselves the persecution they
suffered".

Many of the internees had been helped to get out of Germany,
some from concentration camps, by the Society of Friends in
London. Dr Sydney Morris, president of the European Emergency
Committee, visited the Hay camps for four days (1 to 4 November
1940) as a representative of the Society of Friends, of which he was
a member. He reported that living conditions, though in many
respects "very primitive", were bearable, but would probably be
much less bearable in January, February and March when heat,
flies and dust-storms would prevail:

> The only redeeming feature of this arid area is the
> Murrumbidgee River which in this part of the State is not a
> very imposing stream. It seems that this uninviting district
> must have been chosen for the reason that should any
> internee manage to escape his only means of survival would
> be to keep to the river. His line of escape being strictly
> limited by physical geography, his capture would be the
> more certain and speedy.

At its nearest point the winding river was about three quarters
of a mile from the camps.

Dr Morris's report continued:

> Nearly 400 youths between the ages of 16 and 19 are in the
> camp...They were at schools, universities, agricultural
> colleges and similar institutions under a scheme of training
> sponsored by the British Government. Their parents, in
> many instances, are still in Central Europe, and the mental
> anguish and anxiety of these lads would melt a heart of
> stone. It must have been some ghastly mistake to have

uprooted these boys and to have despatched them to this
distant land.

Dr Morris noted that the only clothing of many of the
internees was in great disrepair, and that the great shortage of shoes
forced some to go around barefoot. "The lack of personal
requisites is very sorely felt," he said. "It is depressing to see
youths with 10 days' growth on their faces owing to the lack of
shaving equipment. Very few have toothbrushes and most are
forced to clean their teeth by means of a moist finger dipped in
sand or grit. I was deeply distressed by the utter helplessness of
these unfortunate people, who seemed to despair of the possibility
of obtaining the minimum essentials wherewith to maintain some
semblance of decency." And to show that the "milk of human
kindness had not entirely vanished" Dr Morris spent £4 on
toothbrushes, safety razor blades, shaving soap and brushes,
toothpaste and similar requirements, for distribution to the most
deserving.

"Most of the internees require dental attention," Dr Morris
said. "Equipment has been requested from the military authorities
but so far has not been supplied. There are a number of dentists in
the compounds, some of them having had large practices in
England, who would be able to do this work if they had the
necessary equipment. It was rather pitiful to see one of these
dentists endeavouring to do what was possible with the aid of a few
instruments fashioned out of nails..."

He was impressed by the refugees' administration
organisation. "They have even a schematic diagram showing the
co-ordination of all activities which would do credit to an
American efficiency expert," he reported. He was also impressed
by the creative work that was going on. Internees using only pocket
knives and sharpened nails with broken glass as a substitute for
sandpaper, were making exquisite carvings from firewood. Dr
Hirschfeld had constructed a huge xylophone from odd bits of
timber, laboriously tuning each note with his pocket knife. He had
also made an orchestra of wooden whistles. "It is a treat to hear
classical airs and folk tunes played on this excellent combination,"
Dr Morris wrote.

One internee had made himself a guitar, another a violin.
Furniture was improvised from packing cases. Sun helmets were
contrived out of wire from butter cases and old underclothing.

There was a musical union which organised plays and literary
evenings, including readings from Chaucer and Shakespeare. Dr
Morris was invited to attend a vaudeville entertainment called
"Hay Days are Happy Days". The invitation bore the monogram

of the musical union and the title of the show, both printed from a stamp artistically carved from a potato on pieces of perforated toilet roll, the only paper available. The stage had been improvised from tables, the backdrop and curtains from army blankets, the spotlights from kerosene tins and jam tins. The show ended with all singing "God Save the King" lustily. He thought this "somewhat incongruous and unexpected" from men branded "dangerous enemy aliens".

Hour after hour he listened to their heart-rending stories. "It was the most depressing experience that has ever befallen me," he wrote. "After two sleepless nights wondering what must be done, I felt like a life-belt in an angry sea being grasped by hundreds of clutching hands."

Dr Morris's report concluded with a tribute to the camp commandant, Colonel Thane, Captain Carrington and the officers and men. "They are imbued," he wrote, "not only with a sense of duty but also with high ideals of tolerance, justice and fair play."

Gerd Buchdahl, in a poem titled *One Thousand Men in Compound Two*, appealed to the authorities in verse, of which these stanzas are typical:

> *The sun has given every man*
> *A healthy looking brownish tan.*
> *But it is liable to sting,*
> *So hats and specks would be the thing.*
> *And as many an inmate of this camp*
> *Looks torn and tattered like a tramp,*
> *And many a suitcase was not retrieved,*
> *Some clothing would be well received.*
> *Including trousers, socks and pants,*
> *And singlets, boots and shirts for gents,*
> *And tailoring and cobbling gear*
> *To solve the problem of wear and tear.*
>
> *To raise our state of cleanliness,*
> *And give the light to Mr Bass,*
> *To brush our hair, and sweep our rooms,*
> *We need some brushes, and some brooms,*
> *Soap, paste and toothbrush are no less*
> *Essential to our happiness.*
>
> *There are a number skilled in trade,*
> *And many a thing could well be made.*

Including every day's repairs.
We could build tables, shelves and chairs,
And tradesman workshop, hut and stools,
Had we the timber and the tools.
And to pursue our education,
Engage in sport and recreation,
Including: Rugger, Soccer, Cricket
We need a blackboard and a wicket,
And all the other wherewithal,
Such as piano, book and ball.

For all those things there is indeed,
A genuinely pressing need.
Yet he, who made this little list,
May well be called an optimist.
And since we are not paying rent,
With what we get must be content.
Yet hoping that it may come true,
We now submit this list to you.

Emil Wittenberg, a Viennese theatre architect, wrote in *Boomerang* of the difficulties of constructing a stage out of dilapidated wood, with no tools or nails, not even cardboard or paper. But the stage was finished in a fortnight. The enthusiasm of the workers infected officers and NCOs, who brought along paints and string and other supplies. "My activities in Vienna theatres were easier and more profitable than here," Wittenberg wrote. "On the other hand, we do not have the censor whose ominous presence hangs over the audience like pending disaster." Often the entire staff of the theatre would work for many weeks to produce one stage setting that would be seen for only a few minutes.

Wittenberg was one of four internees who designed the scenery for the camp's 1940 Christmas revue, "Snow White Joins Up". The others were Klaus Friedeberger, Fred Schonbach, Bim Meier and Heinz Richauer. The revue, an elaborate production in three acts, was written, produced and directed by Doc. K. Sternberg. The lyrics were perhaps no sillier than many contemporary pop songs. For example:

Hay Days
Hay Days, Hay Days,
Make your Hay Days your play days,
Sing on every day doodle-oodle-aye,
Smile with never a care.

Hay Days, Hay Days,
Make your Hay Days your gay days,
Yours is all the fun,
Yours is all the sun,
For it shines everywhere.
Long as we're all pals
And we're together,
Never mind the rain and stormy weather,
I know, you know,
Troubles come but they do go,
Doors will open up, you'll be right on top.
Live your life your own way,
Calling every day: HAY DAY.

Major H. McNeill Simpson, a leading Hay solicitor, was the camp's staff legal officer. He recalled a production by internees in English of "Journey's End". "One of the leading parts was taken by a German who spoke no English at all," said Major Simpson. "He had learnt the part parrot-like and gave an impressive performance. The next time I saw him he greeted me with 'Guten morgen!'"

Internees who worked on *Dunera* according to a voluntary roster, scrubbing decks, carrying food from the galleys, etc. had not been paid, but in camp a scale of wages was drawn up in which the more unpleasant jobs were the highest paid. Latrine cleaners earned five shillings a week; potato peelers and kitchen assistants, two shillings; waiters, one shilling. The "fonctionnaires" — camp spokesmen, librarians and teachers — were unpaid.

Payment of wages and transactions in the canteen were inhibited by a lack of currency and Camp 7 decided, with Major Simpson's permission, to issue its own notes. These were designed by an accomplished graphic artist, George A. Teltscher, and issued in denominations of two shillings, one shilling and sixpence. The design included a continuous border pattern of coiled barbed wire behind which could be read: "We are here because we are here because we are here." The notes, which looked like engravings, were serially numbered, and closely resembled the real thing. When a Sydney newspaper published a reproduction of one, keen nostrils in Sydney's Criminal Investigation Branch sniffed a breach of Commonwealth currency legislation. Gavin Johnston, proprietor and editor of the *Riverine Grazier*, who printed the notes — about 2000 of each denomination — recalled how five heavy-footed detectives tramped into his office, questioned him closely, and warned him of the fearful consequences of his act. "If a man can

Camp "money", issued by the internees at Hay, attracted the attention of the police, and was withdrawn.

produce notes like these in an internment camp," said one, "what could he do when he gets out?" Johnston was instructed to return the blocks and the original drawings to the military. Simpson, too, was questioned about his part in the affair.

Boomerang analysed the ages, nationalities, religions and marital status of the 922 internees in Camp 7 at Hay.

AGES

17 — 20	22.78%
21 — 25	19.63%
26 — 30	12.8%
(17 — 30	54.%)
31 — 35	11.17%
36 — 40	12.47%
41 — 45	13.45%
46 — 50	6.08%
51 and over	1.62%

NATIONALITIES

Germans	577
Austrians	239
Stateless	82
Various	24

RELIGIONS

Jewish	747
Roman Catholic	55
Church of England	19
Protestant	89
Unspecified	11
Methodist	1

MARITAL STATUS

Married	234
Single	688

It is interesting to compare the treatment of the many young internees with that of the 20 members of the Vienna Boys' Choir, a Nazi-backed group, whose director, George Gruber, joined the Nazi Party soon after Hitler's annexation of Austria. He organised a choir that flaunted swastikas and sang Nazi progaganda. Most of the boys were Nazis.

In 1939, the choir toured the United States, Hawaii, Fiji, New Zealand and Australia. On Saturday 2 September they gave a concert in Perth and were booked to give another performance before catching a ship for Europe on the following Wednesday. But on Sunday, 3 September war was declared and Gruber and his deputy were promptly interned. The boys were released after a brief internment through the intervention of the Catholic Archbishop of Melbourne, Dr Mannix, a brilliant, controversial Irish-born churchman of whom it was said that "he believed in God and Ireland, not necessarily in that order". Mannix had the boys billeted with Catholic families, and they sang in a choir in Melbourne's St Patrick's Cathedral. (Apart from this act and his intercession on behalf of the Wolkenstein brothers, Mannix does not seem to have shown any interest in the internees.)

Gruber remained interned at Tatura. In February 1946 he escaped, but was soon picked up at Nagambie, 52 kilometres away. When he was released, he settled in South Africa, presumably because he did not want to be repatriated to a democratic or a socialist Austria. Seventeen of the boys remained in Australia after the war.

CHAPTER ELEVEN

At the beginning of December 1940, Sir Geoffrey Whiskard forwarded his Government a 7000-word report on *Dunera*, which had been compiled at his request by the 922 internees of Camp 7. It was a horrifying record of man's inhumanity to man. The document, which was accompanied by a letter to Sir Geoffrey, read:

> ...The memorandum is based on experiences which were collected and scrutinised as to their accuracy by responsible men in this camp...who are prepared to substantiate their evidence in any British court of justice...We are in the abnormal position that nobody in Australia (...Not even the Lord Chief Justice) declared themselves competent to act as an intermediary between us and the British Government.

The statement concluded: "We have refrained up to now from describing our treatment on board HMT *Dunera* as we were afraid that these facts might be used for enemy propaganda. We are now, three months after our arrival, giving this statement for the use of the authorities."

As the Hay internees were about to celebrate their first Christmas in Australia, two of them — Dr A. Wiener and P. Auerbach — in the name of their comrades, addressed an appeal to the Earl of Lytton, president of the advisory council set up to examine the position of interned refugees.

The lengthy document declared it was paradoxical to regard them as having German nationality. No doubt existed as to their loyalty to England. They were racial or political refugees from Nazi oppression, 90 per cent of them of the Jewish race:

It is a maxim of English public international law not to
recognise foreign law in so far as it is incompatible with
fundamental English principles. English law, for instance,
has repudiated the notion of slavery...English law also has
not recognised the Nuremberg marriage laws, nor the more
drastic provisions of the German currency restriction laws.

The document listed the restrictions imposed on the internees
because apparently they were regarded not as refugees, but as
prisoners of war. They were allowed to write only two letters of 22
lines a week, on regulation paper bearing printed instructions in
German and Italian, obviously intended for prisoners of war. All
their letters were marked "Prisoner of War Service". They could
see visitors only through a wire netting and for 15 minutes only,
and they were forbidden to send cables.

The document stressed the climatic unsuitability of the camp
site, the inadequate protection against inclement weather provided
by the huts, and the absence of trees that might provide shade.
"Despite the very decent treatment we get from the Australian
officers and men," the document continued, "we feel the very
gravity and hardness of our plight pressing us to draw the attention
of your Lordship to the before-mentioned facts."

Finally, the document submitted a number of suggestions:

That the restrictions relating to communication be removed.
That the censorship be relaxed and other delays avoided.
That married men and their wives be freed from the
uncertainty as to their future by an early statement from the
Home Secretary.
That applications for release be reviewed speedily.
That those of us who as a result of deportation lost their
asylum be assisted and sponsored in finding a new home, if
possible in Australia.
That pending arrangements for a new home...our youth
whose education and training have been suddenly
interrupted be given a chance to continue their education
under a training scheme similar to that which was granted in
Great Britain.
That our many experts and skilled workers be given leave to
enable them to do useful work and to make a contribution
to the war effort.
That the camp be transferred to a place with a more suitable
climate and not on such desolate ground.
That the camp be taken over by civil authorities and be
carried on along the lines of the well-known Kitchener
Camp.

The reply of his Lordship is not on record. But nothing was done to make life more tolerable for the internees until the arrival from England three months later of Major Julius Layton as a special representative of the Home Office.

In his capacity of assistant to the official visitor, Dr H. O. Lethbridge visited the Hay camp at the end of January 1941. Dr Lethbridge had been government medical officer for 30 years at Narrandera. "I have no hesitation in saying that the climate is healthy," he said, though the temperature might drop as much as 25°C in a few hours. "It was difficult for anyone who has not lived in the western area (of NSW) to believe that the cold of the winter was very much greater than east of the divide."

He noted in his report that the palliasses in the huts were so worn that they let the straw through. "This," he commented, "is inconvenient for the individual occupying the lower bunk. Equally inconvenient to all occupants of the huts was the prevalence of lice." Generally Dr Lethbridge found the morale and health of the camp "excellent" with the exception of a rather serious epidemic of endocarditis and of a foot sore which usually turned poisonous. It led to complications, such as lymphangitis and lymphadenitis and was very resistant to treatment. "Both the many glass fragments (the camp is situated on a disused town dump) and the character of the ground are to blame," Dr Lethbridge wrote. The obvious remedy was to supply army boots, but there was a great shortage of these and no boot repairing material had been supplied by the Army. Dr Lethbridge made a curious observation under the heading "Comfort in Sleeping Huts". The situation of the bunks was bad for the summer, he wrote, and those in the lower bunks complained of dust dropping from above. "Each pair of bunks," he wrote, "is shut off from any movement of air in three directions. This will be looked on as beneficial during winter... when cold winds sweep across the western plains. I would therefore not recommend any alteration of their present position for the time being."

Sir Frederick Jordan responded rather testily to this report. "I do not agree with this," he wrote in forwarding Dr Lethbridge's report to Army HQ in Melbourne. "Before the cold weather arrives, the internees should be supplied with sufficient blankets to keep them reasonably warm at night; and should not be expected to rest content with being huddled up together, packed one above the other, so as to be kept warm by the animal heat engendered by their own proximity, dust, exhalations and lice. The present arrangement of the bunks runs counter to the most elementary requirements of hygiene." Sir Frederick also commented on the absence of proper footwear for the internees and the fact that some were suffering from infected feet. "I must express my astonishment," he wrote, "that notwithstanding that in my report dated 6 November last, I pointed out the necessity for supplying boots and clothing, and referred to the fact that it is a breach of Article 12 of the Geneva Convention not to do so the state of things referred to by Dr Lethbridge should still be allowed to exist. (Between 1 January and 10 May 1941, more than 850 pieces of footwear had received first aid. "We urgently need more equipment," said an article in *Boomerang*.) Sir Frederick added that it was essential for the internees who required it to be supplied with warm clothing and boots, as was required by the Convention.

"I wonder if the Jewish community are satisfied they are doing all that can be done for these unfortunates?" said Dr Leon Jona in the *Australian Jewish Herald* after visiting Tatura.

The Jewish community in general showed little concern for their interned brethren, perhaps because of a fear that any publicity about them would stir up the latent anti-semitism never far below the surface of Australian life in the 1940s. But the Victorian Chief Rabbi, Jacob Danglow, as senior Hebrew chaplain of the Australian Military Forces, visited the Tatura camps periodically.

In January 1941 he wrote to Menzies about the plight of German and Austrian internees who, he pointed out, "owing to the absence of any duly constituted tribunal, to which their cases can be referred, are, so-to-say, nobody's children, without any hope of any amelioration of their sad lot".

None of these internees, as far as Rabbi Danglow could ascertain, had given any cause for criticism or suspicion, but the tribunals so far created in Australia to which interned aliens could appeal dealt with only those internees residing in Australia at the outbreak of war. He asked Menzies to give "kind consideration" to the plight of the *Dunera* and Singapore internees, and to institute machinery for considering applications for release by them. "Alternatively," Rabbi Danglow concluded, "may I venture to suggest with all respect that you take up with the Home Office the position of the above internees in your forthcoming visit to England." This letter was acknowledged by Menzies on 25 January 1941 and further communication promised, but no record of this is available.

Menzies, who dominated the Australian political scene for many years, was a brilliant after-dinner speaker, a ruthless politician, an ineffectual statesman and an ardent monarchist of whom it was said that he had a first-class 18th-century mind. One assumes that he was more interested in the royals of Buckingham

Palace than in the refugees of Tatura. Nothing, of course, came of the rabbi's suggestion.

On 1 May 1941 the Bishop of Chichester, who represented the English Inter-Church Committee, wrote to Bishop Pilcher:

> I have been trying to get an interview with Mr Menzies, who has promised to see Colonel Wedgwood and myself about the internees in Australia, although he is so extremely busy on urgent war duties here, I am hoping to get some talk with him. But I have been urged by a Christian lawyer who is in touch with a great many refugees, to try and get the interest of likely people in Australia, on the position of the anti-Nazis who are interned there. It is really not only a humanitarian, but a legal question that is involved, and it is suggested that the ordinary official reply which suggests that the Australian Government can do nothing because it has no jurisdiction is not soundly based.

The Bishop of Chichester had asked his lawyer friend to draw up a memorandum, which he enclosed. "I believe the memorandum will be very useful," he wrote. "The advantage of having a legal argument at this time is that it is sometimes very useful where one has the good chance of meeting an official who is already convinced on the score of justice and needs argument for his own department. It is of first-rate importance to note that the British Government has...given full power of release to the Dominions."

The memorandum began:

> It is common ground that this is a war against oppression. It is obvious that the first victims of Nazi oppression are of German and Austrian nationality and that their free co-operation with the British is, or ought to be, part of the war effort...Internment of anti-Nazi German or Austrian refugees therefore raises not only problems of public faith and morality, but has a bearing on the very issue of the war. The point was at once grasped by Hitler, who, in spring 1940, said to his people: 'The enemies of Germany are now the enemies of Britain too. The British have detained in concentration camps the very people we found it necessary to detain. Where are those much vaunted democratic liberties of which the English boast?...'

The memorandum commented that red tape rather than bad will had obstructed efforts to restore freedom to all friends of Great Britain. The situation of deported anti-Nazis was particularly complicated because of a continuous shift of responsibility between the Home Office, the War Office, Admiralty, Dominion Governments, high commissioners, United States consulates, etc. Australia had full power to release any internees which it held. Not only had Australia refused to exercise this power, it was detaining even those released by the Home Office, until England took them back.

By the common law of England, the memorandum continued, in force in all British settlements, an alien of enemy nationality was *prima facie* not an enemy, as long as he was resident in His Majesty's Dominions. He owed allegiance to the King. In times of war, the King might but need not, under the prerogative, arrest a subject of an enemy country and make him prisoner of war, apart from prerogative any person might be detained under statutory powers, subject to being given reason and a right of appeal.

Nearly all the people transported were interned by virtue of a general internment order, issued under the prerogative, not under statutory powers. Internment, therefore, was not a measure following from the status of an alien, but a procedure which the King, advised by a Secretary of State might or might not follow...as he thought fit. If he decided to drop it...it was illegal to detain the prisoner or prisoners. One would think that once the friendly character of an alien was established, he should be released.

The memorandum continued:

> The English-speaking nations are rightly proud of the rule
> of law. The fundament of the rule of law is that no one
> shall be detained except for reasons provided by
> law...Apart from statutory powers the law is the same as
> during the Napoleonic wars where nobody thought of
> internment of the French refugees...What strikes me is not
> so much an infringement of formal law, but the very
> reversal of the principle. In a war waged for the
> fundamental rights of man, people friendly to Great Britain
> should not be denied the most primitive right of man
> granted a hundred years ago to transported convicts and two
> hundred years ago, while slavery was legal in the colonies, to
> any negro slave who touched English soil.

The memorandum shrewdly suggested that Australia was not motivated by considerations of military security but was using this as a cloak for its immigration policy. "The question was: is the abandonment of the principle of personal freedom of friends not too high a price to pay for the enforcement of immigration policy? Moreover, making release dependent on shipping accommodation was clearly detrimental to the war effort as shipping was very much needed for other purposes. It also put further responsibility on the British such as was incurred in the sinking of the *Arandora Star*."

Bishop Pilcher sent copies of the lawyer's memorandum to Lord Gowrie, Menzies, the Minister of the Interior, Senator Hattil Foll, and to Spender, a King's Councillor.

The memorandum seems to have stirred a great flutter in political and Army dovecots. The minute replying to it, issued by the Department of the Army, was circulated widely from August 1941 to July 1942.

The unidentifiable author of it contended that it was based "more on political and sentimental considerations than on legal arguments. It was true," he wrote, "that the constitutional concept known as the rule of law embodied the principle that no one should be detained, except for reasons provided by law, but there was ample legal ground, both for the original internment of these aliens in England and for the continuation of their internment in Australia." In support of this, he invoked Halsbury's *Laws of England*, 2nd Edn, Vol. 1, p. 447, in which an enemy alien was defined as "one whose sovereign or state is at war with the sovereign of England". The same work on page 455 stated that "an alien enemy has no rights at all".

Moreover, the minute argued, as *Dunera* internees were interned by virtue of a general internment order, issued under the prerogative, the same prerogative would justify their transference to Australia and "might justify their continued detention here as a matter of administrative convenience in the special circumstances of this war, which makes comparison with previous wars unprofitable". The minute concluded that the position had been made quite clear in Australia by the issuing of internment orders against each internee under the National Security (Aliens Control) Regulations.

This casuistical justification of Australia's obduracy seemed to satisfy all concerned. It ignored the fact that in England the prerogative was no longer in force, as the internees had been released by the English Government, and it did not question the validity of the internment orders issued in Australia. Bishop Pilcher's resolute crusade had failed and the politicians and brasshats were no longer to be irritated by this turbulent priest.

A peculiarly English institution, the Pit Ponies Protection Society, had some distinguished names on its executive. The president was Sir Robert Gower, the vice-presidents Fenner Brockway MP, Clemence Dane, Augustus John, Eden Philpotts, H. W. Nevinson and Hugh Walpole.

On 5 February 1941, the secretary, Dr Geoffrey Williams,

wrote to Clarke of the Society of Friends in Australia:

> ...I agree that at the time there was a real *fear* of invasion
> and of Fifth Column people...It is true the refugees
> themselves thought it but fair to agree to internment at the
> time in very large numbers of cases, and some had suitcases
> packed in advance. But there was undoubtedly at the head
> of things an atmosphere of panic and the War Office simply
> had its way...It is an eternal black mark against our Home
> Office.

In January 1941, on their way back to Melbourne after attending a
Friends' general meeting in Sydney, Clarke and Miss Pierce visited
the Hay camps, 7 and 8. They were received courteously and talked
to 12 internees, though interviews were officially limited to one
internee each morning or afternoon. The interviews took place in a
"visitors' hut", in which the visitor faced the internee across a
long table with 2 centimetre wire netting separating them. The
visitor and guard sat or stood on one side of the table and the
internee on the other. The internees were brought out under armed
guard from the compound, which visitors were forbidden to enter.

All the private soldiers whom Clarke and Miss Pierce spoke to
had a high opinion of the German and Austrian internees, but this
friendly feeling towards the internees did not seem to be shared
fully by the officers. "It should be noted," they reported, "that the
officers do not come into such close contact with the internees as do
the men, and the officers are naturally in closer touch with the
official attitude, which seems to regard all internees as potentially
dangerous 'enemy aliens', whether they are refugees, Nazis, or
otherwise."

Some of the higher officers resented the fact that the internees
had numerous visitors and well-wishers, while no one seemed to be
interested in them.

Clarke had an interesting talk with a local contractor whose
truck, loaded with sand, had just come into the camp. The truck
had been loaded by internees, who had gone out on a voluntary
working party accompanied by an armed guard. As the truck
stopped, the guards and internees climbed down and the internees,
having neatly stacked their shovels, went into the compound
through the double gates in the barbed wire. The contractor
remarked that the internee working party (several of whom were
bespectacled middle-aged men) were poor shovellers. A private
standing by asked if the contractor would "shovel his guts out were
he an internee". "No," said the contractor, "I'd be blowed if I
would." The private agreed, and expressed his admiration for
"brainy men like the internees being willing to do shovelling work".

Oswald Volkmann, the camp's most prolific versifier, wrote a lighthearted poem, "Gravel Party":

If we are tired of the camp
And fond of motor travel
We say we like to do some work
And volunteer for gravel.
  Our only chance to travel
  Is fetching sand and gravel.

With us they send an armed guard
Of fiercely looking diggers,
Three soldiers and a corporal
Their fingers on the triggers.
  Our only chance to travel
  Is fetching sand and gravel.

We climb upon the heavy truck
Where twenty stone of sergeant
Sits ready at the steering wheel,
He seems to be quite urgent.
  Our only chance to travel
  Is fetching sand and gravel.

And off we go the open road
At fifty miles. How pleasant!
We see the cattle, sheep and pigs,
We never see a peasant.
  Our only chance to travel
  Is fetching sand and gravel.

When we are driving back again
The fiercely looking diggers
Have changed into a company
Of kindly, smiling figures.
  Our only chance to travel
  Is fetching sand and gravel.

When Mr Justice Davidson again visited Hay, he was not pleased by what he found. He complained of delays in forwarding the internees' mail; in some instances letters took 11 days to reach him in Sydney and the envelopes were marked "passed by the censor". Some months earlier he had been compelled to draw attention to the Regulations which provided that the letters of internees to the official visitor should not be subjected to censorship. This was an infraction of the regulations. He was also greatly "disturbed" that certain work for the benefit of the internees mentioned in his report of 1940 had not been carried out. Some of the items for which this assurance was given were dining room utensils, soap, clothing and blankets. There was also a gross delay in delivering parcels to the camp. "I can only draw the inference," he wrote in his report, "either that in some quarter there has been deplorable inefficiency, or that there has been a distinct breach of faith with myself as official visitor, and with the internees . . . such a position is entirely intolerable . . ."

> As official visitor, it is my duty to see that the provisions of
> the Geneva Convention are being observed and to make
> such recommendations that are necessary . . . I cannot
> tolerate for one moment being used as a mere blind to
> enable the public to be deluded with the idea that the
> proprieties are being observed, and *unless I can ascertain*
> *that something is being done at once in connection with the*
> *matters I have mentioned, I shall have to resign as a protest*
> [his italics].

Davidson said he appreciated the courtesy he had received from the Military Board, the camp commandant, and from every official connected with internment matters, but he intended to write also to the Minister for the Army *separately*.

His complaint went the familiar round of government offices, and collected the usual decoration of rubber stamps and illegible annotations.

About the same time, a number of internees whose release had been authorised by the British Government on the grounds of their loyalty to the Allied cause and their special skills, wrote to Dr Lethbridge seeking his help. Some were exceedingly anxious to return immediately to England. Others felt they could better serve the Allied cause by working in Australia. The Australian Government had recently issued a new regulation to the effect that in exceptional cases this would be permitted. The internees asked that their cases be reviewed as soon as possible. Some had already been waiting two months since their release had been authorised. And some who had planned to migrate to the United States were the victims of a "Catch 22" situation, though that valuable term had not yet entered the language. The Australian Government required an internee to be in possession of a landing permit before he could be released. The American authorities would not grant a visa until the internees had been released.

A popular song which was said to have originated in an English camp had this refrain:

You can scream and you can shout,
They'll never let you out
It serves you right, you so-and-so,
Why weren't you a naturalised Eskimo?

The song also circulated in Canadian internment camps.

François Lafitte, a versatile young student of philosophy, politics, economics, anthropology, eugenics, sex and population problems, son of an East London schoolteacher and adopted son of Havelock Ellis, in September 1940 wrote a book titled *The Internment of Aliens*. His interest in the subject derived partly from the fact that many of his refugee friends who had combated Nazi tyranny in Germany and Austria, were then locked up in Britain as "enemy aliens".

Lafitte's work, a comprehensive, compassionate and fully documented study of official muddle and stupidity, and an eloquent plea for a more humane and realistic policy, was published as a Penguin Special.

A copy reached the Hay camp at the end of April 1941 and readings from it were arranged by the camp school. "The large gatherings of listeners were extraordinarily attentive," wrote "Observer" in *Boomerang*, "and this is hardly astonishing for the book is topical in the extreme."

"Observer's" review continued: "A final word of praise must be said for the British censors, the one who allowed the book to get into this camp, and particularly the one who permitted it to be published at all. The fact that this book was not suppressed speaks volumes; it shows that democracy is still alive in Britain."

Concluding his review, "Observer" wrote: "Reflecting on our own experience and reading Mr Lafitte's description of the methods of internment and of conditions in the camps, we naturally tend to become emotional. The author suggests that internment has not demoralised the majority of refugees, but it has taught them never again to trust the word of an English officer. This is certainly an overstatement. We realise the cruelty on the part of the authorities was hardly ever deliberate (except possibly on *Dunera*) but was due chiefly to lack of efficiency and organisation. We realise also that the present British Government, and particularly the new Home Secretary, Mr Herbert Morrison, are much more friendly towards us and have indeed adopted a 'new' policy. We hope that Major Layton will give expression to this changed policy, and that he will allow many of us to help actively in the British war effort."

CHAPTER TWELVE

At the end of January 1941, Colonel Wedgwood received a letter from Lord Gowrie, which included a report on *Dunera* drawn up by the Society of Friends members who had visited refugee camps in Australia. By the same mail he received a considerable number of other letters and newspaper cuttings. He took the correspondence and cuttings to the Secretary of State for the Dominions, Viscount Caldecote, who advised him to take them to the Home Office. Thence they went to the War Office, and immediately the Secretary of State for War, Anthony Eden, decided to appoint a court of inquiry into the whole affair, as soon as those responsible returned to England.

Colonel Wedgwood asked Captain Margesson, an Under Secretary of State for War, whether he would see that evidence would be taken from the Jewish internees who were on board *Dunera*. Captain Margesson replied equivocally that the first thing was to set up the court of inquiry and it would be for the court to get the evidence in the best way it could. (In the event, no Jews were invited to give evidence.)

Colonel Wedgwood, in a later debate, urged the Government to do three things. In the first place, there must be a certain degree of publicity. Only that would satisfy public opinion in Australia and England:

> It is important that we show the world that when anything of this sort has been done by people in British service, direct action is taken by this House and by the Government in order to prevent it happening again, to punish the offenders and to compensate the victims. Do not let this be a hole-and-corner affair...We must show the world that we are not afraid of people knowing what has happened.

Colonel Wedgwood also urged that the court of inquiry should comprise not merely government officials, but some "independent person of judicial mind". And thirdly, and perhaps most important of all, evidence should be given not only by defendants, but by their victims. "They cannot be compensated for the inhumanity," he said, "but they can be compensated for the injustice, and the watches, wedding rings and money that have been taken from them should, as far as possible, be restored."

And before the court of inquiry was held, he concluded, steps should be taken to get some money to the refugees who were penniless. "To have no money even to buy razor blades, cigarettes, newspapers or postage stamps was a terrible position for them."

The Financial Secretary to the War Office, Mr Richard Law, did not agree with Colonel Wedgwood that the fullest publicity should be given to the *Dunera* inquiry. "It is perfectly true that this is a democratic country," he said, "but unfortunately it is not a democratic world, and if the allegations are proved to be well-founded, I can foresee certain definite disadvantages in washing our dirty linen in public in a world which contains enemies as well as friends. Details of the ill-treatment of internees would be construed in enemy propaganda as an admission of guilt applying generally to the British character and the British way of waging war."

The *Manchester Guardian* did not agree with Law. In a leading article on what it called "The Scandal of the *Dunera*", it commented: "If the enemy says that this is a country where such things happen, let him also say and let everyone see, that this is a country which repudiates them, and will publicly expose them, and make amends rather than have anything like that happen again."

When the National Council for Civil Liberties in London, the Australian Council for Civil Liberties and other organisations raised the question of the *Dunera* men the British Government acknowledged that most of them should never have been interned. Winston Churchill somewhat hypocritically described their internment and deportation as "a deplorable and regrettable mistake". "No ordinary excuse," Major Cazalet said, "such as that there is a war on and that officials are overworked, is sufficient to explain what has happened...Horrible tragedies, unnecessary and undeserved, lie at the door of somebody...Frankly, I shall not feel happy, either as an Englishman or as a supporter of this Government, until this bespattered page of our history has been cleaned up and rewritten."

The court of inquiry was held in secret and its findings never disclosed. But as a result, on 20 May 1941 three members of the

Dunera guard faced a field general court martial at the Duke of York's Headquarters in Chelsea.

Scott appeared on two charges. The first was that he had improperly addressed his troops on *Dunera*, saying he would turn a blind eye to petty pilfering. This was in his "belly buttons" speech. Major Mothersole, who commanded a company of Pioneers, told the court how he had instructed Lance-Corporal Walton, a professional shorthand writer, to take down Scott's speech. Scott was also charged with having failed to ensure a proper inquiry into the violent treatment of one internee.

Major Mothersole gave evidence that he saw internees' cases burst and the contents lying about the ship. He suggested to Colonel Scott that the cases should be guarded. Colonel Scott, he said, replied: "Are you telling me what to do?"

Scott admitted saying that he was only too well aware that were they in the position of their guests (meaning the internees) after being searched, they would be lucky if they had their belly buttons left. He also admitted saying, "I am an old soldier, and I know that the British Tommy looks upon a time like this as an opportunity to help himself to any unattended trifles," but he said he meant this as a deterrent for them not to follow the example of the Lascars, whom he blamed for the pilfering. Scott denied having said that he would close a blind eye "to petty offences of purloining of articles", adding that if he were going to close an eye, he would not have mentioned it.

With brazen effrontery Scott claimed that Mothersole and Walton had conspired to fabricate this part of the speech. The court martial accepted this extraordinary explanation without calling on Mothersole or Walton to deny it.

Answering the second charge, that he failed to ensure a proper inquiry was held into the violent treatment suffered by one internee, Scott said he was quite satisfied there had been no violence towards the interned man.

Despite Walton's evidence and Scott's own admission he was found not guilty on the first charge. On the second charge he was found guilty and "severely reprimanded".

In Scott's defence the court was told that he had served through World War I and had been discharged with 40 per cent disablement pension.

Sergeant Helliwell faced four charges. He was then the Senior Provost-Sergeant. The first charge alleged that on the seas on about 1 August 1940, he assaulted an alien; the second accused him of assaulting an internee at Melbourne on 3 September, therefore occasioning bodily harm. The third, alternative to the second, charged him with failing to safeguard from ill-treatment an interned alien in his charge who had attempted to escape; and the fourth, that he disobeyed a command from a superior officer in that he did not provide the alien with blankets and water when ordered to do so.

Helliwell pleaded not guilty to all the charges.

The prosecution alleged that on 3 September an internee, arrayed in the uniform of the escort's regimental sergeant-major, was seen to emerge from a porthole of *Dunera*, slide down a steel hawser and jump to the quay. Helliwell and another sergeant immediately captured the internee and carried him to the gangway. An officer directed Helliwell to confine the internee to the ship's cells. The officer did not notice any injury to the internee, but other officers visiting the cells some hours later saw "a scene of injury and blood". The prosecution added that the internee was left lying in his cell clad only in a blood-sodden shirt. His eyes were puffed and black, his nose was injured and his face covered with blood. He was without water or blankets, although an officer had previously ordered Helliwell to supply these.

The prosecution suggested that the court was entitled to conclude that Helliwell caused the injuries to the internee. It was also alleged that Helliwell once tore a ring from a middle-aged internee's finger with such violence that one soldier shouted, "You swine."

Sergeant Helliwell was found guilty only of disobeying orders and was severely reprimanded.

Acting Regimental Sergeant-Major Albert Bowles MM, who had 26 years' Army service, faced 21 charges relating to the property of enemy aliens, including the charge that while in possession of money belonging to the internees, he had given 10 shillings of it to each of a number of sergeants, claiming that he had kept none for himself. Bowles admitted that he had internees' property in his kit, but said that he had found articles loose on the deck, in a "dump", and taken some of them as it would have been impossible for them to be returned to their owners. He said he purchased a number of articles from young soldiers, but did not know how they had acquired them.

Scott, for the defence, said that Bowles was "an invaluable warrant officer with a character beyond reproach" and that he stood to lose £6.1.6d a week in pension and emoluments.

Bowles was found guilty on two charges only. He was reduced to the ranks, sentenced to 12 months' imprisonment without hard labour and dismissed from the Army.

No internee was called to give evidence nor was Lieutenant Brooks or any member of the ship's crew. In view of this and of the tender treatment meted out to Scott and Helliwell and of the fact that equally culpable men such as O'Neill and others were not charged, some members of the House of Commons, not surprisingly, described the court martial as a "hushing-up operation".

Colonel Wedgwood also asked whether there had been any charges against Scott for looting from the internees on board. The question was not answered. Neither did he get any satisfaction when he asked: "Are we to understand that the net result, as far as the commanding officer is concerned, is that he is severely reprimanded and promoted from captain to major?" Margesson replied: "The House will realise that I am in no sense responsible for a sentence passed by a court martial." Silverman asked: "Is the House to understand that there was no evidence at the court martial from any of the people against whom the alleged offences were committed? In that case was the court martial qualified to come to the conclusion at which it arrived?"

The responsible British press gave full reports of the court martial, but in Australia only short, disjointed accounts appeared.

CHAPTER THIRTEEN

For years before the war, Julius David Layton, a distinguished Jewish banker and stockbroker of London, had been actively associated with Jewish refugee organisations in England. He had made many visits to Germany to select refugees and had twice visited Australia to arrange for their resettlement.

When Hitler seized Austria in March 1938, Goering announced in Vienna: "We don't like Jews and they don't like us. We will make them glad to go away." The Nazis inaugurated a system of taking bus and train loads of refugees and dumping them over the nearest frontier. There were then 179,000 Jews in Vienna alone. Layton went to Vienna and arranged for the emigration of 3500. (Austrian Jews were committing suicide at the rate of about 130 a day. On one day in July, 800 were said to have killed themselves.)

In Vienna, Layton always had to report to the arch-murderer Adolf Eichmann, head of the Nazi emigration office, whom he met in the sombre, crowded quarters of the Kultus-Gemeinde, a Jewish cultural and religious association to which all Austrian Jews had to belong, and which became the voice of the Jewish community. Eichmann had declared his task was "to purify Vienna and Austria from Jews in the quickest possible way". While he was in charge of Vienna, Nazis beat up Jews in the street and by September 1938 the Jewish hospital was so full that there was no room even in the corridors.

"I had to report whom I was going to select, and how I was going to select them," Layton recalled. "He approved of my mission. From his point of view I was doing what he wanted done — getting Jews out of Vienna, so he wasn't unpleasant to me. In fact, when the German diplomat Von Rath was assassinated in Paris in 1938, he telephoned me and said he wanted me to keep out of the Jewish quarter that night, as there would be reprisals against the Jews, so I stayed in my hotel. It was a ghastly night..." Next morning, on the urgent advice of the British consul, Layton left Austria. (On 7 November a 17-year-old Jewish boy shot and mortally wounded the third secretary of the German embassy in Paris, Ernst Von Rath, which led to the worst pogrom in Nazi Germany.)

After the collapse of Germany in 1945 Eichmann escaped to Argentina, where he lived under an assumed name. In May 1960, he was kidnapped by Israeli commandos, tried in Jerusalem for his war crimes and hanged.

At the outbreak of war, Layton was in charge of the 3500 internees in the Kitchener camp. As commandant, he had selected 500 to go to Australia, and, years later, recalled with pride that all were successful in their new country.

After the fall of Dunkirk, the refugees in Kitchener camp were moved from Richborough to the Lingfield camp on the Isle of Man, and Layton, now a lieutenant in the Pioneer Corps, went with them. At Lingfield camp, according to one occupant, "he put an end to the gradual starvation of its inhabitants and successfully advocated the release of many transmigrants".

Layton's work for refugees had brought him into close contact with the Home Office and with Major A. J. Wheeler — migration officer at Australia House, the London headquarters of Australia's High Commissioner. Wheeler reported to Layton that his Government wanted the Home Office to send a representative to Australia to sort out the "dreadful muddle" of the *Dunera*.

A representative of the Home Office, Sir Alexander Paterson, the famous chairman of the Prison Commission, had been sent to Canada to select internees eligible to return to Britain and to facilitate the emigration from Canada to the United States of those who had American visas. A conference was held at the Home Office on 12 December 1940 to consider whether similar arrangements could be made for dealing with the internees sent to Australia.

The conference was attended by three representatives of the Home Office, a representative of the Directorate of Labour, War Office, and a representative of MI5. The Australian Government was represented by Major Wheeler, and the internees by Lieutenant Layton. Major Wheeler said that Layton's appointment as the Home Office representative would be welcomed by his Government.

The conference agreed that enlistment of internees in the Pioneer Corps should be confined to category "B" and "C"

Germans and Austrians, and not extended to Italians, numbering about 200, because all had been members of the Italian Fascist Party. As soon as the Australian Government approved of the proposal, Layton would proceed to Australia by the quickest available route. In the meantime, the Australian Government should be asked to display a notice in the internment camps calling for volunteers for the Pioneer Corps, and to obtain from applicants the particulars required by MI5 for "vetting" purposes.

The conference also suggested that it might be possible to make use of these men in the Middle East, thus avoiding the long journey to England. Returning internees would leave Australia as free men, without military escorts.

The Australian Government agreed to the proposal, and in January 1941 Layton left England for Australia, by way of Canada. He had been seconded to the Home Office with the rank of major, and carried a warrant from Herbert Morrison, "one of His Majesty's principal secretaries of state".

The warrant read:

I hereby appoint Major J. D. Layton to be my
representative in Australia for the following purposes:—
1. To consider the cases of civilian internees transferred to
   Australia and to recommend which of them should be
   allowed to return to this country if they so desire;
2. to make any necessary arrangements with His Majesty's
   Government in Australia for the purpose of securing the
   return to this country of the internees selected for return;
3. to facilitate the emigration of internees who obtain visas
   authorising their emigration to other countries;
4. to make any necessary arrangements with His Majesty's
   Government in Australia for securing shipping
   accommodation to the United Kingdom or other suitable
   destination of internees found suitable for enlistment in
   the Pioneer Corps of the British Army.

Layton arrived in Sydney on 24 March 1941. Welcoming his expected arrival at Hay, an internee wrote in *Boomerang*: "I can hardly imagine a man who would be better suited for this job. He has devoted much time to refugee work, and has become widely known in Bloomsbury House [a Bloomsbury hotel that had been taken over by the principal refugee organisation] as an agile and intelligent man whose sympathy and generosity never failed..." Looking back on his mission, Layton said: "Being interned was a ghastly experience, but my appearance seems to have injected the internees with a spirit of hope that they would soon be released. I am afraid it was a long-drawn-out hope but you cling to anything when you are in that unfortunate position."

The Australian Army Minister, Spender, was quick to reassure his countrymen that Layton would not be opening the door to a horde of aliens. Layton was in Australia to consider the case of aliens who alleged they were wrongly detained, he announced. Australia was only acting as the custodian of internees:

> If the British Government desires that any of these aliens should be released, they will be released from Australian detention camps but only so that they can then at once be returned overseas... *They will not be permitted to be at large in Australia* [author's emphasis].

(Spender had been personally involved in a case of wrongful internment. At the outbreak of war, his brother-in-law, Philip Hentze, a Belgian wool appraiser, born in Germany but brought up in Australia, had been picked up with his wife and child at midnight but released after a few hours on Spender's intercession.)

Immediately after Layton's arrival he was sent for by Lord Gowrie, who continued to interest himself in the internees at Hay. He was greatly perturbed about the "disgraceful happenings" on *Dunera*, and asked Layton to look into it before he did anything else. But Layton had received an urgent request from the Home Office to report on 60 Italians in the Hay camp who were suffering from throat trouble. Would their continued internment there be detrimental to their health?

At Hay, Layton had two memorable encounters; one with a "willy-willy", the other with an obstructive Australian Army officer. (The latter experience was to be repeated many times during Layton's four years in Australia.) Layton was advised to keep his mouth tightly closed until the willy-willy passed. When he could open it, he insisted on inspecting the kitchens and found everything in them covered with a thick layer of dust. He decided that Hay was an unsuitable camp site, not only for the sick Italians but for all the internees. But the medical officer was uncooperative. Sending the Italians back to England, which Layton said might be necessary, would only add to England's food problems, he said. In any case, he denied that there was anything wrong with them. "I think you are allowing your private views to interfere with your military duties," said Layton. "Are you doubting the word of an Australian officer?" the medical officer asked. "If you care to put it as crudely as that," Layton replied, "that is exactly what I am doing!"

Layton reported this spirited exchange to Army headquarters in Melbourne and insisted that Hay was not a suitable camp for

Europeans. He arranged for the internees to be moved to Tatura.

(In November 1945, when Layton was completing four years of arduous work on behalf of the Home Office, he received a cable from it which read: "A query has been received from the War Office as to whether you were provided with a sleeper at public expense on a journey from Adelaide to Melbourne on 7/8 July 1944. Any assistance you may be able to give will be appreciated." Unfortunately, Layton's reply to this urgent inquiry is not on record.)

At the end of March 1941 Spender again reassured his countrymen that the arrival of Major Layton would not cause any change in the Australian Government's treatment of the *Dunera* men. "Internees who came here from Great Britain were interned for a variety of reasons which, in the opinion of the British Government, justified their being kept in custody," he said. This statement suggests that he was astonishingly ignorant of the facts. And he continued:

> It is true that since they came to Australia Mr Morrison, the
> Home Secretary, has made certain statements which have
> since been incorporated in a White Paper. The
> Commonwealth is merely the custodian of these internees:
> it is not in possession of the details of the grounds upon
> which they were interned, nor has it the means of checking
> those grounds. There has recently arrived from Great Britain
> a gentleman representing the Home Government who will
> consider the case of some of these internees, after which he
> will, no doubt, make representations to his Government.
> Should the British Government decide on their release, the
> Commonwealth Government will comply with any request to
> release them, provided that the persons concerned are kept
> in custody until a vessel is available to take them from these
> shores.

Layton offered to repatriate internees who wished to return to England, provided they were willing to join the Pioneer Corps, and were acceptable to the British authorities. Conditions for enlistment in the Pioneer Corps were posted in the camps. Applicants had to be between the ages of 18 and 50 and physically fit, though "slight disabilities" and defective eyesight did not matter. They would be sent to England at the cost of the United Kingdom Government for non-military service in Great Britain or elsewhere if required. Rates of pay and allowances were the same as for the infantry of the line:

Private	2/6 per day
Corporal	4/6 per day
Sergeant	6/6 per day

Family allowances:

wife	18/- per week	3rd child	4/- per week
1st child	7/6 per week	every additional child	4/- per week
2nd child	5/6 per week		

An article by John Cashel in the Melbourne *Herald* of 15 June 1941 described the work of the Pioneer Corps in England. It was headed, "GERMANS HELP TO CLEAR LONDON DEBRIS". "I was for a day virtually a member of the strangest foreign legion in the world, the Pioneer Corps of the British Army," it began, "aliens who also served behind the British front in France before the Nazi 'breakthrough'. I experienced the inspiring sensation of seeing exiled Germans, good freedom-loving patriots of the true Fatherland all of them, cleaning up the ruins of British homes bomb-blasted by other Germans of a different sort."

> The Pioneers wielding the demolition spade and pick-axe were 60 per cent Germans, 30 per cent Austrians, the remainder Poles and Czechs, and an odd Lithuanian or two. 'Hard work?' I asked. 'No, child's play,' was the answer. 'Try it.' I helped him for a time laboriously, as huge lumps of conglomerated brick overweighted my shovel, and the remnant of a gaping wall threatened any moment to engulf us. I should like to know what the private-contractor demolition chaps are paid for the same toil!
>
> Their company is a democracy in itself. Shovelling side by side among the rubble are lawyers, doctors, journalists, engineers, ship-brokers, chemists, dentists, farmers, wholesalers, clerks, agricultural labourers. Ex-college boys jostle with the less-educated. Some once rowed in English varsity eights! Others had commissions in the German and Austrian armies and high positions in the Reich. One sergeant speaks 10 languages.
>
> The Pioneers I saw, like all others of the corps, British and alien alike, assist the Royal Engineer Service. They may today be clearing up London, tomorrow constructing roads, building camps, felling trees.

About 400 internees immediately took advantage of Major Layton's offer, returning to England in varying numbers, as shipping became available. Two hundred more, who had been promised that their wives would follow them to Australia, were also sent back, and about another 200 on the grounds that they could help England's war effort.

Repatriation of internees to England began on 2 June 1941 when 139 sailed in *Largs Bay*, followed by 58 two days later in *Themistocles*, and on 7 July, 16 in *Glennifer*. The next large batch, 338, sailed on 12 October in *Sterling Castle*, followed two days later by 106 in *Ceramic*. Thereafter, with the exception of 298 who sailed on 19 July 1942 in *Themistocles*, only small numbers were repatriated. The total number at the beginning of January 1943 was 1141. As a result of enemy action 47 lost their lives during the return voyage.

Applicants for the Pioneer Corps had to fill in a long and searching questionnaire. One of the questions asked was: "Did you leave (Germany or Austria) for any of the following reasons:

(a) racial
(b) political
(c) economic."

"To reply 'Because of Nazi oppression' is insufficient information," the printed application form warned sternly (and incomprehensibly). Surely to most of the refugees it was a more than sufficient reason for leaving their native land.

Not all the internees were prepared to join the non-combatant Pioneer Corps as a condition of their release. Peter Stadlen, for example, awaiting Layton's arrival, wrote to the Society of Friends: "I sincerely hope that no pressure will be brought to bear on refugees here to join the Pioneer Corps as the only means of getting released. Quite apart from other considerations, I would consider it very unfortunate if there was put before them the decision either to join up or forgo their liberty for the duration..." Their viewpoint was expressed vigorously in an article that appeared in *Boomerang* soon after Layton's arrival. It was written by a young internee who had been educated in England and served in the Officers' Training Corps. He pointed out that an amazingly high proportion of the internees had been in Nazi concentration camps, and commented: "Had the Governments of Europe hated the Nazis half as much as we, there would have been no Nazis left to fight the war." It was ludicrous, he continued, that men like Ward Price should be at liberty while known and tested fighters against Nazism were interned. And:

> We are informed that we may join the Pioneer Corps, and
> thereby demonstrate our loyalty...but unconditional
> enlistment will not demonstrate so much loyalty as
> desperation...Many...are eager to join the fighting forces
> proper. We don't want to be merely tolerated, allowed to enter

a corps in which we bear no weapons, be privates, but not officers...It is up to the Government that they trust us, and that they intend to do us justice. Sufficient humiliation has already been inflicted...As equals we would be happy to brave the storm, but we will not be suspect, nor will we be inferiors. For those who serve in England's battles surely deserve the privileges of Englishmen. Let these not be withheld from us.

An internee who was able to "brave the storm" was young Tim Bleichröder, a member of the well-known German Jewish banking family. As a parachutist in the British First Airborne Division ("The Red Devils") he took part in the disastrous drop at Arnhem in September 1944, was captured and, it is presumed, executed as a traitor.

Layton also had authority to arrange for internees to migrate to the United States. Between 800 and 1000 men wanted to go but were prevented by a change of policy announced in Washington on 1 July 1941. This denied an entry visa to any person who had blood relations living in German-controlled territory.

Among the internees who left the camp on 25 May 1941 to embark on *Largs Bay* was a doctor from Lancashire, who in November wrote to friends still interned in Australia:

As a matter of fact, it is only too easy to adapt oneself to normal life again and to forget unpleasant experiences. But I assure you we have you constantly in our minds. You will reply that our efforts on your behalf have been unavailing and have made absolutely no difference to your position, and you are unfortunately right. But the pictures of all of you crowding behind the barbed wire and waving to us when our coaches drew away from the camp on that fateful 25 May will always be remembered by us and will see to it that we shall never abandon our efforts for you who are helpless.

The doctor described some of the efforts. Members of Parliament including Sir Alexander Maxwell, Permanent Under Secretary of State in the Home Office, had been interviewed and statements made in the House of Commons were undoubtedly due to these efforts.

Doctors had no difficulty in getting jobs as assistants to general practitioners, the Lancashire doctor reported, but not all the returning internees were so well off. "Private Epstein is at present engaged in washing dishes and peeling potatoes, and I wonder whether he sometimes wishes he were back in his old proud position as the leader of the camp of a thousand men."

Charles Bastian of the Royal Australian Air Force travelled to Greenock in *Largs Bay* with a small contingent of Australian Air Force and naval men, miscellaneous passengers and returning internees. He remembered:

> ...a small band of crazy Noumean French naval reserves who had a cache of absinthe, a dear old lady who had been for many years a missionary in Japan, and drooled about their wonderful manners...two young ecclesiastical embroideresses...one sexy-looking woman...who drank the Navy sub-lieutenants into bankruptcy before succumbing to the wiles of their senior escort officer (crafty b--- he was, *and* patient!!!) and a stinking cargo of hides...

Two of the internees, Dr Marcus (awarded an Iron Cross in World War I) and Julius Schott, undertook to improve Bastian's rudimentary German in case he was captured, and gave him addresses of people in Germany who would be friendly. Another internee, Weiss, was an accomplished accordionist "who loved beer, but was flat broke":

> So, after we had finished our evening PT parade, and the bar was opened, we thirsty few would ply Weiss mit grog while he played until his fingers lost co-ordination, when he would subside into grinning, blissful sleep in our bar corner...When the bar closed, we'd carry him down to his quarters...

The internees told Bastian that they had had "a pretty rough time on the *Dunera*", did not complain about this, but had harrowing tales to tell about their treatment in Germany:

> ...One was unable to speak intelligibly because of a mangled tongue. Another had an ugly depression in his cheekbone, and a useless mashed eye from an interrogation session...None of the other passengers including the RAAF peasants treated them in anything but the most friendly fashion. They frequently expressed their amazement and pleasure at this...

When the British Government agreed to compensate the *Dunera* victims for their losses, Layton, in addition to his other exacting tasks, had to interview claimants, and authorise payments. It was not always easy to assess the validity of a claim. One internee, for instance, said he had invested his entire savings — £800 — in a bar of platinum bought from a London firm, which he named. Layton asked the Home Office to check the story. It was found to be true, but the price of platinum, alone among the precious metals, had fallen during the war. The Home Office made the necessary adjustment, and authorised an *ex gratia* payment of £700. "I do not think any other Government would have gone to so much trouble at such a critical time," was Layton's comment.

Another internee claimed £200 for the loss of an unpublished novel. Layton asked him on what he based his valuation. "I made £100 on my first novel," the claimant replied, "and the second is twice as good."

Ultimately the British Government paid more than £35,000 in compensation.

CHAPTER FOURTEEN

Many *Dunera* passengers managed to keep diaries. Some, like the camp constitution, were written on purloined toilet paper, but one of the most interesting, because it gives a schoolboy's reaction to internment in England and deportation to Australia, was written by Oswald Wolkenstein, later a Sydney businessman, in small notebooks that had escaped the predacity of the guards.

The Wolkensteins are one of the oldest families in Austria. An ancestor, the poet Oswald von Wolkenstein, born in 1377, has been compared with Goethe. Austria commemorated him on a special stamp issued on his 600th anniversary.

In July 1938 Count Wolkenstein and his five sons fled from Vienna, and after seven months escaped to England by way of Italy and Yugoslavia.

Oswald and his elder brother Christopher were sent to Ampleforth College, Yorkshire, while the three younger brothers went to Stonyhurst, also in Yorkshire. Only Christopher and Oswald were interned. In the crazy capriciousness of the internment policy their father throughout the war worked in an English munitions factory.

On the first anniversary of his arrival at Ampleforth, Oswald wrote: "Today one year in England. Very happy. In the afternoon I tobogganed for one and a half hours." A few days later he is learning "weapon tactics" with the Officers' Training Corps. He practises map-reading, commands a squad, shoots at the range, takes part in route marches. His diary for 1940 is a typical schoolboy's record of tobogganing, cross-country runs, tennis, gym, ping-pong. He attends High Mass, and reports on the weekly film night: "*The Mikado* is rather an opera than a film. Quite good...*Brother Rat* — not very good but quite funny. *Turn of the Tide*. It was quite good but not very interesting. *Q-Planes*. Very interesting. The best film of the term, *The Spy in Black*."

He boxes for his House, runs in the half-mile and the hurdles, hunts and records a kill. He does well in English, Greek, maths. The war across the Channel is very far away. Then, on Friday, 10 May 1940, he wrote: "Germany invades Holland, Belgium and Luxembourg. Many air raids. Mr Chamberlain resigns as Prime Minister and Mr Churchill succeeds him." Two days later, on Whit Sunday, the entry reads: "I went in the morning to Holy Communion. After my breakfast, the policeman came with the frightful news that I am going *to be interned*" [his italics].

The boy's first internment was in the big hall of the Infantry Training Centre near York. "Barbed wire is around us and there are about five guards. Washing accommodation quite nice but cold. There are 25 other Germans (mostly Jews). We get up at five o'clock and go to sleep at 10.45. We are not allowed to write home."

At first the food was "quite good" and quite plentiful. After a week, he was allowed to write home "or anywhere" and visitors were allowed. Then on 25 May he wrote: "No more visitors. Food is getting less. We always get the same things." At the end of the month he was moved to Huyton. "Food is quite good," he wrote on 31 May. "At lunch we got an *Eintopfgericht*. No newspaper or knives or even 10 shillings are allowed. No news from Papa." He played bridge, and ate well. Dunkirk fell. Nothing much happened in camp. "I am pretty lazy," he wrote. In June, teaching began and he attended lectures. One was by Captain Rintelen: "Quite interesting. The German Crown Prince is as well here."

On 12 June, he wrote: "Today I am a month interned. Pretty awful." Two days later he was moved to Douglas on the Isle of Man. He recorded his routine: "Mass at 6.45. 7.30 first roll call. 8.30 breakfast. 10.45 inspection. 1 pm lunch. 6 pm high tea. 9 pm second roll call, and 10.15 pm lights out."

3 July 1940: "At 11 o'clock, after some notice, I had to be ready with my luggage probably to leave for Canada. I am searched for money." Next day, he arrived by ship in the Clyde, near Glasgow, and "took decision to go to Canada", but 5 July found him back at Douglas. "Slept very well after my excursion to Canada," he wrote.

7 July: "Rumour news. Rumania was attacked by Russia and Bulgaria. A great sea battle for Gibraltar but driven back with 89 per cent losses. The Q-ship *Arandora Star* full of refugees to Canada was sunk. Very many were drowned."

Wednesday 10 July: "After a trip on a small ship (*St Helena*) we arrive at Liverpool in the evening. Then we board our transatlantic ship, HMT *Dunera*. We were searched quite cruelly at 11 pm below deck."

Thursday 11 July: "At about 3 am we leave Liverpool for Canada. All my luggage was taken from me and my pockets were empty too. So we could not wash ourselves after a very bad night."

Friday 12th July: "Our treatment is still very rotten. It is just too awful. The sea is quite rough. I get six times seasick. I help those pickpockets to empty our trunks. Then at 9.15 am a terrific bump occurs. I was up at the deck. Food is quite good because most people are sick."

Saturday 13 July: "As we have been told later that bump was not from the engine but a torpedo which struck our ship but did not explode. But they are not sure about it."

Sunday 14: "Food is getting less and worse."

Memo at bottom of page: "Brought into HMT *Dunera*. Treatment very bad. Pockets searched and trunks captured. People are kicked by soldiers. No washing material. Ablutions and lavatories rotten."

Diary entries became fewer. Some days there were none.

21 July: "We are allowed to take 20 minutes' walk on deck and that is very unpleasant."

22 July: "Frightfully hot day. I sweat very much especially down here where we 'live'." They sight land after 14 days at sea. "It is Freetown. Lovely trees, especially palms we never saw in the open air growing wild."

25 July: "Food quite good again. Get sometimes apples which are often exchanged for cigarettes. Every day a walk. No definite news of where we go — certainly not to Canada."

27 July: "Takoradi. We take fresh water."

28 July: "Still at Takoradi. Treatment a little better."

29 July: "After breakfast (9.45) we move off Takoradi. Going home day at Ampleforth. (Nice, isn't it!!!) Only salt water to wash with. Take often warm salt-water shower."

1 August: "Got apples. Sea rough."

5 August: "My name day. Christopher made a very touching parcel with three cigarettes in it, and he gave it to me as a little present. After four weeks at sea — Cape Town, lightened, lovely, no black out." They load stores, water and fuel oil.

11 August: "First Mass. Went to communion. It is a great gift. The Mass was said on deck. Many people came. It was touching. Nice day. Quite warm."

15 August: "Yesterday we were for the first time allowed to go for the deck walk with shoes on. We could not before. The ship rolled and pitched. Very uncomfortable."

21 August: "Stormy weather. At our exercise on deck someone (J. Weiss) jumped overboard and drowned. Ship stopped but too late. First suicide."

24 August: "Storm at night. The ship rolls and pitches so much that our plates fall from the tables and break. Those who fetch food spill our meals on the stairs. Evening better. One person dies in hospital."

25 August: "Sea quiet at last."

27 August: "Eighteen days from Cape Town arrived at Fremantle. Short walk on deck. Saw Australian soldiers for first time."

29 August: "Went to doctor as a little ill. Got apple. Twice a week we get apples or some other fruit."

1 September: "Fingerprints were taken and cards filled out for the Germans and Italians. *Memo*: Now we know quite definitely that we are going to stay in Australia. How long?"

3 September: "Melbourne. The Germans (Nazis) and Italians are put out and we stay quite alone."

4 September: "Leave Melbourne. Someone was knocked out in a quarrel, and died immediately, because he fell unluckily."

5 September: "Excitement everywhere. Groups arranged for disembarkation."

6 September: "Fifty-eight days on *Dunera*. Arrive at Sydney after two days. Lovely city like New York. We are landed and put on a train and went away. In the train we got a lovely packet with sandwiches and fruit, and coffee later on. Go quite fast. Sleep in train. Play bridge."

7 September: "At 6 o'clock in the morning arrival at Hay. End station of railway line. Got a good breakfast. It is rather hot, and the camp is also not very inviting. The treatment is good."

8 September: "Roll call again (twice a day) which we did not have on the ship."

HAY CAMP

Oswald and Christopher move to Hut 2, with Father Koenig.

12 September: "In the evening I experienced my first SANDSTORM. It was frightful. The whole hut sandy and dirty. The lights went out. Later rain came. Night was rather cold."

14 September: "Suitcases which are still intact were given out today. One could see many disappointed faces. Seven days in Hay."

15 September: "To my great joy, I got my suitcase and Christopher too. Nothing was taken from mine. But everything is damp and a little bit foul from the sea air."

He played bridge, read some newspapers, and listened to Professor Meyer lecture on music. Food was tasty and plentiful. Choir practice (first bass).

20 September: "Wrote application for release to Archbishop Gilroy [Catholic Archbishop of Sydney]. Terrific rain. Half an inch. Camp under water. Very cold. Could see your own breath.

"Can write two letters a week with limited two pages (150 words)."

26 September: "Wrote long letter to Papa telling him everything at last. Mr Brand of Sydney Jewish Welfare Committee not well informed about us either.

"Compounds I and II were divided. No communication allowed.

"Father Carrol of Hay very kind and helpful. He arrived with presents: toothbrushes, ink, pencils, penholders, soap etc."

29 September: "First Mass in Hay. Father Carrol supplied everything for it.

"Japanese-German pact."

4 October: "Saw a whirlwind. It was a grand sight going into the air 500 feet."

6 October: "Community singing with Ray Martin and Eric Liffman, in the evening around a campfire. Sergeant-Major and another behaved and enjoyed themselves very much."

7 October: "Getting quite hot (93 degrees). Minced meat for the first time."

12 October: "Very much to eat because most Jews fast. Very hot. Water restricted owing to shortage."

Candles arrived and daily Mass resumed. More campfire singing. Newspaper pasted on wall.

15 October: "Camp school officially opened by Dr Wolff."

16 October: "Articles in papers about indiscriminate and hasty internment of aliens."

20 October: "Very good food. Lunch: soup, potato and minced pie, custard and pears. Supper: mixed pickles, corned beef, salad, bread and butter, tea and stritzel.

"Nearly every day a warm shower."

3 November: "*Food.* Very good breakfast: jam, stritzel with raisins, bacon, eggs, salad, bread, coffee.

"Choir under Professor Peter Meyer."

14 December: "Wrote to Archbishop Mannix [Catholic Archbishop of Melbourne] for his kindness to take charge of us."

24 December: "Am in Christmas mood. Had a party. Our choir sang. Speeches were delivered. Very nice. Got presents. Then we celebrated...in the dark hut.

"Very touching Christmas midnight Mass."

26 December: "Premiere of 'Snow White'."

11 January, 1941: "List of 62 men to go to Orange. Some refused. Didn't want to be separated from friends."

22 January: "Wiener schnitzel and kartoffel salad."

4 February: "*Dunera* case was brought up in the House of

Commons. Learning Pitman's shorthand and Spanish."

17 February: "Mr Brand of the Australian Jewish Welfare Committee addressed us and warned us of our tactless manner, especially the Jews to keep their faith. Everybody discussed his speech in the evening."

20 February: "My fingerprints were taken by a detective. Took bridge lessons. Choir practice as usually."

The flies were "very tiresome". Oswald wrote of terrific rains in March. He sat for a portrait by Kaemerer and saw Professor Hoffman's paintings.

On his 17th birthday — 8 April — Oswald got two packs of playing cards, a bridge-scorer and calendars from his father, and from his camp mates books, cigarettes, a tie, a shirt, cigarette holder, a belt, milk, coffee and sugar ("so that I can make coffee for myself"), a salami, a cup, a plate, sweets and biscuits.

12 April: "Have eaten my birthday salami. It was very delicious. Dentist. Dr Woldsechs."

"Fistball, football, chess, ping-pong."

18 April: "Started the camp school for matric. I take English, German, French, Latin and maths."

5 May: "Got up at 5 am because 100 people leave for Tatura."

9 May: "Bade goodbye to Stephen Kuffner who is released for Cuba. He gave me his one pound and an English orange marmalade."

10 May: "Major Layton addressed the hut captains. He excused himself for the deplorable mistake."

18 May: "Got ready for leaving. In the evening...a most enjoyable hut feast. Everyone made a little speech. Then we sang and ate. Had also wine which was made ourselves. Dr Ullman made verses on each member of our hut.

"Left 19 May after 255 days at Hay. Started at 5.20 am, changed at Tocumwal, arrived at five. Twenty-five-minute journey in bus." *TATURA*

22 May: "Got up at 7.15 as we have roll call at 7.45. The treatment is not very good. We have got roll call at 7.45, 10.30, 5 pm, 10.30. It is very harsh and we are treated like prisoners of war, who must have four roll calls. Everything is very strict and exactly after regulations.

"But lunch and supper plentiful."

25 May: "Saul...and others left for England."

30 May: "The *Age* reports that the Council for Civil Liberties, at its annual meeting, had complained that thousands of innocent alien refugees from England, many of them anti-Fascists, were interned in Australia. The secretary, Brian Fitzpatrick, said 2000 refugees had been sent out and were in two internment camps, but the authorities would not release them, even on the best of recommendations. There were about 400 between 16 years and 19 years of age, who had been attending English public schools and universities at the outbreak of war, but their release could not be secured. Archbishop Mannix informed the council that he was interested in two boys who were Austrians, but he had been unable to induce the authorities to allow them to continue their education. The treasurer (Mr Fadden) promised to take the matter up with the Minister of the Army, and the Leader of the Opposition (Mr Curtin) and other Federal members consented to inquiries.

"Mr J. McKellar said one of the internees was a former editor of an anti-Nazi newspaper, who had to leave the continent when France fell. He was a member of the PEN Club and the PEN Club of New York would be pleased to receive him, but the man was not allowed to write to the club to make the necessary arrangements."

15 June: "Major Layton giving interviews.

"Learning the flute."

7 September: "ONE YEAR IN AUSTRALIA. The first year in Australia was not too bad. Reviewing the last year, I can copy Christopher's statistic: We spent £9.10.2. We received about 225 letters and postcards (168 from Papa). We wrote 225 (100 to our dear Papa)."

4 October: "Peter Stadlen with a choir of 55 and an orchestra of 10 gave Handel's 'Israel in Egypt'."

30 October: "Layton came again. More interviews."

31 October: "Says only 250 for USA. Every White Paper man can return to England...so-called skilled workers can return.

"Father Koenig, Christopher and I were interviewed by Layton. Layton very kind and the outcome was positive.

"(1) no difficulty for our release from British Government,

(2) there has not yet been a change of policy,

(3) he was well informed about our case."

22 November: "Army Minister Forde with Major Carnera, group commandant, and another MP. He was very nice and inquired about the people. Hans Feder recited poems which were nice and pleased the Minister."

24 December: "Xmas supper: soup, schnitzel and kartoffel salad, plum pudding, beer, biscuits, pineapple and coffee."

On the last day of 1941, there was the first performance of "Snow White Joins Up". At 10 pm coffee was served with krapfen, and wine "made from a queer mixture of apples, oranges, bananas etc...it was very good".

Oswald's hut mates at Tatura (Hut 14) included George Nadel (who described Oswald as "my greatest friend" and "the sole light in my internment"), Walter Koenig, Dr Paul Schatzki, Paul

Kaufmann, Professor Peter Meyer, Richard Ullman.

"Christopher got £3.18.0 for *Dunera* claim."

5 January 1942: "My first job in camp. Joined Christopher in the lavatory cleaning party, five shillings a week. One hour each morning."

Oswald had just finished a game of chess with Paul Sculz on Saturday, 10 January, when someone came into the hut and told them they were released and should be ready to leave on Monday. "I could not believe it, so that I was both happy and sad."

12th January: "RELEASE.

"My happiest day since long. It was the 12th of May 1940 when we were interned, exactly 20 months ago. It is really a lovely feeling, and I am sure that I will soon forget the internment and appreciate freedom twice as much...It was a sad picture when we went out of the gate as free men to see others behind barbed wire who shared the same fate as we did..."

At 7 pm that day, Father Meagher, Father Provincial of the Society of Jesus, who had met him at Spencer Street Station, presented him to Archbishop Mannix. "He was very kind, tall and white hair. Then I went to bed and slept very well in a decent bed again", at Burke Hall, Xavier's preparatory school.

He entered in his diary: "Having been interned for 610 days (87 weeks, 20 months), in Australia 493 days (70 weeks, 16 months). Correspondence (during 493 days): wrote 269 letters; to Papa 139; to others 130. Received 316 letters: from Papa, 251, from others 65."

In December 1942 Oswald matriculated in English, Latin, English history (1789-1914), maths I and maths IV, with honours in German. He won seventh place in Victoria. His brother, Christopher, passed first year medicine at the Melbourne University.

10 August 1942: "Wrote to Professor Peter Meyer, congratulating him on his achievement to become a member of the Royal College of Music in London for his work 'De Profundis' composed in camp."

The following are extracts from the diary of Austrian-born Albert Karoly, who in June 1940 was a student at Nottingham University College studying for the Inter BSc examination and living at the Nottingham home of Dr E. M. Barker as a sponsored refugee:

> On June 25 there is a two-hour air raid alarm. I get to bed around four in the morning. At 6.30 there is a knock on my bedroom door, Dr Barker and a policeman tell me that I am to be arrested. I am a German passport holder and Britain is

at war with Germany. Although I had been to an Aliens
Tribunal and had a favourable classification, the
Government apparently has decided that all 'enemy aliens'
are to rounded up... The policeman tells me that maybe this
is only for a day or two. But I pack a suitcase.

Karoly was transferred to various internment camps, and on 3
July found himself at Douglas on the Isle of Man. On 9 July he had
to sign a paper volunteering to go to Canada. On 10 July he
boarded *Dunera*.

We go up the gangway, carrying our luggage. As soon as we
reach the top, the suitcases are taken away, we are searched,
valuables are taken away. Those resisting are pushed, rifle
and bayonet butts are used. All of a sudden I am almost
thrown down the steps of one of the many staircases leading
to the front of the ship. I land on top of someone who
introduces himself as a relative of Sigmund Freud. We sort
ourselves out into three groups. 1. German ships' crews. 2.
political refugees and anti-Nazis. 3. Italian nationals. Their
language is their bond. I stay with Group 2... We form a
sort of ship's university... there are a large number of
lecturers from London, Oxford and Cambridge on board,
who start teaching on any subject. I lecture on the Viennese
Boys' Choir, of which I was a member from 1929 to 1931.
As days go on, the ship seems to be going due south. I
mention this to a number of fellow passengers and I
immediately get abused. 'Did we not sign a paper stating
that we volunteer to go to Canada. Are the British not a
race of gentlemen?' At Freetown I see palm trees and
coloured folks around the dock area. I am told, 'Don't you
know that there are negroes in Canada?'
    At Takoradi, West Africa, we volunteer to carry
provisions on board... and we also manage to organise
additional food. We bring this back and share it with the
people from our mess table. I learn to have accidents while
carrying a case of fruit later in Cape Town. I 'slip', fall, the
case falls, all the fruit spills out and before anyone can do
anything we have put all the fruit (apples) into our
pockets... On the move for nearly four weeks and lecturers
in full swing. Anything and everything is being taught.
Mathematics, physics, astronomy, chemistry, languages,
bridge.
    Bridge becomes the obsession.
    Melbourne, where the craziest rumour is spreading. We
are after all, going to Canada, the port will be Vancouver.

Friday 6 September 1940 we land in Sydney, on to a
train standing ready to take us somewhere. Strange names
appear, I write them down as we pass the stations:
Hurlstone Park, Canterbury, Campsie, Cabramatta,
Liverpool (is the end the beginning?). Our guards are now
Australian soldiers with strange hats, broad brimmed, one
side turned up.

Hay. This is it...We see two camps, later known as
Hay Internment No. 7 and 8. I am assigned to 8. In the
kitchen there is the most wonderful food. Fresh white bread,
good tea, butter, corned beef. We all eat and eat.

Extract from the diary of a young internee rescued from *Arandora
Star*:

11.7.40. The escorts are very strange, they regard luggage as
their property and take even wristwatches and fountain
pens. Perhaps because of the newspaper reports, we are in
their bad books and they are looking for an opportunity to
fire into us. Or perhaps there will be a hand grenade down
the stairwell some time...the constant fear that any moment
might come a 'crash'.

12.7.40. Night very disturbed; in a half-awake state there is
always the vision of the explosion and subsequent panic.
Trembling like an animal. Every bang or loud breaker
makes one feel like leaping up...Twice complete panic
because of the blocked exits. Wincing with every loud noise.

24.7.40. Cannot get water at Freetown, therefore rationed,
not for washing, and that without a single piece of clothing
beyond what we are wearing. Start making pair of shorts
from a palliasse...Had a dream of typical pre-war freedom
— one now lives more for the night than for the day.
Started making trousers.

31.7.40. Haunting vision of catastrophe strong again.

3.8.40. Early morning in grip of terror as of old; then
suddenly a quotation from Shakespeare's *Julius Caesar* —
something like

> *The coward dies a thousand deaths,*
> *The brave but one.*

and that strangely 'helped'.

18.8.40. The tub rolls a lot, seems to be top heavy — which
brings fearful memories of the metacentre, especially in seas
which would render the launching of boats very difficult. If
anything happens, most of us will cop it.

25.8.40. News...of three air attacks on London, 'some

damage'. So it would not be very important if we popped
off here.

30.8.40. Bridge and fed-up. Completed equation of
logarithmic spiral on sphere...

3.9.40. Melbourne disembarkation directly on to
train...very nice older guards. Soon departure for Tatura.
En route lunch reception. One is no longer used to that sort
of thing and appreciates friendliness very much...One has
the 'man-nourishing-earth' again under one's feet and can
slowly start to learn that not every bang is a torpedo.

An extract from another internee's diary:

Freetown...Everybody streamed to the portholes to see land
for the first time. At Takoradi, the portholes in the
washrooms were firmly closed, only the portholes in the
latrine open and there was a great rush to have a look
through them. An orderly approach was organised while one
toilet was being used for its normal purposes; there was a
queue to have a brief look through the other, by clambering
across the toilet. Normally one of the toilets was used as a
smoking room, as smoking, even owning cigarettes was
strictly prohibited, and the people who controlled the queue
also watched for the approach of the guards.

CHAPTER FIFTEEN

The plight of the internees received little attention in Canberra. One or two Labor Members showed a mild interest in them. The United Australia Party and its partner in the governing coalition, the Country Party, showed none. (The United Australia Party in 1945 revived the name of "Liberal Party", an impudent misnomer for "Tory".)

The internees were first mentioned in Federal Parliament on 12 December 1940, when Mr Rowland James, a rugged New South Wales Labor representative, in a debate on the estimates, said: "Recently a considerable number of enemy prisoners arrived in Australia from Great Britain for internment in this country. Included among them were many Jewish refugees who had run away from the wrath of Hitler and obtained domiciles in England where upon the outbreak of war some of them were interned":

> Among these people are some members of the German
> Christian Socialist movement. An Anglican clergyman of my
> acquaintance had some money for one of these Christian
> Socialists, but it was only after most exhaustive inquiries
> that he was able, with my help, to find out which camp the
> man was in. This man was strongly opposed to the Hitler
> regime, and it seems to me to be unjust that he should now
> be interned. The representations made to the Government
> for the release of an internee named Ziebold should be
> carefully considered. Ziebold was interned some time ago,
> but, at the instigation of the late member for Kalgoorlie
> [A. E. Green], he was subsequently released. He was
> afterwards re-arrested and again interned. I believe that
> action was taken against him because of his political beliefs.
> There was no suggestion that he was engaged in subversive
> activities.

Mr SPENDER: I think the honourable Member must be in error in that regard, for our advisers in these matters confine their attention to subversive activities. A person would not be interned simply because he held certain political beliefs.

Mr JAMES: I understand that the report in regard to Ziebold stated that he was a German Communist. No section of the German people was more opposed to Hitler than the Communists. Ziebold has been in this country for years, and he married an Australian girl. Although I disagree with the views of the Communist Party, its members should not be interned merely on account of their political beliefs.

Later that day, during a debate on the right of aliens to appeal against internment, the House of Representatives, for the first time in its history and for no comprehensible reason, went into secret session. Army Minister Spender had under statutory rules set up tribunals to hear these appeals, and a private Country Party Member, Archie Galbraith Cameron, gave notice of a motion to disallow them. Cameron, a farmer from Barker, South Australia, with a "Hitler" moustache, was the most notable eccentric in the House. But he was not an amiable eccentric. A Presbyterian converted to Catholicism, sometimes described as a Catholic-Calvinist, he was truculent, bellicose, intolerant, and puritanical, as famous for his elastic-sided boots as for his inelastic mind. When angry, he would remove his boots and throw them around. At times he could be seen padding around the chaste and cold halls of Parliament House in his socks.

Cameron gave details of a number of cases which had become known to him as an Army intelligence officer. At the request of the Army, and on the authority of the Speaker, Walter Nairn, these names were deleted from *Hansard*. Cameron then threatened to bring about the defeat of the Government if he were not allowed to state his case. (Two Independents, Arthur William Coles and Alexander Wilson, held the balance of power.) He suggested a secret session; and during the midnight supper adjournment, Menzies and the Leader of the Opposition, John Curtin, agreed to this. Frank Green, Clerk of the House from 1937 until 1955, described the incident:

When the House resumed after supper 'strangers' were spied and the public and press galleries were cleared, but Senators sat tight in their gallery, and the question was raised as to whether they were 'strangers'. Menzies settled that question by saying that while Senators were undoubtedly *strange*, they were not *strangers*, so they remained.

The secret session lasted till 2.50 am. Cameron said nothing of importance and Spender had nothing to answer. "Somebody described it as 'a damp squib that barely fizzled'," said Green.

Spender defined the Government's policy on the *Dunera* internees on 26 March 1941, when Charles Albert Aaron Morgan, another New South Wales Labor Member, during Question Time said:

> I understand that a number of German socialists and anti-Nazis were brought to Australia from Great Britain in July last and interned here. Since then, the British Government has reversed its attitude to many of these people. Some of these internees were persecuted by the Nazis before leaving Germany, but later they escaped from internment there. I now ask the Minister for the Army whether the Government proposes to follow the example of Great Britain in regard to these people and give to them the right of appeal against their internment.

Spender giving his stock reply said that Australia was "merely the custodian of these internees", and he continued: "There has recently arrived from Great Britain a gentleman representing the Home Government who will consider the case of these internees...Should the British Government decide on their release, the Commonwealth Government will comply with any request to release them, provided that the persons concerned are kept in custody until a vessel is available to take them from these shores."

The question that preceded Mr Morgan's was of much greater importance to politicians and public. A Member asked the Minister for Trade and Customs, Eric John (later Sir Eric) Harrison, whether his department would "deal with those brewery companies which decline to supply hotelkeepers with beer because they have refused to charge additional prices for beer following the additional taxes imposed on that commodity by the Budget?".

On 2 April, Cameron returned to his attack on Spender. Standing Orders were suspended to enable him to move this motion:

> That the Minister for the Army has lost the confidence of this House because of his handling of the internment, trial and release from internment of certain enemy aliens.

In his speech to the motion, the fire-breathing Member for Barker enunciated clearly his attitude towards all Germans, whether Nazis or anti-Nazis, supporters of Hitler or his victims: "Such persons enjoy no rights whatever in enemy territory," he thundered, denouncing what he described as "the kid glove 'pansy' method" of handling them. And he reached an extraordinary conclusion: "Certain Jewish refugees also have been interned, and a lot of 'hot air' is being talked about them," he said. "I have heard talk of 'friendly aliens'. I do not know what a friendly alien is. I know that when my country is engaged in a life and death struggle with Germany and Italy, any man of German or Italian birth is an enemy alien. If he is friendly to this country, then he must be a traitor to his own, and I do not think it is our part to encourage treason."

The motion lapsed for want of a seconder.

Hansard does not record whether, at this stage, Mr Cameron removed his boots.

A young internee reading a report of Cameron's speech wrote:

Statements like this can only be excused if one considers
that the maltreatment and humiliations to which we were
subjected by the Nazis go beyond anything an Englishman
could even imagine anybody to inflict on his own
countrymen...

Bearing this in mind I come to the conclusion that the
majority of Englishmen are not fully aware of what
internment means to us. They do not realise that every day
they make us spend behind barbed wire is an insult to us.
They do not realise that in suspecting us of Nazi-sympathies
they make no allowance for such things as honour and self-
respect. To call us anti-German is no offence, to call us pro-
German is. Maybe this is incomprehensible for anybody who
has not himself been a victim of Nazi-persecution...

No one will believe that at a time when England was
standing with her back to the wall, she sacrificed precious
shipping space in order to send perfectly innocent people to
the remotest corners of the world. There must have been
some reason, and this suspicion is further aggravated
through the fact that originally the scheme had been
intended for dangerous Nazi prisoners and the first few
shiploads did largely consist of such people...

The principal point is that during all these months the
Government has done practically nothing to rectify these
initial offences against us. It is possible to regard the whole
series of events last summer, wholesale internment,
indiscriminate deportation, maltreatment on the *Dunera*,
misinformation to the Australians as to our real status, as
an unfortunate accumulation of individual blunders without
any consistently hostile force behind them, blunders such as
are bound to happen at a time of great political and military
tension. 'Mistakes have been made'...We have heard that

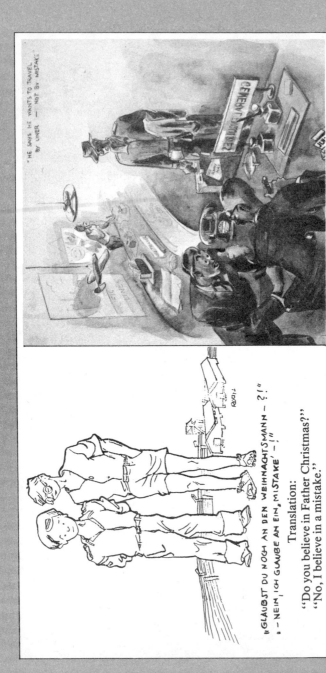

Translation:

"Do you believe in Father Christmas?"
"No, I believe in a mistake."

Embittered comments are expressed in these drawings by the internees.

(Schonberg Graphics)

so often and we are only too keen to accept such an explanation since it allays possible fears of more sinister motives.

Moral rehabilitation is our principal need and we feel all the more justified in putting forward this claim as it can be fulfilled without sacrifice of money or shipping space, in fact without putting any strain on the war machine...An authoritative statement...would clear our record...It would reassure those of us and of our friends in England, who, as a result of what happened to us, have begun to doubt whether Britain has the right to pose in this conflict as the champion of democracy, justice and tolerance...

British policy was defined during a debate in the House of Commons on 16 October 1941 when Eleanor Rathbone asked Morrison whether, in view of the fact that the Australian public apparently believed the aliens interned there were dangerous, he would make a statement "calculated to remove this misapprehension and to explain the real facts".

Morrison replied:

Some 2500 internees were sent to Australia of whom about 400 were persons detained on security grounds, while the remaining 2100 were Germans and Austrians who had been classified in categories 'B' and 'C' and were interned as a precautionary measure, in pursuance of the general policy of internment which was adopted in the summer of 1940. I have frequently explained in this House that the fact that a person was interned in pursuance of this policy and not on security grounds personal to himself was not intended to make, and does not in fact make, any reflection on his reliability or reputation. The circumstances in which His Majesty's Government sent to Australia refugees who could not be regarded as dangerous from the security point of view were explained to the Government in the Dominion more than a year ago, but if amongst members of the general public in Australia there is still misapprehension as to the character of the internees, I hope that this answer may help to remove it.

It did not.

But the Wise Men of Canberra were slowly coming to realise the absurdity of keeping behind barbed wire internees who might be helping to win the war. A Victorian Labor MP, E. J. Holloway, told Parliament that the Australian Labor Party had received letters from prominent members of the English Labour Party, including the Minister for Labour, Ernest Bevin, and Sir Walter Citrine, General Secretary of the Trades Union Congress, inquiring about the continued detention of the *Dunera* internees. Holloway referred to these enquiries when he reminded Spender on 20 June 1941 "of the unfortunate plight" of the internees, many of them highly skilled tool makers and optical instrument makers, of whom a great shortage existed in Australia. Spender replied that internees from Britain whose *bona fides* had been established by the British Government, might soon be doing war work in Australia. "It would be foolish," he declared as a man making a profound revelation, "not to use the services of these men even if they had come here as internees." He did not admit that until then his Government had been guilty of this very folly. And his leader, Menzies, added, "Obviously, no man could be used if there were any doubt about him. Therefore we will confine ourselves to those who have been wrongly interned and about whom no doubt exists."

Less than five weeks before — on 16 May — Spender had stated firmly: "Aliens who are being released from internment camps on the decision of a specially appointed British Officer [Major Layton] will go direct from the camps to ships." He again emphasised that the aliens would not be permitted to remain at large in Australia at any time.

CHAPTER SIXTEEN

The Rev. W. H. Twigg (later Archdeacon of Riverina), of Griffith, a New South Wales town 150 kilometres from Hay, was another churchman who interested himself in the welfare of the internees. He discussed their problems with a Victorian Member of Parliament, W. H. McKenzie, who was visiting Griffith, and on McKenzie's advice on 26 May 1941 wrote to Dr Herbert Vere Evatt, a Labor Member of the House of Representatives, about them. With his letter, he sent a copy of Lafitte's *The Internment of Aliens.*

Evatt is the great enigma of Australian politics. As a brilliant jurist sitting on the High Court, he had been a staunch defender of civil rights and the liberty of the common man. But when he resigned from the Bench to enter Federal politics he left his idealism behind and became an expedient, devious politician, lusting for power at all costs. It was to Evatt the libertarian that Mr Twigg optimistically addressed his eloquent appeal on behalf of the internees.

"These people," he wrote, "are being guarded, fed and clothed by the Army Department which has no further interest in them...They are kept behind barbed wire, not allowed parole, only allowed to see visitors through canary cage wire, and no matter how responsible a citizen of this country a visitor may be, he has to sign a paper that he has only discussed matters relating to their spiritual and personal welfare." Twigg made it clear that he was not criticising the administration of the camp, nor its "kindly garrison", who were only carrying out orders. But he suggested that the Federal Government should reconsider its attitude towards the internees:

> We want fighting men; there are hundreds of internees who
> have every reason to fear a victory from Hitler and want to

do something to prevent it. We need skilled men and men of science; there are many behind barbed wire. Meanwhile, a perfectly good garrison is being wasted to guard men who have no desire to escape and whose most fervent hopes are in a British victory.

Twigg suggested that a question in the House as to whether the Government had considereed releasing internees known to be loyal might bring matters to a head. But he added perspicaciously: "Public opinion is so ill-informed that it might however bring down a torrent of abuse upon the questioner."

It was Evatt the politician who received this letter and ignored its wise suggestions. No question was asked in the House. Even when five months later (October 1941) Labor came to power, neither Evatt nor any of his colleagues risked a "torrent of abuse" by showing interest in the fate of the internees.

The Minister for Labour in the Labor Government was Edward John Ward, a former Sydney tramway fettler who had become the militant, incorruptible and eloquent leader of the left wing of the Labor Party. For nearly 30 years in Federal Parliament he vociferously championed the oppressed and the needy but his sympathy ended at the gates of the internment camp, as Alfred Jacob Stern, a Tatura internee, discovered.

Stern was a German who had worked on farms in many parts of Germany. He had testimonials to his skills as an agricultural worker, and to his technical knowledge, organising ability and knowledge of machinery. (One was from Count Zeppelin who had employed Stern on his farm at Aschzusen.) In December 1941, he wrote to Ward, saying that he had been classified as "C" in England, and now wanted to be released to do farm work in Australia. A week later Ward replied that the question of release came under the control of his colleague, the Minister for the Army, Frank Forde, to whom Stern's letter had been referred.

A month later, the camp commandant told Stern that his "representations concerning employment in Australia" would receive consideration. Eight months later, Stern was still interned, and he wrote to Clarke:

> May I take the liberty of putting forward some of the
> problems confronting me at the present? Within two long
> years of waiting, I experienced one blow after the other. My
> wife, being about to leave Germany, got prevented from
> doing so at the last minute, was subsequently deported to
> Poland, while my father-in-law, an old man of 72 years, left
> quite alone, for Cuba. Furthermore, in spite of all my
> endeavours to ascertain my mother's whereabouts, I didn't
> succeed yet. And so I am without a word from my family

for nearly 10 months. That is only half the story and a most depressing one. The other part has been no less dejecting. I am a farmer able and willing to do useful work for the country in this capacity...to reach this goal I am striving for nearly a year...Would you have the kindness to get in touch with Major Layton and try to bring my case to a final conclusion? Just in this very moment when a call for rural manpower sounds throughout the country, when the last able-bodied man is badly wanted, immediate steps should be taken to bring home to authorities concerned that a lot of refugees of this camp could be employed in rural industries. This is a matter of justice and common sense.

But justice and common sense were equally rare commodities in Federal Parliament and Army headquarters. Stern remained in camp.

Another experienced Tatura agriculturist was A. Knudsen, a Dane with a German passport who had lived in Algiers where his neighbour and close friend was the sheriff of Morocco. Knudsen was in England in 1940 and, at the age of 70, was embarked aboard *Dunera*. From camp in March 1944 he wrote to Miss Pierce acknowledging the gift of a jar of honey:

I am, I daresay, the biggest gardener here. I had so much sweet corn that I had to feed the horses with it, because nobody in our camp wanted to eat any more of it. Of cucumbers I have harvested more than 1000 Early Fortune alone, the smaller kind I never harvested. I have learned in the course of these four years what can be done with this beautiful soil even without using artificial manure.

His watermelons, which weighed as much as 16 kilograms each, were very sweet and had a "peculiar aromatic taste", which he believed was due "to the constant radiation of the searchlights at night and of the sun at daytime".

In another letter, Knudsen wrote that going through his papers, he had found an old and tested secret Arabic recipe (given to him by the sheriff) for curing stomach ulcers, by boiling down certain parts of a sheep. He thought that as Australia was a country with plenty of sheep, he could sell it at a very low price.

In March 1945, he wrote:

I wonder if I will ever see liberty again after five years' internment and being told so often that I could be released as soon as satisfactory arrangements can be made for my support.

That of course can never be done as long as I am

interned, Everybody who is urgently in need of a man in his
factory says: 'Absurd, a man of 75 years of age, he should
be buried and can be of no use or value to me.' That is
quite natural. However, unfortunately, my people live up to
90 or 100 and are healthy and strong like myself. A few
days ago we received fodder for the horses (you know, I
feed and groom six horses for over one year, my special
hobby!) and by receiving 90-pound and 110-pound [40 and
50 kilograms] bags (bales) from the truck, I found that I
was handling just as many bales as the young soldiers at the
stables and just as fast...In addition to my stable duties I
am tanning rabbit skins and making a trunk...

Five months later, Knudsen was released to work on a poultry
farm for 30 shillings a week and keep.

The last issue of *Boomerang* appeared on 16 May 1941, just before
the move to Tatura. In it, a writer compared the condition of the
departing internees with their condition eight months before:

Those of the inhabitants of Hay who sat on the fence
opposite Hay station on the morning of 7 September 1940,
saw a procession of 'prisoners of war', pale, half-starved,
clad in rags with hardly any luggage, and being marched to
a desolate-looking camp. Those inhabitants (if any) who will
sit on that fence in the near future, will see something rather
different. There will be a procession of sun-burnt, well-fed
(sometimes over-fed) and well-dressed refugee internees, also
known as 'Mistakes', marching back to the station, with
piles of luggage following behind. Had this change been
brought about merely by better food and clothing? The
answer was 'No'. It was due to the 'Spirit of the Camp' —
a realisation of their helpless situation combined with a
spirit of defiance in face of it.

"So chins up," the article concluded, "and let the people of
Hay notice the difference."
    A factor contributing to the "Spirit of the Camp" was surely
the excellence of the camp cuisine, presided over by accomplished
European chefs. In the same issue of *Boomerang*, Rudolph Mohr,
an appreciative internee, paid light-hearted tribute to them. "I have
often wondered whether our community is sufficiently grateful to
those British authorities who, in their inscrutable wisdom, have
assured us of the company of first-class cooks." He named three:
Ferdinand Lang, an expert in sauces, mayonnaise and "the more
romantic egg dishes", Hans Edelman, an expert in the luscious

Austrian sweet, *mehlspeisen*, a famous alloy of flour and sugar, while English cooking at its best was represented by Walter Salamon, a specialist in fish dishes and salads.

Ferdinand Lang, who began his career at Vienna's restaurant Hartmann, was a cook on the Blue Train before graduating from a cooking college at St Cloud. This was followed by appointments at Monte Carlo. He was chef at the Hotel Prince de Galles, and when war broke out was in Paris officiating over the stomachs of a wealthy American family with whom he fled to England after the invasion of France.

Mr Hans Edelman had started his culinary career at the age of six.

The youngest of the trio was Walter Salamon, aged 21, who, after leaving school in England, spent three years at the Westminster Technical Institute in London, before becoming a chef at the George, in Colchester, and Laurence Hall, in Richmond, where he was cooking when he was interned. "If Mr Salamon could be considered a typical disciple of modern English cooking," Mohr commented, "one could confidently look forward to the elimination of indigestion."

There were three kitchens — ordinary, vegetarian and, for the Jewish internees, *kosher*. Internee gardeners contributed to the cuisine by growing herbs and vegetables then little known in Australia —borage, angelica, fennel, chives, celeriac and soya bean.

"It is well to emphasise two points..." *Boomerang* concluded. "The first is that life and work in the camp has been surprisingly harmonious, in spite of little outbursts of petty squabbling now and then; any such occurrences can be explained by the strain imposed by circumstances. The second is that there is a genuine and widespread desire, cheerfully to make the best of a bad job."

On the first anniversary of their internment the refugees issued a passionate but well-reasoned "Appeal for Justice and Humanity" to the Australian Government. The document of more than 4000 words contrasted England's attitude towards anti-Nazi refugees with the attitude of the Australian Government, which despite its promises at the Evian Convention was still keeping friendly aliens behind barbed wire. It quoted what Lord Cecil had said in the House of Lords on 6 August 1940: "I feel most strongly that the history of what has taken place with regard to these unhappy aliens is one of the most discreditable incidents in the whole history of this country." The document pointed out that "the skill and capabilities of the engineers, scientists, doctors and experts in our midst are rotting behind barbed wire...if we were allowed to participate in the common effort, we would cease to be a burden and problem, and become an asset to Australia."

On the train that took him from Hay to Tatura, Henry Mayer wrote:

Australian Journey
The thirsty earth gives us the cue of discontent,
It stretches, void of lumps, miles onto miles,
Is broken by a solitary windmill
Sheep grazing.
No flatness could exceed its own.
Conscious of waste and sand it folds its arms,
And through its fissures — as the child
Is torn from the dry breast and pulls
It exhales a vacuum, charged with frustration.

Screeching parakeets — rainbows in miniature
Dissect the grey horizon.
Dry, as your palate on the morning after,
Is the land.

We left the wire, spiked with adverse menace,
We marched by shanties of glistening tin,
We felt the sun, promising incandescence, within
Our bodies. It painted our weary, sleepy faces.
The wire bides its time and waits.

CHAPTER SEVENTEEN

Camps for the internment of aliens resident in Australia were set up in Tatura in the early days of the war, to the great discontent of citizens of the neighbouring township of Rushworth, who had hoped to share the construction cake. Tatura is situated 180 kilometres north of Melbourne, in the western Goulburn Valley, and the four internment camps were approximately 16 kilometres from the township. It is a pleasant district of thriving farms and orchards, with sheep and cattle grazing in lush pastures, an earthly paradise after the aridity of Hay, though summer shade temperatures can reach 46°C, and winters are often severe.

The Nazi internees showed great ingenuity in listening to broadcasts from the Third Reich.

Two internees who worked on stage machinery and stage sets in a small workshop dug a shaft nearly four metres deep under the recreation hall and at the bottom made a small dugout. It was lined with timber, heated, ventilated and electrically lit. In it they installed a short-wave radio receiver which some of their colleagues had constructed, using valves taken from the camp's talking picture equipment, acid jars cut from bottles, and sulphuric acid made from sulphur filched from the camp's medical stores. Silver paper from chocolates was melted down to make plates for the batteries and earphones; condensers and rectifiers were improvised from assorted bits and pieces.

After six months of patient experiment and failure, they picked up an American station's call sign, and soon were able to receive German, Japanese, English, American and Russian bulletins. German and Japanese broadcasts invariably proclaimed great Axis victories, and the texts of these were secretly typed out and circulated.

The German prisoners in camp 1 also devoted considerable effort to planning escapes. Early in 1942 they received permission to convert a corrugated iron army hut into what they called the "Welbech Cafe". A stonework promenade over a metre high was built around the entrance, on which stood plants in large tubs, tables and chairs. On summer nights a seven-piece orchestra played while smartly dressed waiters served black coffee and German cakes. Inside the cafe, where there were tables and chairs for 30 diners, the panelled walls were adorned with gaudy pictures of the Rhine, and of Berlin. Behind the counter were stocks of preserved foods and delicacies.

The cafe also served as a gambling den, and as the headquarters of a well-organised escape society. When, after several escapes, an Australian search party pulled a large loose nail from the flooring, a small section apparently of solid concrete swung downwards on a hinge, revealing a number of small compartments. In these, the escape society had accumulated money for distribution to escapees.

The anti-Nazi internees of compound "D" also had their cafe, the "Grand Cafe Tatura". Less elaborate than the "Welbech Cafe", it consisted of a "terrace" with a few home-made benches and tables, and an inside room similarly furnished. Among the pictures on the walls was a caricature of Hitler, Goering and Goebbels looking at the anti-Nazis in their compound and laughing exuberantly at their plight.

The manager of the "Grand Cafe Tatura" was Felix Danzig, who before the Anschluss had owned the Kater Restaurant and the Union Bar in Vienna. Black coffee or a dubious sandwich cost 1½d, a glass of lemonade or a piece of cake 1d, scrambled eggs, the dearest item on the menu and little called for, cost 5d. The cafe was open from 10 am till noon, and from 2 pm till 10 pm.

There was scope also for smaller enterprises. One resourceful entrepreneur fashioned a toasting-fork from fencing wire and contracted to make morning toast for his colleagues for a fee of 6d a week. He was so successful that he was able to employ two assistants, and with the proceeds, open a small coffee-house.

Money sent by the Society of Friends in London helped to provide three camps with a radio, but the programmes were controlled from the guard room with loudspeakers in the compounds. An internee wrote: "I wish you would have been able to see the mess hut...in deep silence hundreds listened to the wonderful performance of Beethoven's third and ninth symphonies."

Internees at Tatura were allowed to subscribe to any

Australian newspaper providing it was at least three days old, but listening to news broadcasts was not allowed. Here again the military's attitude was incomprehensible.

As soon as the Hay internees were settled in Tatura, they set up a number of camp schools or "universities". One in camp 4 was proudly named the *"Collegium Taturense"*. Its first president was Dr Bruno Breyer, a slightly bald, sandy-haired, 41-year-old doctor of medicine and industrial chemist whose life epitomised the fate of the 20th-century Jewish intellectual caught up in the turbulence of pre-war Europe.

He was born in Zagreb, Yugoslavia, and studied chemistry at the University of Bonn, where he took his PhD and became an assistant lecturer. In order to take a job in Germany he acquired German nationality and worked for two years for the German industrial giant A. G. Farbenindustrie. When Hitler came to power he fled first to Zagreb, where he continued his studies, and then to Italy where he took an MD, and became a research scientist at the University of Padua.

Again racial laws caught up with him and he had to move to Switzerland. He continued his chemical researches at the University of Freiburg until April 1938, when, unfortunately as it proved, the Refugee Organisation of British Scientists helped him to go to England. Here he joined the Colloid Science Department of the University of Cambridge. The Royal Society of Medicine and Trinity College gave him membership. He did research on local anaesthetics and advised an instrument company on building England's first polarograph. (A polarograph is a machine for making swift qualitative and quantitative analysis of many organic and inorganic compounds.)

"At the outbreak of war," he told Emery Barcs when they met at Tatura, "I was engaged in vital research work with Professor E. K. Rideal, who asked me and my wife to stay with him so that we could proceed with our investigations in a quiet and secure atmosphere." But on that fateful day in May he was rounded up and moved from camp to camp until he found himself on *Dunera*. "Before sailing," he told Barcs, "I had received a firm assurance that wherever they took me I would be allowed to continue my work. We arrived in Australia in September and I have been here ever since."

Dr Breyer was later released from Tatura to resume his work on polarography, a subject on which he was a world authority. Both the University of Cambridge and a private firm in Sydney wanted him to help in the construction of an advanced polarograph. He chose Australia and from 1945 until 1950 was

Associate Professor of Agricultural Chemistry at the University of Sydney. He returned to Italy in 1951 and was Research Professor in Pharmacology at the University of Milan until his death in 1967.

"I am very happy to be in this camp," wrote a theological student who arrived at camp 1, Tatura, on 24 May 1941.

> The camp university has a proper theological seminary... I have an opportunity of taking the German matriculation exam at least in some subjects. Our timetable consists of history of religion, dogmatics, and history of dogmatics, introduction into the New Testament, and New Testament theology, Greek grammar and Greek New Testament, and philosophy. You see that the possibilities here are tremendous, besides there are regular lectures on general topics, weekly cinema, two orchestras, a huge library and regular sports provide ample entertainment and exercise. Outwardly the camp makes the impression of a small garden colony, with flowers, lawns and trees everywhere...

The camp school at camp 2, Tatura, Compound "A", had 220 students learning English, 40 learning Spanish, 10 Portuguese, 20 French and 20 Hebrew. Fifteen were studying social sciences, 11 philosophy, 16 the history of art, 13 psychology, 8 ancient philosophy, 45 architecture and building, 40 agriculture, 26 general science and medicine.

An educational officer assisted the internees in their educational work, and arrangements were made for a number of the young boys to take their Leaving Certificate examinations at the camps, and for a few men to sit for some of the arts course examinations.

One of the teachers at Tatura was the Jewish barrister Richard Flatter, a versatile man of letters who had been legal adviser to the *Wiener Zeitung*, the Austrian state paper. In that capacity he had represented the editor in several trials, and had also written a great number of articles attacking Hitler and Hitlerism. "On account of this," he wrote, "after the annexation of Austria, I had to flee my native country, leaving behind me my aged mother, my friends and my fortune." With difficulty he managed to cross the border into Czechoslovakia only 11 hours ahead of the Gestapo. He had translated Shakespeare's "Sonnets" and several of his dramas, some of which had been produced at the Vienna State Theatre by Max Reinhardt, and had written a book on the problem of Hamlet. He had also translated English poetry from the 14th to 19th century, and two of his own plays had been translated into

English. In December he sent one of his own sonnets to Clarke, apologising that "it is the only Christmas gift at my disposal".

In about a dozen packing cases two separate collections of books, most supplied by the Australian Students' Christian Movement, were sent from Hay to Tatura. The library was set up in the HQ hut of Compound "A", a well-lit room where the few available tables were occupied for 14 hours every day. Mr John and Gerd Buchdahl were chief librarians. It was the first camp institution run jointly by both compounds. It consisted of 3866 books, 733 in the "fiction library", 3133 in the "school library". "Because of the shortage of text books," Hans Buchdahl wrote to Miss Pierce, "the typewriters work all the time making copies of them."

The Friends were tireless in their help to internees, sending them books, technical magazines, clothing, tools, coffee, typewriters, musical instruments and sporting equipment...A typical purchase made by Miss Pierce at Posner's Store, Russell Street, Melbourne, included razor blades, shaving sticks, soap, hair oil, boot polish, pencils and Solvol. The Friends were also supplying two shillings a month pocket money to men who were penniless. They also sent £5 to Dr Danziger to buy urgently needed syringes and stethoscopes for the camp hospital.

"Perhaps the most influential of the internees were a group of liberal, upper-middle-class Jewish intellectuals, not more than 30 or 40," recalled Peter Herbst. "But there were also very Orthodox Jews, Jewish mystical sects, young Zionist left-wingers, devout Catholics, hard-line Communists and Austrian aristocrats, pleasant, cultivated and urbane."

Of greater interest to him than the hardships of internment was the social interaction, the cross-fertilisation that took place between enormously diverse groups — businessmen, rabbis, priests, middle-of-the road socialists, farmers, gardeners and chefs.

Looking back on his internment he said: "We had to come to terms with diversity, and to live together as a community...It was a two-way transaction, though the refugees provided a lot of talent for Australia, they had an opportunity for concentrated study and later employment opportunities that they might not have had in Europe...War produces madness. We would have fared no better in other hands."

In a series of articles published in the Australian periodical *Quadrant*, Dr Emery Barcs, a distinguished Hungarian journalist, who had come to Australia before the war and been interned at its outset, recalled his experiences in Compound "D". He wrote of the "fairly homogeneous social fibre" of the majority of the 180 or so internees and, like Peter Herbst, who was teaching English full time, acknowledges the influence of the central European middle-class, mostly Jewish intelligentsia.

> By and large we spoke the same 'language'. We had in common *Bildung* — a term which cannot be translated into English. *Bildung* is what remains after one has forgotten what one has learned. It is the residue of a variety of studies outside one's professional specialisation. It is the opposite of knowing very much about very little. People with a broad *Bildung* usually find something (and often many things) of mutual interest. 'D' Compound literally swarmed with people with *Bildung*.

Bern Drent recalled some of the more idiosyncratic occupants of Compound "D":

> The greatest mixture of individuals you could meet on God's earth:...fair dinkum escapees from concentration camps and across borders, ex-Reichstag MPs, a real Hohenzollern prince, anti-Nazi writers, actors, etc., all or most of whom had families, or relations in Germany. The last thing they wanted to do was to remind the Nazi authorities of their existence...Doubtful characters, and opportunists of 22 different nationalities, Finnish sailors, Rumanian crooks, Hungarian coffee-house sitters, a little Russian of Estonian extraction who in turn claimed to be pro-Russian and pro-Esthonian. French Foreign Legionnaires of German origin who had deserted in order to join the fighting French, Polish leftists in disagreement with the exile Polish Government in London, Italian adventurers (I remember one whose latest job had been smuggling arms for the Chinese and Japanese in turn, whoever paid him the most. He was a double, double-crosser). Engineers and farmers from the east, rubber millionaires from Malaya, some of the *Arandora Star* survivors — and Australia's most distinguished safe-breaker, a Dutchman I think, a very amiable and quiet fellow.

Dr Borkenau continued to interpret world events in frequent briefing sessions. In May 1941 he gave an accurate forecast, "when things looked pretty black for the Allies". "If an invasion of England is successful or if Britain collapses before America can successfully intervene, it's not the end of chapter, but the end of story...If Britain survives this year, she has overcome the danger, but it will take years, assisted by America, to defeat Hitler's Germany."

According to Brent, Borkenau "loved to report sick to the camp's hospital (a first-aid post with beds) since he could then take to a bed and be waited on". Brent earned a shilling a week by taking in his breakfast.

The frustrations of the refugees increased as there was no change in their situation. "One is not surprised that the mood of some of the people is explosive and is reflected in anti-British utterances," wrote the 17-year-old Brent in his diary on 13 June. "We have been recognised by the British quite officially as refugees and friendly aliens. Many have been released by the Home Office and could be working for the war effort...and yet..."

About a dozen young internees escaped from their inactivity by volunteering as "guinea-pigs" in anti-malarial experiments conducted by the Australian Army at Cairns, Queensland. Each later received a letter of thanks from the commander-in-chief, General Blamey.

When Maltby visited the Tatura Camp, he was irritated by complaints of inadequate washing facilities and exclaimed: "If you fellows complain about trifles like this, one must wonder about the credibility of your stories about the treatment in Nazi concentration camps."

Dr Hirschfeld remained interned until March 1942 when, through the intercession of Dr (later Sir) James Darling, headmaster of one of Victoria's great public schools, Geelong Grammar, he was released to become its art master. Hirschfeld was a conspicuous success and had an enduring influence on Victorian art. Soon after the war his friend Walter Gropius, who was then chairman of Harvard's Graduate School of Design, offered Hirschfeld a much better paid and more important job in America, but Hirschfeld refused to leave the school and the country that had befriended him.

In 1953 he held an exhibition of the work of his pupils in Melbourne which has been described as "unique in Australian art and education". It demonstrated for the first time in Australia the Bauhaus principles of the Study of Materials. Hirschfeld also conducted a Study of Materials workshop for art teachers, and in 1963 Longman's published his short account of the Bauhaus for students' use, *The Bauhaus — An Introductory Survey*. When he visited Germany the following year, he was invited by the Bauhaus Archiv to demonstrate his reflected light plays, which he had devised at the Bauhaus in the 1920s. Hirschfeld died in Sydney on 7 January 1965. "He inspired dozens of boys with his integrity, and enthusiasm," said Sir James. "He was an almost perfect man, physically, mentally and spiritually, a beautiful character and an original teacher."

One of his pupils, who acknowledges his debt to Hirschfeld, was Daniel Thomas, later curator of Australian art at the Australian National Gallery in Canberra.

CHAPTER EIGHTEEN

Australia, a country with an enduring tradition of xenophobia, and not a little anti-semitism, had no desire to become permanent host to a crowd of foreigners. The Government repeatedly made it clear that it was acting only as their custodians for the duration of the war. The lofty promises of Evian were conveniently forgotten.

The Government's views were endorsed by the influential Returned Soldiers' and Sailors' League, an organisation not noted for its liberal outlook. At its congress in November 1941, it demanded the deportation at the end of the war of "all interned aliens" to their countries of origin.

The Australian Government was unwilling to discuss the possibility of even releasing on parole internees who could find useful employment in Australia. And there was no doubt that the authority to do this rested solely with Australia. The British Government was reluctant to interfere. "The obvious reason for this attitude," said a report from VIREC dated 17 November 1941, "is that the British Government does not wish to ask the Australian Government to bear the brunt of bungling for which it is alone responsible. Such a request might create a dangerous precedent at a time when the harmonious relations between the two Governments must be maintained, even at the expense of justice being done to some hundreds of refugee-internees."

Australian trade unions have historically been opposed to foreign migrants, partly because they have shared the traditional Australian xenophobia, and partly because they have shared Sir Frank Clarke's belief that foreigners posed a threat to Australian working conditions. So it is surprising that in August 1941 the Trades and Labour Council of Queensland addressed a letter to Menzies protesting against the treatment being meted out to the *Dunera* deportees:

Our information is that these internees, who are all anti-Fascists, were interned in England as a result of hysteria during the collapse of France, and at a later date were deported to Australia on the vessel *Dunera*, and the treatment meted out to them was so bad that certain military officers on that vessel were court martialled by the British Government. A large number of these people have since had their release ordered by the British Government, but so far such release orders have not been put into effect by the Commonwealth Government.

The council requested that the Australian Government "take immediate action to put the release orders of the British Government into effect". Menzies' reply is not on record. But the request, of course, was ignored.

The Armed Forces urgently needed "optical munitions" which were not available in Australia. In July 1941, Dr Richard Woolley, then Government Astronomer at Mount Stromlo in the Australian Capital Territory, suggested that his observatory should devote all its resources to manufacturing these requirements. (Dr Woolley was later knighted and became Astronomer Royal at Greenwich.)

An optical munitions panel was established and Dr Woolley set about organising an experienced team of technicians. Major Layton accompanied him to the camps where four skilled workers, all *Dunera* men, were recruited. They were Gus Krentler, George Frohlich, Hans Meyer and Ernst Frohlich. (Ernst Frohlich after the war set up a steel business in Canberra, took up law and became a successful barrister.)

Another recruit was Hans Buchdahl, released to assist Professor Leicester MacAulay, then Professor of Physics at the University of Tasmania, who was working on the design and construction of optical systems.

The observatory at Stromlo did not make optical glass but concentrated on optical instruments such as gun-sights, range-finders and, later, thousands of precision prisms for the Americans. The glass was made at the University of Melbourne under the direction of Professor Hartung, and the lenses ground at Mount Stromlo. "We were a happy close-knit group," said S. C. B. Gascoigne, who joined the team in August 1941 and later became Professor of Astronomy at Mount Stromlo. He recalled bicycle races round the billiard-room table, and swimming excursions to the Murrumbidgee River.

Mount Stromlo is approximately 16 kilometres from Canberra, and Mr Justice Simpson, then Director-General of Security in the Australian Capital Territory, placed a four-mile (6.4 kilometres) limit on the movements of the Mount Stromlo team, which meant they could not visit Canberra in their free time. When Layton heard of this "crazy and incredible" limitation, he urged Simpson to lift the ban, and finally threatened to send the men back to England. He had arranged for their passages before Simpson relented. "Simpson was not only difficult, he was almost impossible," said Layton.

Layton had yet another brush with authority in Melbourne when a similar four-mile ban was placed on Dr Eirich, an eminent chemist who was released from camp to do important war work. "He used to come to see me," said Layton, "and at Princes Bridge, Melbourne, would say, 'I can't come any further.' He would turn round and go back." Dr Eirich had been camp leader at Hay and Tatura, and was released in August 1941 to work at the University of Melbourne as a special investigator for the CSIR (Council for Scientific and Industrial Research). He later returned to his previous lectureship at Cambridge and in 1947 went to America to become Professor of Chemistry at Brooklyn Polytechnic Institute, consultant to the detergent industry, and president of the Rheology Society.

"Some of the refugees who were sent out on the *Dunera* as prisoners of war in the panic of last summer (who were treated on the voyage out I should not say as criminals, but as no criminal should ever be treated), are now back in this country," said a contributor to the *New Statesman* of 6 September 1941. Conditions in the camp were fairly satisfactory — food and clothing were adequate — but internees hoped something would be done about the cold, for living quarters were still unheated.

Their chief complaint was that they were still treated as prisoners of war with severe restrictions on communication overseas. Many were convinced that details of their detention had been passed on to the Nazi authorities, because threatening letters from Germany, passed by the Australian censor, had reached them in camp. The article continued: "Release in Australia is apparently out of the question, and chances of emigration are slight indeed. Thus the great number are left without hope. Internees in Australia are severely penalised for the bad luck of having been selected, without any criterion or discrimination, for deportation to Australia at the time of the Fifth Column scare."

In October 1941 the new Army Minister, Francis Michael Forde, submitted to Cabinet a "confidential agendum" dealing with the treatment of "overseas refugees from Nazi oppression" then interned in Australia.

The "agendum" reminded Cabinet that these refugees had been accepted by the Australian Government solely on condition that they would not be released in Australia. The only deviation from this policy had been the release of eight internees who possessed "specialist qualifications of an exceptionally high standard and could do work of national importance". A few similar cases were under consideration. And what of the remainder? Forde suggested that a policy of limited release might be adopted, having regard to five factors:

   (a)   the justice or otherwise of holding in detention refugees from Nazi oppression.
   (b)   the attitude of the detaining administration.
   (c)   security considerations.
   (d)   public reaction.
   (e)   the utility of those released.

Analysing these factors, Forde concluded that the first one required no comment. As to the second and third, the Australian Government had full powers to release interned aliens at its discretion, and the military had no objection, provided that those released could contribute to the war effort, or were able to support themselves.

The fourth point was the most difficult: "There is a distinct possibility that public opinion may react unfavourably to any proposals for a large-scale release of internees," Forde wrote:

> And it can be expected that this state of feeling will be made
> acute by certain sections of the vernacular press. This
> reaction could probably be prevented by the issue of an
> official statement explaining fully the motives prompting
> whatever policy of release is followed and indications that
> all necessary economic and security safeguards will be
> adopted.

Forde also suggested that minors numbering roughly between 250 and 300 be released to continue their studies, providing they had private means or could be supported by welfare organisations.

Forde's final submission showed that however bitter their other differences, on one point the Labor Government and the Opposition were in complete agreement:

> The final submission is made that Cabinet approve of the
> principle that release in any case shall not imply in any way
> that the individual concerned will be allowed to remain in
> Australia after the war.

CHAPTER NINETEEN

Japan attacked Pearl Harbour on 7 December 1941, and early in 1942, when her forces were thrusting southwards through Malaya, Layton persuaded the Australian Government to allow internees to join an employment company of the Australian Military Forces or, if they had special skills, to work in essential wartime industries.

On 21 January, Forde announced that refugees held on behalf of the British Government and regarded as "safe", could volunteer for service in labour units of the Australian Military Forces:

> It is only reasonable that aliens, including refugees, should, to some extent, contribute to this country's defences, in return for the protection they have received, and for the economic and social opportunities they have enjoyed in times of peace.
>
> I believe that the aliens affected will welcome the move. Considerable numbers of them have already expressed their desire to perform service. I have received a telegram from the Migrants' Consultative Council in Sydney stating that the council, representing Jewish refugees, welcomes the proposal that their services should be utilised.

Forde seems to have forgotten that for more than a year *Dunera* internees had been frustrated in their desire to participate in Australia's war effort, but he remembered to repeat the now familiar assurance that the release of refugees did not imply that they would be permitted to remain in Australia after the war.

Before Japan entered the war, the question of aliens in Australia being compelled to perform non-military service had not arisen. But according to National Security Regulations issued in February 1942 any "refugee alien" under the age of 60 who had not volunteered to serve could be called on by the Minister of the Army to perform such non-military work "as might be directed by the Minister for Labour". The definition of a "refugee alien" was fairly complex. He was "an alien who has no nationality, or whose nationality is uncertain, or who is an alien enemy in respect of whom the Minister of State for the Army, or a person authorised by that Minister to act on his behalf, is satisfied (a) that the alien was forced to emigrate from enemy territory on account of actual or threatened religious, racial or political persecution, and (b) that he is opposed to the regime which forced him to emigrate".

Dr Max Gellis, camp spokesman of camp 2, Tatura, expressed the feelings of many of his fellow internees when he wrote to Clarke: "In spite of the long internment, we have not lost the true measure of our hardship, as against the events of the world." But he wished to draw Clarke's attention to the "over-aged" (over 60) and the "unfit" (rejected from the labour battalions). There were indications that employers were reluctant to employ these men because of their unfitness. "May I allay this misgiving," Dr Gellis wrote. "Military unfitness is not identical with lack of ability to do civilian work."

The Australian War Cabinet in March decided that all refugee aliens who had not volunteered for other services and all enemy aliens should be made available to the recently created Allied Works Council (AWC). This was the constructing agency for a great number of national defence projects, many of them in remote and inhospitable areas of central Australia. They included building strategic roads and airfields, gathering timber, charcoal burning, and stone breaking. The tasks allotted to those called up were chosen indiscriminately, and often, it seemed, vindictively. Moreover, in some labour camps anti-Nazis and Nazis were forced to live together.

The Director General of the AWC, appointed by Curtin, was E. G. Theodore, and his deputy in New South Wales, Frank (later Sir Frank) Packer.

Once a miner in Western Australia, Theodore had been a union organiser in Queensland, a Queensland Labor Premier, and a brilliant Federal Treasurer before his involvement in a Queensland mining scandal contributed to his political extinction. Subsequently in association with Packer he had made a fortune in Fiji gold-mining, and in 1936 he and Packer had acquired the moribund Sydney *Daily Telegraph*. Packer, an unscrupulous entrepreneur, used the paper to voice his unpredictable whims, prejudices and dislikes. Neither partner had any sympathy for the refugees. Theodore's lack of sympathy was the more remarkable because he came from a Rumanian immigrant family whose original name was Theodorescu. "I got little help from Theodore," Layton recalled.

A typical example of the AWC's attitude towards refugees was the experience of a man named Cast, who wrote to the Society of Friends that he suffered from flat feet and required new arch supports when he was sent to Alice Springs, 600 miles (965 kilometres) north of Adelaide, South Australia. The medical authorities of Alice Springs would not give him new supports on the grounds that exercise was all he needed. He was constantly in acute pain but after a week in hospital was recommended to return to full duty. The camp manager once said in his hearing that he had no pity for any Germans as all of them should be re-interned, and he asked Cast, "How would the German Gestapo treat you?" Cast was ordered to do pick-and-shovel work and, failing to comply with orders, was prosecuted. He consulted a solicitor and after months of adjournments won his case on technical grounds. During the months of waiting, he received no pay or rations, not even razor blades. Cast appealed to Dr Pilcher, who brought his case and others to the attention of Curtin, but without success. A year later Cast was again ordered to pick-and-shovel work with a road-making unit. He refused and was again arrested.

Another pick-and-shovel worker was Dr N. G. Howard, an eye specialist at the noted Koenigsberg Hospital before being forced to leave Germany. As a special concession the University of Adelaide gave him permission to qualify as an eye doctor, but the AWC flatly refused to release him. A Melbourne solicitor who had himself done pick-and-shovel work asked the Society of Friends to intervene "to rectify a situation which deprived Australia of a very well qualified medical man".

Refugees now had an ardent champion in Brian Fitzpatrick, described by his biographer, Dr Don Watson, as "variously radical journalist, historian, adviser to governments, and chief publicist in Australia for the Australian Council for Civil Liberties". He had a unique platform in a regular column in *Smith's Weekly* — unique because his views were at complete variance with those of the paper. Again, to quote Watson, *Smith's* was "chauvinistic, racist, bigoted, salacious, and after 1946, McCarthy-ist". Fitzpatrick's column always carried the disclaimer "Without Prejudice to *Smith's* Policy". His achievements have yet to be adequately recognised by his countrymen, especially by the academic élite.

In his column Fitzpatrick quoted other examples of petty persecution of refugees.

I know one man who was a labour lawyer in Vienna, did underground work against Hitler after Nazi occupation of Austria, speaks, writes and types three languages, kept his

wife and small child by practising a tanner's trade he learned
here and who for months now has been pushed about north
Queensland and central Australia with Nazis and Fascists in
a Civil Aliens Corps quarrying gang...

"I know another refugee, a Czech," he continued,

who runs a chemical business on war work, and who, for as
long as he was allowed to, did a second full-time job using
his knowledge of seven languages for Department of
Information purposes. So far we have struggled successfully
for his body against Mr Theodore, whose men ordered him
first to cut firewood at Beaufort, Victoria, then to do
likewise at Mildura, then to do some unspecified manual job
at Alice Springs. He is blind in one eye, and the other is
susceptible to glare.

When refugees were accused by the AWC of evading service
and black-marketing, Fitzpatrick publicly challenged Theodore to
produce a single instance of this. The challenge was not accepted.
And when the *Daily Telegraph*, a strident calumniator of the
refugees, published an editorial headed "Refugees Who Shirk
Duty", a farrago of lies, it refused to publish a correction written
by A. Landa, a member of the New South Wales Legislative
Assembly, in reply.

Landa pointed out that the refugees working for the AWC
were paid only six shillings a day, thus undermining Australian
working conditions. A few years before Sir Frank Clarke had
accused refugees of posing a threat to Australian standards. Now a
government instrumentality was forcing them to do just what Sir
Frank had fulminated against. In his *Smith's Weekly* column,
Fitzpatrick wrote:

I say that somebody in authority has it in for refugees,
wants to do them as much damage as possible in public
regard, wants to deny them an economic place in the
community, wants to give them another taste here of the
Gestapo experiences many of them had in Europe in Hitler's
concentration camps of Dachau and Buchenwald.

A watchful Victorian patriot, W. H. Janson Holloway, wrote to
Prime Minister Curtin in March 1942, complaining that "enemy
aliens" in internment camps such as Tatura and Murchison were
buying from Melbourne stores very expensive goods such as clothing
and suitcases. "I am advised," he wrote, "that shirts at £3 each
and ties at 10.6d each and more are being bought...It seems to me
incredible that such persons be allowed to obtain such unnecessary
luxuries and if they have so much money to spare, should they not

be compelled to invest it in the War Loans or put it to some nationally useful purpose?''

The Prime Minister's Department duly advised Mr Holloway that the information had been brought to the attention of the "appropriate Commonwealth authorities". What authorities were responsible for controlling the neckwear of internees was not revealed.

The camp spokesman for Compound "A" in camp 2, Tatura, E. H. Meyer, voiced the feelings of many of the internees when he wrote to Miss Pierce in December 1944:

> How is it possible that men known not only to be Hitler's enemies but his first victims, and sympathetic to the cause of the Allies who — being four years and four months in Australia — are still interned as we in this compound are? Their only 'fault' consists in the fact of having been brought to this country, as those who were left in England have been released long ago.
>
> It is true, one can apply for release from internment by volunteering for the Employment Company or the Civil Aliens Corps; but, be it because people do not wish — after having lived in camps for so many years and knowing that they could be usefully employed in factories, on farms, etc. — to continue the same type of life in new surroundings, or because they do not wish to forfeit their chance of returning to England before the end of hostilities with Japan. . .or for any other reason, some people here do not see their way to avail themselves. . .to apply for release. . .on the above basis. Is that surprising? I find it surprising in the highest degree that people known to be innocent are kept prisoners. . .and every day these people are detained adds to the injustice done to them.

CHAPTER TWENTY

Because orchardists in the Goulburn Valley, Victoria, were desperately short of labour, 286 *Dunera* internees volunteered for fruit picking prior to their enlistment in the 8th Australian Employment Company. Most of the volunteers were sent to pear and peach orchards near the township of Shepparton about 180 kilometres north of Melbourne. Orchardists examined the men carefully, sometimes feeling their muscles, before selecting them. The atmosphere reminded some of what they had read of the slave markets of America's deep south.

The work was hard and tedious, and the fruit-pickers were restricted to an area of 16 kilometres around Shepparton, but after the regimentation of the internment camp, with its guards, its censors and its barbed wire, it was a delicious taste of freedom. "It is a kind of half-release," Edgar Bogden wrote to Miss Pierce in February. Bogden, an Austrian, was a graduate of the University of Vienna and had a PhD for a thesis written under the supervision of the cancer expert, Professor Ernest Freund, on an unknown phospho-proteid of the thyroid gland of cattle. For six years he worked as an analytical chemist in his father's firm, and for one year at the research laboratory of the Clinical Therapeutical Institute of Arlesheim, near Basle. He escaped to England in June 1938.

Sitting on a fruit case, with another fruit case for a table, after a hard and hot day, he wrote to Miss Pierce his first uncensored letter ("a grand occasion"). In it he told her that when the fruit picking was over in April, he hoped to be able to do some specialised work that would help Australia more than carrying boxes or digging trenches in a labour unit. He had two professions: firstly, as an analytical chemist, secondly as a teacher of abnormal children. He had worked with backward children in many

European countries, and in England. Could Miss Pierce or her friends help him? He apologised for making a request in his first letter written in freedom. "Dear Miss Pierce," he concluded, "I have to close as it gets dark, a good night to you. Excuse this confused letter with the difficulties of a new-born farmhand and fruit-picker."

Bern Brent wrote to his mother: "The pay is good (£4.6.0 for 48 hours). After spending 16 shillings for food, we are left with 70 shillings. The only thing to do on Saturday afternoons is to go to Shepparton, nine miles [14.5 kilometres] away. Farmers and farm workers all flock into town, the goal for most of them, young and old, is the pub...when the pubs close at six o'clock the town provides a rather odd picture."

Another fruit-picker, Henry Mayer, again expressed his feelings in verse:

> *randy ration*
> *here we are. free in a free country.*
> *peach fluff on our arms, pear stalks in our ears.*
> *carrying ladders that seem to reach*
> *to doom; cursing fate that took action,*
> *dazed, feeling Rip-van-Winkleish,*
> *kissing the cheeks of peaches, red*
> *and slowly blushing...fifty boxes a day.*
>
> *after two years the wire has fallen —*
> *on the road to eternity, walking, cavorting*
> *you have no limit but the stars*
> *and the size of your shoes.*
>
> *it was too late, too soon, too slow, too sudden...*
> *the solemn warning list in a whirlpool*
> *the bell's clamant clangour never heard*
> *pear stalks as our phallic symbols*
>
> *there, in the small provincial town*
> *the cut embraces, carefully censored*
> *girls...on the screen.*
> *and we embrace our peaches.*
>
> *now that the bull-frog's ugly bellow*
> *expresses our randy desires*
> *now that we should, by all canons*
> *rush, rape and revel*
> *we are silent and frightened of life.*

Professor Henry Mayer.

Mayer, who became a distinguished political scientist, had an undistinguished scholastic career. The son of indulgent German parents, he was, in his own words, "a very reluctant pupil" at many schools in Germany, Italy and Switzerland. He came to England in 1936, in the care of his relative, Sir Robert Mayer, well known in London musical and financial circles, but chose an independent career as a freelance journalist and writer of pseudonymous short stories for pulp magazines. He also read palms in Soho for two shillings and sixpence a seance, became public relations man for the jazz band at the Frivolity Night Club in Leicester Square, wrote anti-Nazi articles for various papers and ghosted talks for the BBC.

Mayer's academic record is impressive. After demobilisation he graduated at the University of Melbourne and was appointed to the Chair of Political Theory at the University of Sydney in 1970. His main work has been in the fields of mass media and communications. He has been a Rockefeller Foundation Fellow and Visiting Professor at the University of California (Berkeley) and the University of Illinois. His many publications include *The Press in Australia* (1964), and *Marx, Engels and Australia* (1964).

Walter Kaufmann was among the Shepparton fruit-pickers. "Even in the evening," he wrote, "the hut held the heat of day like an oven":

> They had carried water up from the irrigation ditch, and
> flooded the corrugated iron roof with water. It had not
> helped much. The air was still; and down by the ditch the
> mosquitos had proved a curse. They were almost as much of
> a curse outside the hut. Their whine pierced the distant
> croaking of the bullfrogs and taunted their eardrums. They
> stung their faces and the backs of their hands. There was no
> escape, except by the open fire where the smoke kept the
> insects at bay. They were tired, work-weary, but it was
> impossible to sleep in that stuffy heat on those palliasses
> inside the hut. Better by far to squat on a log by the fire, to
> boil the billy on the fire — hot tea against the heat, the
> drink of the bushman. Tea quenched the thirst, drove out
> the sweat all over you, and afterwards you felt cooler.

When his stint of fruit-picking finished, Kaufmann joined the 8th Employment Company and, after discharge, did odd jobs around Australia. He was a labourer on Melbourne wharves, a builders' labourer at the abattoir, a tug-boat deckhand, a street photographer and a seaman on an Australian coaster. In Melbourne, he joined the Realist Writers' Group and, encouraged by writers Frank Hardy and David Martin, began work on a novel about underground fighters under Hitler. It was published in 1951 under the title *Voices in the Storm*. Kaufmann returned to Germany in 1955 and became a successful novelist and short story writer.

Sigurd Lohde's English career had ended when, on the way to the Isle of Man, he had been mistakenly deported on *Dunera*. His Australian career began when he joined the 8th Employment Company and loaded trains and lorries with shells, jam and bully beef. Discharged from the Army, he acted in radio plays and had one good film role — Frederick Vern, ex-officer in the Royal Hanoverian Guards, in the Ealing production *Eureka Stockade*.

But the Australian film industry was moribund. The theatre offered little scope for a type-cast actor of military roles, and radio actors were poorly paid. To augment his inadequate earnings Lodhe again set up as a radiotherapist, and when the stars were favourable, for he believed in astrology, bought a few tickets in the New South Wales State Lottery. One day in June 1946 he won £1000. He invested it in a Sydney milk bar and changed his name to Sid Loder. Subsequently he returned to Berlin, opened a tavern called "Das Kangeru" and resumed his acting career.

The 8th Employment Company was a remarkable body and its commander, Captain Broughton, who created it, a remarkable man. He was a half-caste tattooed Maori, born in Ngapuke, New Zealand, on 6 August 1884, and christened Edward Renate Mugunga Broughton. At the age of 16, by falsifying his age, he enlisted in the New Zealand Mounted Rifles, and served in the South African war. Fourteen years later he fought with the Maori Battalion on Gallipoli, was mentioned in despatches, and commissioned. After the evacuation of Gallipoli, he served in France, and with a Russian regiment.

In June 1940, he enlisted as a private in the Australian Imperial Forces, again falsifying his age. This time he reduced it by 16 years. Discharged from the AIF in September 1940, he was commissioned into the militia with the rank of lieutenant and raised to captain the same day. In May 1942, he was given administrative command of the embryonic 8th Employment Company. His task was to weld an extraordinarily diverse assortment of German and Austrian refugees into an effective working unit. He not only achieved this, he also endeared himself to his men. "He knew every member of the unit by name, and their personal histories," wrote Irwin Frenkel (ex-*Arandora Star* and *Dunera*, later succesful Melbourne businessman) when Broughton died in 1955:

Captain Broughton, commander of the 8th Employment Company.

Keenly intelligent, well-read, endowed with a superb sense of humour, completely untainted by any racial prejudice... deeply interested in human beings, he did not only gain immediate respect and obedience, but also the love and affection of the unit. He enjoyed hugely being at its head, learned and meticulously respected Jewish customs, and was immensely proud of the unit because of the splendid work it did, humbly unaware of the fact that it was only he who could have turned these people into willing manual labourers.

...For years after he had been retired from the Army...he kept in touch with the boys like a benevolent father. He engaged in incessant publicity war on our behalf and fought hard to have our status changed, only to be booted out by the Army eventually...After being shoved around as flotsam and jetsam for many years he managed...to make us feel like human beings again. He restored our faith in man, as something more than 92 per cent water and a few chemicals. He was a scholar and a gentleman.

A page taken at random from the roll of the 8th Employment Company shows a great diversity of occupations. They included:

stove setter	tool maker	textile apprentice
merchant	handbag designer	artist
engineer	chemist	student
butcher	locksmith	wool sorter
mechanical engineer	physics student	upholsterer
uniform presser	farmer	agriculturalist
civil engineer	clothes cutter	mechanical welder
foreman	gardener	textile mechanic
factory manager	bookbinder	agricultural science
cowman	mechanic	student
baker	silversmith	knitter
clerk	hotel manager	company director
commercial traveller	turner, cutter	stone engraver
bootmaker	music student	shipping clerk
commercial artist	accountant	milk tester
chartered accountant	radio engineer	farm labourer

Members of the 8th Employment Company were employed in loading and unloading on the wharves in Melbourne and at Albury and Tocumwal railway junctions, where there was a break of gauge between Victorian and New South Wales railways. One of them, Private Hans Blau, wrote and composed a song, "Tocumwal, City of My Dreams". Possibly the only time in its modest history has this township been hymned in words such as these:

Tocumwal, Tocumwal, City of My Dreams,
Lovely in the sunshine
And when moonlight beams
Kindly the people, the girls,
And so the boys
Lovely the surroundings and painted like toys.

In July Gracie Fields, entertaining troops in camps throughout Australia, visited the city of Blau's dreams on her flight from Melbourne to Sydney.

Another musical member of the team was Felix Werder. His father was a Berlin opera singer, Boas Bischofs-Werder, and to the musical household came notable musicians such as Arnold Schoenberg. His father's operatic career had to be abandoned when Hitler came to power, and he became an Obercantor — leading singer — in a Berlin synagogue. In 1932, when Felix was 10, the family escaped to England. Felix was studying architecture when he and his father were interned together. He started writing music in camp. Often under his direction a working party would burst into madrigals. After the war he composed operas and concerti at an enormous rate. He told an interviewer in 1973 that after reading Nietzsche he had burnt 200 of his works and started again. Subsequently he turned to electronic music with great success.

In 1943, while he was still serving in the 8th Employment Company, Private Fabian exhibited his crayon drawings in Melbourne, Sydney and Adelaide. Melbourne's National Gallery bought his "Shower Bath".

Camp Pell, Royal Park, where the Employment Company was based, was close to the University of Melbourne, and internees were able to take courses at night. Some 50 graduated.

"They Don't Forget" was the title of an article about the 8th Australian Employment Company which appeared in *Salt*, the Australian Army magazine, in April 1942. "You will find them on the docks, in warehouses, depots, dumps — the men whom Hitler hated," the article began. "First victims of the Nazi madness, the men...wear the Australian uniform pridefully, voluntarily. This is their war as well as ours."

The article paid tribute to their commanding officer. "Broughton knows each man, his past, his ability, his worth to the unit — and to the nation. He has graded his unit according to health, strength and age...the men appreciate this." It continued:

An 8th Employment Company working party, under the direction of
Sergeant Doc. K. Sternberg, unloading goods at a military warehouse in
Melbourne.

(John Fairfax & Sons Ltd)

The job of an Employment Company is seldom a sinecure. There is no grim glory about it, but it is hard, back-breaking, monotonous...many of the company are professional men with fine brains and specialised training. They have learned to use their muscles. They are bent on helping to win this war because Fascism to them had a real meaning.

They have seen history made, but they do not talk easily of the past. Occasionally they will tell some bloody tale of Dachau and Sachsenhausen. On their scarred bodies and in their eyes they carry the worst story of our times. One young lad tells this story. He was in Vienna in 1938 when the Nazis came...He was just 16. His parents had to flee; for not only were they Jews but liberal thinkers. Dodging frontier guards they made their way to Luxembourg; there the police caught them. For three days they were shuttled between frontiers, unwanted, targets for sudden bullets. At last they were given 12 hours' grace in which to leave Luxembourg.

Came 1940 and the family were in Brussels. On 10 May the Nazis marched...Soon Nazi bombers rained hell on the city. All was confusion. The lad and his mother tried to reach the French frontier by train; the father had already been interned by the Belgians. Stukas dive-bombed and machine-gunned the train. At the border the lad was parted from his mother and hustled back to Brussels and prison. He has not seen her since. From the prison window the boy could see long columns of trudging refugees. Hundreds died beside the road, victims of the strafing Huns. Then prison guards thrust him into a bus, which made its way to one of the bomb-harried, shell-struck French ports still in Allied hands. Finally he reached England and Pentonville prison. Now he is in Australia. He has a debt to repay.

Another case history recorded by *Salt* was that of a German doctor of economics who spent four-and-a-half years behind electrified barbed wire. "He saw his friends killed simply to raise a Nazi guffaw. Miraculously, he survived to escape. He is very quiet now and does not like to speak of the terror. Frail and no longer young, he tackles hard jobs with silent patience."

Salt's article concluded:

This Company wants combatant service. Those eligible for the AIF in age and health have already volunteered. So far they have not been accepted but to become diggers is their highest ambition. To these men their Australian uniform is a

symbol of tolerance, and decency. Australia and Australians
have revived their flagging faith in mankind. We can be
proud of that.

Melbourne saw its first sophisticated revue in April 1943, when
members of the 8th Employment Company, celebrating its first
anniversary, presented at the University's Union Theatre "Sergeant
Snow White, a Happy-go-Lucky musical revue of bad old and good
new times". It was an ambitious production in three acts and 22
scenes with a cast of more than 50.

The revue, written and directed by Doc. K. Sternberg, skilfully
blended the comic and the tragic. It told how Snow White leaves
her land of fairy tale, passes through a concentration camp in
Europe, frustrates the designs of Fascism (represented by the
wicked witch) and finally joins the Australian Army. In the last
scene, "Calling All Cobbers", when the Queen is presented with a
flower-bedecked "V-for-Victory", she exclaims impassionedly,
and to the delight of the audience, "Ah! V for Vinston!"

The show deployed an abundance of talent. The choreo-
grapher and solo dancer, Corporal Peter Schmitz, was a former
member of the Russian Ballet in London. Sergeant Sigurd Lohde
displayed versatility in a variety of parts. A magnificent tenor,
Private Eric Liffman was well known to radio audiences in England
and Holland. Private Erwin Fabian designed masks for the ballet
and Privates K. Friedeberger, Bim Meier and F. Schonbach did
much of the striking scenery and decor. (Subsequently, Fabian and
Friedeberger each had successful careers in England, Meier in
Melbourne and Schonbach in the United States.) One of the six
accordionists had played by command for the Duke of Windsor.

Melbourne critics, like the audiences, were enthusiastic. "It
expresses the personality of these young men far from their own
countries and deprived of all they possess, who yet can laugh at
their troubles," wrote Catherine Duncan, a leading Melbourne
radio-actress and playwright. "But more important it is
Melbourne's first taste of European wit blended with the
Australian idiom...Here is the nucleus of a cast that can put on
something new in entertainment — something that can make a real
contribution to the Australian theatre." Her review carried the
headline "Novel Show as Pointer to Theatrical Future".

Layton continued his patient repatriation of refugees. By the end of
1943, 1148 had been returned to the United Kingdom, 154 to other
countries, including Brazil, Cuba, Argentina, Leeward Islands,
Mexico, Venezuela, Ecuador, Canada and China. Five hundred
and forty-nine had enlisted in the employment units, 205 had been

The 8th Employment Company's revue, *Sergeant Snow White*, was warmly received by Melbourne audiences. The programme cover for the production was designed by Erwin Fabian.

In a macabre ballet (choreographed by Peter Schmitz), the ghosts of Nazi-terrorised nations rise up and overthrow the "hangman of Europe", Hitler.

(John Fairfax & Sons Ltd)

Villains of the piece included the wicked witch and a wolf-headed storm-trooper.

released for work of national importance, 474 were still interned and there had been 12 deaths. About 40 had married, and Layton again raised the question of allowing internees who had been released to remain in Australia, but was told that the time was not appropriate for the Australian Government to make this decision.

By November 1943, 121 internees had been sent to Palestine in small groups as shipping became available. The voyage from Tatura to the Promised Land was slow and often perilous. A group of 13 who sailed from Australia in March 1942 did not reach Palestine until July. Their ship had been bombed on the approaches to Bombay and their naval escort sunk.

With 297 other internees, Pelz left camp in July 1942 for repatriation to England. He was wearing a light brown limp coat that flapped round his calves — a valedictory present from the Australian Government. In Melbourne, "with its bustle, its smells of soot and rubber and perfume, its women with very short skirts and incredibly high-pitched voices", he embarked in *Themistocles*, heavily laden with copper. His cabin-mate was Herr Nowothy, a "fair, long-faced gipsy scholar who had studied Homer and psychology, Virgil and T. S. Eliot by Swedish roadsides, in Italian vineyards and Polish gutters". As they left Durban, they heard that seven ships had just been sunk outside Freetown. There was a U-boat alarm at Freetown, and Pelz wrapped the poems he had written on the ship in oilskin and stuffed them under his shirt. After Freetown, they joined a large convoy, and on a rainy October day reached Liverpool.

Pelz's subsequent career in England was remarkable. He worked again as a farmhand, and as a navvy, student teacher and boiler man, while studying as an external student at London University. Converted to Lutheran Christianity, he attended theological college, and for 10 years was vicar of a Bolton parish. In 1961 he and his Viennese wife published *God Is No More*, a book that was widely acclaimed.

In addition to work and study the young members of the 8th Employment Company now enjoyed a busy social life, meeting Australian girls and being entertained by their parents. Two men helped to prepare them for their entry into society. A monocled dancing master of the old school gave expert instruction while grizzled guards looked on in wonder. He stood in the centre of a ring of eager students, monocle pressed into one eye, while his charges, both arms raised appropriately, moved slowly round the floor, anti-clockwise, to the beat of "In a dream I kiss your hand, Madame". "Later," Bern Brent recalled, "as we progressed, we would dance with other fellows, changing from male to female at our instructor's command, that is, unless we happened to be dancing with one of the camp's 'queers' who were quite content to remain 'damen' dancing on their toes.''

The well-known author Alan (*I Can Jump Puddles*) Marshall briefed them on the technique of talking to girls. The important thing, he stressed, was not to exhaust your conversational gambits — jokes, anecdotes, books, music, theatre, etc. — at the first meeting. Some should be conserved for subsequent meetings, which were likely to be difficult if the young man "unpacked all his goods at the first date, leaving him with an empty conversational larder''.

Australian girls gave Brent his first experience of Australian society: ''. . . whether they were servicewomen or students, farmers' daughters or office girls, I salute them. For I suppose it was they who gave me a glimpse of Australia which I grew to love so that when the time came to return to Britain and Europe, I couldn't. Today, I particularly salute their parents. They offered hospitality when it was not yet fashionable to be nice to foreign migrants. . . when food and petrol was rationed. If the Army taught me all about mateship, vomit in wet canteens, doing one's dough at two-up pay days, and four-letter-word vocabularies, there was also rowing in Studley Park, tea and toast in front of the fire, home-baked birthday cakes, hiking in the Dandenongs and washing up in the kitchen after tea.''

Several fully qualified doctors joined the 8th Employment Company hoping that they could be attached to an AIF medical unit, but they succeeded only in being transferred to medical aid posts attached to working parties.

The Australian Medical Association followed the lead of its English counterpart in opposing the entry of refugee medical practitioners.

After more than two years' service in the 8th Employment Company, a number of refugees sought government approval to remain permanently in Australia. Full Cabinet in March 1944 agreed to this in cases where

(a) The applicant has been classified as a "refugee alien".

(b) Nothing detrimental is known against him.

(c) The Minister is satisfied that applicant is likely to make a desirable citizen of Australia if permitted to remain here.

Anglo-Saxon democrats of the Returned Soldiers' and Sailors' League were moved to protest. The Jimna (Queensland) sub-branch of the League sent Curtin a copy of its recent resolution:

> We, the members of this sub-branch of the RSL...view
> with concern the impending disaster to our returned fighting
> men, should the action of the Minister of the Interior to
> favourably consider the applications for release of internees
> in Australia, be fulfilled.

"We would be extremely grateful if this matter would be reconsidered at the next sitting of the House," wrote the sub-branch secretary.

When a similar protest was made by the Gayndah (Queensland) branch of the RSL, the Prime Minister's Department assured the branch that the approval of release applied only to certain internees who had been classified as "refugee aliens", against whom no security objection was known, and who had served with a good record in the 8th Employment Company, or in some other useful capacity.

But the RSL's fears of "impending disaster" were not allayed. At its Federal congress held in December 1944 a motion was carried unanimously urging the early deportation of all "enemy aliens" brought to Australia, and the Traralgon (Victoria) branch of the League passed a motion demanding that "enemy aliens" be banned for 20 years. There was, however, a surprising comment in *Mufti*, the official organ of the Victorian branch of the League.

In its January 1945 issue it published a long editorial headed "Should Aliens be Deported?" The editorial began by acclaiming the "intensely patriotic...hearts and feelings" of the League members who had supported the two motions. It continued with a familiar attack on aliens who had opened businesses in Melbourne:

> Along with others in the community, returned men have
> been disturbed to note the infiltration of aliens into city
> industries. Every luxury trade seems to be falling into the
> grip of people who are as yet un-Australian in outlook...
> Dozens of new shops have opened in the city and suburbs,
> and the owners have been aliens. Up to recently, and until
> the League obtained the imposition of a restriction upon the
> purchase of land by aliens, properties everywhere were being
> bought up by men who were not in this country prior to
> 1939...Viewing the advance of alien people — at a time
> when so many Australians are away serving up north — it is
> small wonder that returned men would be voicing fears
> and protests. It is small wonder too, that the resultant cry
> should be one of 'Boot them out'.
> Democracy permits no other penalty.

But, asked the editorial, if the two motions were understandable, were they necessarily sound? One might feel a natural desire to kick somebody, but it might not be politic to do so. In any case it was a sign of a civilised community that national decisions should be based on reason and not on emotion. If it were in Australia's interest that the aliens should be sent back, they should be sent back, "without regard to feelings or to real or imagined right". The editorial then sounded a note of warning:

> Australia needs population. If she does not get sufficient immigrants from Britain she will have to get them from other countries. *But get them she must, or eventually go under.*

What then should be done with the aliens already in Australia and who might want to stay there?

> In the first place, they may be no worse than the men Australia may eventually have to accept. Even those guilty of subversive activities in Australia have been guilty only of serving their own country in time of war — an offence that Australia would expect of its own nationals if caught in enemy country.
>   Briefly, then...if Australia wants a much enlarged population after the war, and cannot gain the whole of her requirements from Britain, she will have to spend money to get people from other European countries; and if that position arises she would be incredibly foolish and illogical to send back the would-be migrants she already has here, who would probably on return to their native land be amongst the first applicants for re-admittance.

The writer of this editorial — the State secretary, Charles W. Joyce — seems to have been unaware of the existence of the *Dunera* men, but he showed foresight in his prediction of Australia's future immigration pattern. Between 1945 and 1978, 3,300,000 migrants came to Australia. Of these only about 42 per cent were from the United Kingdom.

Another patriot who seemed unaware that the *Dunera* men were anti-Nazis deported by mistake was the Victorian Senator General Charles Henry Brand CB, CMG, CVO, DSO.

Mufti, under the heading "Suspects from Britain Admitted to Naturalisation", reported a speech General Brand had made in the Senate in June 1945. During a debate on a re-establishment and employment bill, the General complained that a number of "enemy aliens" who had come to Australia on *Dunera* had since been naturalised although their five years' qualifying period included a stay in an internment camp, and many apparently were not to be returned.

Mufti's report continued:

> General Brand said that scores of the men had since been released for civilian employment — some had joined the Labour Corps and were wearing the Australian soldier's uniform whilst others had opened shops and businesses left by men called up to join the Services.

There was strong suspicion against these men, the General added, "or otherwise the British Government would not have taken the drastic step of deporting them to Australia".

The General's polemic evoked a spirited reply from W. T. Tackaberry, commandant of the Tatura camps from September 1940 until his retirement from the Army at the end of February 1942. "Your article gives quite an erroneous impression of the facts regarding 'Overseas' internees who arrived in Australia on the *Dunera*," he wrote. "I was charged with the close supervision of them...and I claim to know something about them."

> Your article is headed: 'Suspects from Britain admitted to Naturalisation' and I would like to know when has it been the British custom to convict persons on suspicion? As a matter of fact they were mostly classified as Refugee Aliens and not Enemy Aliens and had left Germany and Austria because of their hatred and fear of 'Hitlerism' and 'Nazism'. Quite a number had resided in Great Britain and had never lived anywhere else; also quite a few had sons and daughters in the British Army.

Tackaberry was unable to agree with General Brand's suggestion that men who "were forcibly (though innocent of any subversive act) brought to Australia" should be debarred from the privilege of naturalisation. And with a nice sense of convict history he reminded the General that quite a few useful and respectable citizens were descendants of people who "were forcibly brought to Australia in the past".

The RSL continued its campaign against the refugees. In January 1946 the president of the Victorian branch, G. W. Holland CBE, protested against the Federal Government's proposal that members of the Employment Companies should be included in the provisions of the Re-Establishment and Employment Act that granted preference of employment and training facilities to servicemen. Mr Holland said these companies chiefly comprised aliens and his executive thought that such addition to the number entitled to preference would lower its value and bring this scheme into disrepute. It would have a more serious effect on training. Already there was insufficient accommodation for servicemen. For every alien brought into the scheme, some good servicemen would lose benefits. Friction would be inevitable.

The rights of refugees who had served in the 8th Employment Company became a hotly controverted issue in Federal Parliament.

During one debate in the House of Representatives, ex-Major Maltby (Barwon, Liberal) attacked the Commonwealth Government for releasing some of the *Dunera* internees "whom he classed as dangerous"... Maltby said that he wished to direct attention to what he might term the improper immigration which had taken place since early in the war. In 1940 650-odd foreigners had been gathered up in the south of England after the fall of Dunkirk and moved to Australia in *Dunera* for the safety of England. Many remained in Australia, because they would not essay the journey as their files were of such nature as to mark them as dangerous.

Professor H. Woodruff, chairman of VIREC, replied vigorously to Maltby, pointing out that "as Major Maltby he was in a position to know the facts". Woodruff recapitulated the history of the *Dunera* internees and concluded that "I and many others who know them feel confident that they will, if allowed to do so, play a worthy part in the future of this country".

The controversy became acute in March 1946. More than 360,000 men had been demobilised since the end of the war. Among them were 19 members of the 8th Employment Company who were given "accelerated discharges" to complete courses in universities and technical schools, under the provisions of the Re-establishment and Employment Act. The RSL was now joined by another active organisation, the Soldiers', Sailors', and Airmen's Fathers' Association of Victoria, conveniently known as the "Dads' Association". In a long protest sent to the Minister for Post-war Reconstruction, Mr J. J. Dedman, the State secretary of the "Dads", R. Hugh Palamountain, wrote:

> The accelerated discharges given to a number of enemy
> aliens, mostly Germans, with we are told more to follow —
> in all at least 20, in order to take up university courses
> under post-war reconstruction training, is looked upon by
> the Dads' Association with disgust, and our determination is
> to contest the granting of privileges to aliens with all the
> strength behind our 25,000 members in Victoria.
>
> The nationality of these aliens in our opinion remains
> enemy aliens. Some of them, probably all, according to our
> information, are ex-internees, and to admit these men to the

full privileges granted to our own gallant soldiers under the pretext of their being stateless is a slur on our lads and in direct conflict with the principles for which this association was founded, namely — to watch, guard and forward the interests of our servicemen and women.

We will continue to work in the service of those who serve, and not pander to the nationals of the country or countries that have plunged us into the horrors of war on two occasions during the last 30 years and have been guilty of all the inhuman acts that were associated with their campaign of hate and lust for power.

The issue was first raised in Canberra by a Victorian Country Party Member, Colonel Bowden, who moved adjournment of the House to discuss what he described as a state of affairs which was "an affront to Australian fighting men". The discussion was not conducted on a very high level. Colonel Bowden claimed that these 19 "enemy aliens" had been given preference over Australians with long overseas service, and in a burst of eloquence declared:

Australians are recognised as a tolerant people. They certainly are a reasonable people. In circumstances of this kind, they are a generous people. I claim that generosity should not be carried to the extreme degree of requiring the Australian taxpayer to defray the cost of educating nationals of former enemy countries, and according to them benefits under the Re-establishment and Employment Act, until the last demand of every Australian has been met.

The real issue was whether the 8th Employment men were "enemy aliens", in which case they were not entitled to reconstruction benefits under the Act, or whether they were stateless, and had applied for Australian naturalisation, in which case they were entitled. On this point, Colonel Bowden made an extraordinary comment. He believed there was no legal backing for the use of the word "stateless", and added:

If it is here applied to the members of the Jewish race who left their own country, either voluntarily or compulsorily, in order to escape persecution, it can have no force today, because the tyranny which drove them out no longer exists.

But the garland for idiosyncratic oratory went, as often, to Archie Cameron of the elastic-sided boots:

Some alien refugees approached me in Sydney with a proposition to form an Australian foreign legion. I would not touch their proposal with a 40-foot pole. I have never believed in the French Foreign Legion, although it has been

one of France's greatest weapons in its political and
economic policy.

As for the 8th Employment Company men:

> Taking these people at their best, as enemy aliens, stateless
> or whatever they may be, they did not come to Australia for
> Australia's good or because they had any particular love for
> Australia. They came here because circumstances in their
> homeland made it uncomfortable for them to remain
> there...They did not come here as ordinary immigrants, or
> to settle here, but simply to accept the asylum which was
> offered to them by the Government of Australia.
> Consequently, they have quite a lot to thank this country
> for.

The Government had little difficulty in refuting the charges of the
Opposition. Dedman proved conclusively that not one Australian
serviceman or civilian had been denied the opportunity of going to
the university because of the admission of 21 (the figure had been
increased by two) stateless aliens. Every one of the 911 servicemen
who had applied for admission had been released and admitted.

The Government's claims were endorsed by the chairman of
the Universities Commission, Professor R. C. Mills, and the
Registrar of the University of Melbourne, Mr John Foster.
Professor Mills said that all ex-servicemen reconstruction trainees
could be accommodated at Australian universities, and Mr Foster
said that no ex-servicemen qualified for admission to the University
of Melbourne had been refused admission.

Speaking on the adjournment motion, Colonel Bowden had
quoted the specific case of Lance-Corporal Walter Wurzburger
who, he claimed, was granted an accelerated release to take a full
course in the Melbourne Conservatorium of Music. In a letter to
the Melbourne *Herald*, Wurzburger politely corrected Colonel
Bowden. His application for benefits under the Reconstruction
Training Scheme had not yet been granted. And he added:

> I, like the other students concerned, had volunteered for any
> service in or outside Australia, but we were not accepted for
> the AIF.
>
> My two brothers, just as alien as I, were accepted by
> the British Army and had the chance of fighting their way
> back to Germany to help to bring justice to the inventors of
> the gas chambers through which my parents and another
> brother had to pass.

Another letter to the *Herald* was signed Jack Barry KC, Brian

Fitzpatrick and Margaret Holmes. Barry, a staunch defender of human rights, later elevated to the Bench, was associated with Fitzpatrick on the Australian Council for Civil Liberties. In their letter they wrote of the men of the 8th Employment Company:

> ...the UK Government acknowledged that these men never should have been interned. Winston Churchill described their internment and deportation as "a deplorable and regrettable mistake". In February 1942 the Commonwealth Government gave the men the opportunity of volunteering for service in the Australian Military Forces. Almost without exception, refugees able to bear arms volunteered. Not for labour service, for any service. They were drafted to Australian Employment Companies and served for almost four years. The authorities failed to accede to continued appeals from many of the men to be permitted to serve with the AIF.

Barry had also prepared for the council a submission "on the eligibility for re-establishment of aliens of enemy origin". He made some points which had escaped the attention of Colonel Bowden and his colleagues:

1. There can be no doubt that by the municipal law of Germany all emigrants from Germany and Austria of Jewish birth were deprived of their nationality and thus rendered stateless.
2. Even if it be argued that the soldier's present nationality decides the question of his eligibility, it is impossible in international law to force upon him a nationality against his will. There are American precedents for this which have recently been upheld in an Australian court of law...

   It may therefore be taken as a valid legal principle that "no man may have imposed upon him without his free assent, a nationality that he does not possess or that he has ceased to possess".
3. National Security (Aliens Service) Regulations... promulgated 5 July 1944 read: 'Enemy Alien' means a person who, not being a British subject possesses the nationality of a state at war with His Majesty...*but does not include a refugee alien.*

With demobilisation, former members of the 8th Employment Company sometimes found it difficult to decide whether to become Australian citizens or to return to England. In a diary entry Brent recorded his indecision:

Damn it, I am all confused and muddled up. Sometimes I make a resolution to stay here. Then I say to myself: 'Don't be foolish, old boy! This is a good country, the people are all very nice, the climate is a healthy one, it is a place of untold riches and future possibilities.' The next day I look upon a letter from a reader of the *Sun* complaining about aliens released from internment getting award wages of £3.18 per week while our boys are getting six shillings a day. Then I feel I can't stand any more ignorance, stupidity and narrow-mindedness and want to get away from it all at all cost.

Brent chose Australia. His subsequent career was varied. He was successively a process worker, a street photographer, and a nit keeper at a baccarat school, while studying at the University of Melbourne. After graduation he held a number of important educational posts, including a teaching mission in South-east Asia under the Colombo Plan, and an education officer in Sydney and Canberra with the Commonwealth Public Service.

One of the last voices of protest was that of Walter Meyer, who on 11 January 1945 wrote to Layton pointing out that he was not being treated according to the terms of the Geneva Convention. He quoted articles of the Convention, which provided that rooms had to be sufficiently heated and lit, whereas the internment huts were insufficiently lit and unheated. The long internment had already seriously affected his health and that there were no security reasons to detain him. He added that he was legally entitled to the treatment laid down by the Convention without being subjected to any call-up or service whatever in Australia and that he was not applying for release.

POSTSCRIPT

Anti-semitism and xenophobia lingered on in post-war Australia, nourished by misleading articles and provocative cartoons in right-wing publications — notably *Smith's Weekly*, the *Bulletin, Truth* and the Sydney *Daily Telegraph*. (Some of the cartoonists seem to have drawn their inspiration from *Der Stürmer*.) It was not till 1960, for example, that a Jew was admitted to the Melbourne Stock Exchange. Appropriately, the historic breakthrough was made by a *Dunera* "Old Boy", Herbert Baer.

On 6 March 1947 Arthur Calwell, Minister for Immigration in the Labor Government and architect of Australia's realistic post-war immigration policy, replied to members of the Opposition who had objected to a certain number of relatives of Jews in Australia being admitted on humanitarian grounds. When the old bogy of refugee aliens "flooding" the country was invoked, Calwell pointed out that his Government's policy on refugee migration was identical with that of the conservative Lyons Government, which agreed at Evian in 1938 to admit 15,000 refugees over a three-year period. Because of the outbreak of war, this quota was never filled and Australia was still committed to receive 8525 refugees. "Much of the public misunderstanding of the alien immigration question was due to exaggerated and untruthful reports," Calwell said. "Some of the most extraordinary and brazen inaccuracies seen in many years have been spread by certain newspapers during recent weeks in alleged news statements on the question of refugee aliens." He specified one "brazen inaccuracy", a boldly displayed story in the Sydney *Daily Telegraph* on 11 February stating that 3000 refugees were coming to Australia in three Dutch ships, the *Johan de Witt, Orange* and *Johan Oldenbarneveldt*, chartered by the American and Netherlands Jewish relief organisation.

The story, like many a *Telegraph* "scoop", was, of course, without foundation.

The first reunion of *Dunera* internees, in Melbourne in 1972.

By 1947, of the 2562 refugees deported on *Dunera* "by mistake", 1451 had been repatriated to England, 165 to other countries, 13 had died, and the remainder — 913 — had been permitted to remain in Australia. Most of these settled in Melbourne, where many married Australian girls. A number have made significant contributions to Australia's cultural and economic life. Some of these have been mentioned in preceding chapters, others have changed their names and cannot be traced.

As a trooper *Dunera* took part in the Madagascar operation in September 1942, served at the Sicily landings in July 1943, carried the headquarters staff of the US 7th Army at the invasion of southern France in September 1944 and took occupation forces to Japan in 1945. She was refitted at a cost of nearly a million pounds in 1950-51 and carried troops to Cyprus, Ceylon and Malaya until 1960, when she was again refitted as an educational cruise ship, carrying 194 cabin and 834 dormitory passengers. In November 1967 she was sold to Spanish interests and broken up.

In September 1972, about 200 *Dunera* men held a reunion in Melbourne. "We didn't do it to revive memories of how the British ill-treated us," said the organiser, Erwin Frenkel. "We just got together with our wives and families to have an earbash about old times and to raise money for some of the survivors."

Since then, the reunion has become an occasional event, held on 4 September.

APPENDIX

A DUNERA ANTHOLOGY

Poets, or at least versifiers, flourished in the internment camps. Some wrote only in German, some in German and English, some only in English.

Here is a representative English selection:

The Porthole
Recollection from a prisoners' ship.

The porthole is the polar star we follow.
In it the skyline seems to sink and soar,
First, one feels filled with lead, and then feels hollow,
As the horizon lifts and falls once more,
The head is heavy, and the weary eye
Sees through the porthole nought but sea and sky.

Eternally this voyage seems to last
Since the horizon swallowed up the coast.
Now only water — water grey and vast,
We feel that we are breathing it, almost.
The sentry with his rifle stands near by
And through the porthole, nought but sea and sky.

In that small ring of light the world goes by,
Before the hollow-eyed and hungry crowd
Whose eyes reflect the colour of the sky
And bend their starving gaze on each stray cloud
As if the day of doom at hand might be —
And through the porthole, nought but sky and sea.

Max Zimmering, 1940
(Translated by Barbara Whitehead)

Loyalty

We have been Hitler's enemies
For years before the war,
We knew his plan of bombing and
Invading Britain's shore,
We warned you of his treachery
When you believed in peace,
And now we are His Majesty's
Most loyal internees.

We left in search of liberty
The country of our birth,
We thought to live in Britain was
The finest thing on earth,
You gave us hospitality
When we gave guarantees,
And now we are His Majesty's
Most loyal internees.

When war broke out, we tried to help
The British war effort,
We could not join, but volunteered
For jobs of any sort,
In our registration book
They stamped "Refugees"
That's why we are His Majesty's
Most loyal internees.

When Hitler's troops in Rotterdam
Came down by parachute,
And everybody panicking
The thing became acute,
We were with wives and families
Arrested by police,
So we became His Majesty's
Most loyal internees.

They told us not to be afraid
We might be back at night,
We were not prisoners at all

And would be soon all right,
But after weeks of promising
They sent us overseas,
Although we were His Majesty's
Most loyal internees.

The Censor hinders me to tell
The story of our trip,
It is sufficient when I say
Dunera was the ship,
MPs discussed in Parliament
How we had sailed the seas,
Yet we remain His Majesty's
Most loyal internees.

And here we are, without the means
Of proving our case,
Behind a strongly guarded fence
In a forgotten place,
We wait while the authorities
Consider the release,
Because we are His Majesty's
Most loyal internees.

Oswald Volkmann

Back in London

You have been in Australia for more than a year;
I am sure you can tell me a lot.
As you know I am always desirous to hear
From the man who has been on the spot.

I am eager to listen to your report
Of the harbours and cities there.
Of the beautiful girls, of the cricket sport,
Of the kangaroo, koala bear

I am sorry I cannot fulfil your desire.
I don't know how Australia looks.
I have been in Tatura behind barbed wire,
So you better enquire at Cook's.

Oswald Volkmann

Poem

"Change" has no place
In our dust-sand dictionaries,
Editions 1939.

Compounds are there defined
As place for cattle.
We are milch-cows, it may be true
But profits drawn from such dry udders
Must needs be barren,
Shrivel to nought in the miller's palm.

The wire tears at our souls
which absolutely
refuse to bleed
but only sweat.

Henry Mayer, Tatura, Christmas Day 1941

Mirror — distorted

Above the dome of cobalt,
Gargantuan, otiose, incandescent eye,
Staring at me. . .
Thorns outside not as sharp
As those of cold ferocious steel,
Strung on a weary wire
Which enclose us — symbol, Symbol?

Roads where you dawdle, simian, tetchily,
Build of the same sand which crazily races
—Afraid of you, 'fraid of itself —
To form an esoteric entity with bodies
When they bellyfull and histrionical
Return to bunks — to lie, to drowse
The buggish heat of spring octobrous
Stabbing their brows.

Whispers of night now boomerang
From far-off corners, chase tawny violet
— incredible as pregnant icecream —
Lack softness. You guzzle furiously
Splurgy night air, attempt in vain
To imitate the stridulation of the crickets
Transmuted to the randy croaking of the frogs.
Here solitude is always shared — even at midnight
Octagonal stares of blue-bottles buzzing busily
Assail you.
This crowded isolation frightens.

When daybreak comes the whistle blows,
Misery yawns once more and wakes
All play at shilly-shally, make-believe
And you, merely in fragments, show
A superciliousness towards the demos
Which is on par with rusty parish pumps

Across the sea, crossed through a devious nightmare
Rushing with puffed cheeks to finite doom
Are missiles — holding formulae

That once helped till the fields
Grew red, pellucid globes,
Bursting when harvest-time drew near,
Bursting with pride unbound
Eager to die through sheffield-steel
...stainless and warranted — two bob the set...

There's juice and steel there now
But red now holds, or rather held
The very essence of those lives
...so full of stains, no-guarantee, but 18 bob a week —
Sprawling across the slummy filth,
Grasping in death the earth they never owned
Their bodies lie. An arm, a grotesque spid'ry limb
That once perhaps was he
Whose clever face, rebellious hair
You hated — yet adored.

And yet I'd change and dive
Deep anywhere, deep into hell let loose —
At least my passions might
Intransigent and truculent
Awake once more
To give me blisters in the neck
If nothing else.

A chancy sudden death
Must be preferred
To atrophy of limb after limb
To slow stagnation
Foul, fetish — fecund with fear...

Henry Mayer, Hay, 5 November 1940

In Memoriam

Have you heard my story most brave
of the thousand dead without grave
in that wonderful town
with the moon upside down
and the wires in need of a shave?

Each man is a corpse, as he sits
decaying and doubting his wits
whilst far, far away, where the night is the day
his world is breaking to bits.

They remember the books they have read
and eat and go tired to bed
and — gruesome to tell —
though they frolic in hell
not one of them knows he is dead.

On a stage where the scene is abstract
and the gestures, the shadow of fact,
their time to beguile,
they quarrel and smile
and believe that they are what they act.

And at times when the distant parade
of life sends the laugh of a maid
or the sound of a bell
deep down into hell
they ponder and are afraid.

So the months and the years go by
and the sands of the deserts that fly
heap a merciless brown
on that wonderful town
of the dead refusing to die.

George Rapp, Hay

Let those who fret in petty discontent,
Of grievances and wrongs, of stale mishap
Be petulant in pain nor see the gap
Between injustice done and justice meant.

I cannot witness the approaching death
Of a whole world and still bewail my fate,
While circling overhead already wait
The silent vultures of the aftermath.

George Rapp

Fragment

Don't talk aloud in public, never praise
The Continent. Agree at any price:
The English have so many diff'rent ways —
Drink tea with milk. You must assimilise.

Time marches on and on; months fade away;
You understand this new society,
Its language, habits, many a curious way,
Its constitution and mentality,

So when the country is in mortal danger
And everybody's asking: "Foe or friend?"
Glancing suspiciously at every stranger —
You are interned. At first you understand.

Your case will be reviewed. 'Tis but an error,
A week or two until they set you free.
But they, completely blind and struck with terror
Think otherwise, and ship you 'cross the sea.

There you may scream aloud, appeal for justice,
Lodge your protests in triplicate or pairs,
Type letters, statements, the infernal fact is:
Nobody hears you. Anyhow, who cares?

When you're allowed to wear the rising sun,
The whole procedure proves to be a fake.
You suddenly have ceased to be a Hun.
Two years barbed wire? — Sorry, a mistake.

Bern Brent, Tatura

INDEX